VAGABOND MOON

Cheryl Koshuta

Cheryl Koshuta/Ghost Coyote Press
2580 Goldshire Drive
Driggs, Idaho 83422
www.cherylkoshuta.com

Book Design and Layout by TheBookMakers.com
Cover Photo by Cheryl Koshuta

Vagabond Moon / Cheryl Koshuta. —1st ed.
Paperback: 978-1-0880-1434-9
eBook: 978-1-0880-1441-7
Hardcover: 978-1-0880-1448-6

CONTENTS

PREFACE

In 2014, when I started the journey described in this book, I took for granted that I was able to travel freely almost anywhere I could imagine going. I had the time, the desire, and the internet. The limitations on travel were my own: avoid unstable or warring countries, stay safe as a woman alone, and live within my budget. But, by March of 2020, everything was different, and the limitations imposed by the Covid-19 global pandemic were out of my control.

I was one of the lucky ones though. When the world shut down, I didn't have to worry about making a living or feeding a family. By then, I was living in rural Idaho and could still freely roam in the mountains. My day-to-day life was largely untouched except for mask-wearing at the grocery store. The biggest change for me was not being able to jump on a plane and travel.

But most people were not so lucky. As country after country (including my own), shut down to tourists and local travel, I wondered how the guides and drivers I'd used over the years would get by without clients. And what about the people who relied on their guesthouse income to survive? Or the owners of hotels and restaurants and the workers they employed? The artists and artisans? The small shopkeepers? The big airlines? All those people who made travel possible and enjoyable. What would happen to them? I felt powerless to help, other than resolving to begin traveling again as soon as I could.

Now, in 2021, it remains to be seen how many travel-related businesses will survive and thrive again. I have seen the shuttered storefronts of many businesses that did not make it through. Such a pity. Which sounds so inadequate.

Of the people I know in the travel industry, many have weathered the storm so far. But I'm sure others have had to give up their chosen profession and move on to more stable work during this period. I have no idea how many have had their lives forever changed because they lost a loved one. Or even whether they themselves have died. The joy of travel is in meeting people; the sadness is in wondering what happens to them when disaster hits. Once again, I have been lucky and spared the grief of either losing someone to the virus or even watching a loved one battle it. My heart goes out to all those who haven't been so fortunate.

The pandemic hasn't dampened my yen to travel, despite the new risks and uncertainties, and additional hoops to jump through. In fact, I feel more strongly than ever that I must find ways to keep doing what I love—to support the incredible individuals who work in the industry, to share and learn from other cultures, and to continue meeting people and making friends around the world.

Yes, I'll keep traveling, because now, more than ever, I appreciate the immense privilege it is to be able to do so.

CHAPTER 1

ZAMBIA AND SOUTH AFRICA

NOVEMBER 2014

Talk about the elephant in the room. I was in a hotel lobby on one side of a leather couch with a huge elephant on the other side. Wasn't anybody going to tell me what to do? Stay in one place? Or run? Her trunk came within feet of me, sniffing my sweaty stench. Terrified, but exhilarated, I looked wildly across the room at the receptionist standing quietly and respectfully behind his tall counter. He put his finger to his lips.

I didn't move, not that there was anywhere to go. She blocked the path both to the wide, doorless space where she had entered and the open courtyard just beyond the lobby. She was so massive, her back nearly touched the eaves of the thatched roof, and she was so close I could see her eyelashes and smell the caked mud on her back.

Then a wrinkled baby stumbled up the few steps into the lobby, followed by two smaller adults. Now there were four elephants in the room. Mamas always protect their babies, and I was too close. I stayed still.

After what seemed like an eternity, the matriarch gave a final sweep of her trunk, then lumbered across the lobby's brick floor into the courtyard, where the boughs of a huge wild mango tree were weighed down by ripe fruit. The other three elephants followed her lead, not giving me a glance. In the courtyard, they picked up fallen mangoes with their trunks and fed them greedily into their mouths.

I let out the breath I hadn't realized I'd been holding. Like me, the elephants were simply there for lunch.

"In November, the elephants come to eat almost every day," the receptionist told me once the ellies were in the courtyard. "When the lodge was built around the mango tree, nobody expected the elephants would continue to come to eat from it, even though it had been their food source for decades. But it was their home first, so we manage around it. I hope you weren't inconvenienced."

I was in South Luangwa National Park in Zambia, at the start of a month-long trip to celebrate my sixth zero-ending birthday. I'd arrived in the country the night before and had spent the morning in an open jeeplike vehicle on a long, sweltering, humid ride from the airport to the lodge. Having flown for more than twenty-four hours from my home in Portland, Oregon, I was jet-lagged, hot, and sweaty. Inconvenienced? No way. Being so close to those elephants was a real thrill. I felt energized.

I had been bitten by the travel bug in my early twenties and had seen a lot of the world by squeezing trips into my career-driven professional life whenever I could. But I didn't take my first "once-in-a-lifetime" trip to Africa until about ten years before this one. After that, I was smitten with the wildlife and birds and returned three more times to watch lions, giraffes, elephants, rhinoceros, leopards, and zebras. As a birder, I'd chalked up a few hundred African "life-listers" (bird species documented when spotted for the first time), but there were hundreds more to see. I felt like I had barely scratched the surface of the huge continent that pulled me back time and again.

Including to celebrate my birthday in 2014, which was a strange year for me. The year before, I had become unexpectedly unemployed when the company I worked for imploded financially. I had planned to keep at my fulfilling job for another five years, when I would retire and indulge my two great passions in life: skiing and travel. But with the layoff, I needed a new path. I picked up temporary consulting gigs but realized my heart wasn't in starting anew as the go-getter I had always been. I was ready to be done. But what to do about money if I wasn't going to work?

I had always lived within my means and was also a compulsive saver, partly to address my lifelong fear of becoming a destitute old lady, especially since I had no kids to rely on. Early in 2014, my financial planner gave me the surprising and welcome news that I'd done such a good job of saving, my money likely would last until I was ninety-five even if I kept spending at the same rate as when I was working. If I were still alive at ninety-five, I suspected both my desire and ability to travel and ski would have diminished and I could comfortably live out my days on my small pensions and social security. I finished up the few consulting jobs I'd taken on and took down my shingle.

I'd been living in Portland, Oregon, for the past fifteen years and had a house, nice "things," a solid network of friends, and a comfortable routine. If I didn't work (I still had trouble calling it retirement at that stage), what would I do? For the first time in my life, I didn't have a five-year plan or vision of the future.

I threw myself into finishing and publishing the novel I had started years before and kept my daily routines and lifestyle. I quickly found that I didn't miss the workplace at all and enjoyed going to the gym, golf course, and grocery store when they were relatively empty in the middle of the day. I was always busy and never bored, but by the summer of 2014, my life had started to feel too conventional and unfocused. I wanted to do something unique and unexpected. I'd always loved traveling as a means of understanding myself and the world and started to dream about traveling full-time. Maybe the next year, 2015. Why not?

When Gayle, a friend of thirty years, suggested she accompany me for a sixtieth birthday celebration in Africa, I was all in. An international trip would be just the thing to help me think about a different way to travel. We chose Zambia on the advice of Jayne, a Portugal-based travel planner who'd helped me virtually with previous Africa trips.

"It's very hot there in October," Jayne said, "but by early November the crowds are gone and the temperature drops. The camps close mid-November when the monsoon starts, so that's a good time to fly down to South Africa for lovely spring weather."

Perfect. I'd spend a few weeks on safari with Gayle, then visit friends in Johannesburg. Finalizing plans for the month-long trip energized me to explore the idea of full-time travel from a practical perspective.

I would have to travel solo, since a decade earlier I'd gotten divorced after twenty years of marriage and, two years before, had ended a lousy divorce-rebound relationship. I'd been dating, but none of the men I met were right for the long term, and I'd given up the fantasy of meeting my soulmate. I suspected I could convince friends to meet me in fun places around the world, but mostly I'd be on my own. I was okay with that.

Physically, I was in good shape with no health problems. Sure, I had a creaky lower back that bugged me if I didn't keep it loose with regular yoga. And there was that pain in my right hip that would flare up unpredictably, although neither hindered my activities. I thought the biggest problem would be international health insurance, but a quick internet search and a few phone calls revealed that it would be easy to get decent coverage.

Yeah, but what about money? To stay within my budget, I'd need to be creative. My biggest expense was my mortgage, so what if I rented out my house for a year and used that money to cover lodging costs on the road? I'd have to buy food whether I was home or not, so that was a wash. As for travel costs, buying one-way plane tickets would be more economical than going round trip a few times a year. If I traveled internationally, I could even get rid of my car and its expenses. My regular budget could become my full-time-travel-way-of-life budget.

I consulted my astrologer (yes, I used an astrologer to feed the part of me that believes that everything isn't always rational or logical). She said the coming year was not only a time to let go of old patterns and baggage, but would be a particularly auspicious time for travel and experiences beyond the familiar. Additionally, the next few years were conducive to spending more time alone, especially contemplative time. And, regardless of whether I traveled, there was a possibility of a karmic relationship sometime in the fall of 2015. Well, I couldn't get a better reading than that.

So why not take advantage of having this rare confluence of free time, no companion, and still enough fitness to haul a suitcase around the world? Why not drink in adventure, feed the quirkiness of my soul that had been buried under career expectations, and minimize regrets when I reached my seventh zero-ending birthday?

I contacted a property management company. Could I command enough rent to cover the mortgage and expenses for the house? Yes, and more, the representative said during an inspection visit, before asking about my timeline.

"I'll be in Africa until the end of November, so I'd like to start a lease in March or April," I said. A consummate planner, I'd need a few months to get organized for my year of travel.

"Then let's get it on the market now. The house will be easier to show if you aren't here," he said, pulling out paperwork from his cloth briefcase. "We can lock in a renter in December or January, and you can start traveling in the spring knowing your house is in good hands."

I signed the papers to keep the ball rolling, knowing I wouldn't have to make any firm commitments—including whether to follow through with the idea at all—before I got back to the United States in December. Then I left for Zambia.

A safari day started early at the comfortably rustic lodges and tent camps, with coffee delivery to our room around five-thirty a.m. and a morning game drive in a three-tiered, open-sided safari vehicle at six. Gayle, a svelte marathon runner with flowing gray hair and a dry sense of humor, had also been to Africa several times, and we both loved watching lions sleeping after a big meal of wildebeest, wild dogs trotting in a dry riverbed, and giraffes elegantly stripping leaves from tall acacia trees. It seemed like I never put down my binoculars, spotting one life-lister bird after another. At the end of each day, we celebrated with "sundowners," the traditional sunset cocktail, complete with a view.

But the weather was something else, with temperatures above 100°F every day. The normal signs of monsoon were absent, humidity was sky high, and the wind felt like a hair dryer on my skin. I figured Jayne hadn't accounted for climate change when she told me things cooled down in November. The country was deep in drought, grasses seared brown and regular water holes dried up. Lions, hyenas, elephants, and zebras sulked in the heat, suggesting a TV nature show with dramatic music playing while a deep-voiced narrator warns that the rains must come for the animals to survive. Including us, I thought. Each night, to help us sleep, Gayle and I took the sarong-sized piece of dense fabric left for us at the bottom of the bed, soaked it in water, and wrapped it around our bodies to evaporate.

The temperature was 113°F the day our guide, James, suggested a short nature walk after lunch, promising a cold drink with ice when we returned. Gayle and I gathered binoculars and cameras while James collected the rifle—a necessity for any hike since, really, there were animals out there that could kill you. We were ten minutes into the walk when I felt cool water falling on my head and arms as we spooked hundreds of cicadas from the acacia trees.

"It's raining!" I said.

"Sorry, Cheryl," James laughed. "That's the cicadas. They pee when they take off." Yuck. I wiped my arms, but the heat had already dried them.

James showed us termite mounds, nocturnal animal tracks in the sand, and other small ecosystem details often overlooked in the hunt for big game. "You know, the park has sixty animal species and four hundred sixty different birds," he said. I didn't know that but thought it auspicious to have all those sixties for my sixtieth.

On our last night in the Park, James took us to a sundowner spot on a bluff overlooking the trickle of water in the Luangwa's sandy riverbed. Scores of southern carmine bee-eaters flew in and out of nest holes in the banks, their pink-red bodies, turquoise crowns, and streaming tails a blur of color in the evening light. A full moon rose in the darkening sky as the birds settled into their nests.

Portland felt far away, but I couldn't help returning to the question of whether to rent out my house for a year and travel—whatever that looked like. Could I afford it? Would I get tired of being on the move or being alone? What did I even mean by "traveling"? Seeing the world, living in a foreign country, or simply not having a home base? I didn't have a clear vision and thought maybe I should forget the whole thing, or at least give myself more time to think about it and *plan*. All week I'd been running the same endless loop of questions through my brain, with no answers.

Stop it, I told myself. Be grateful for this incredible moment on the planet that few people get to experience. Be Zen and be here now. Be like Scarlett O'Hara and think about it tomorrow.

The brilliantly colored bee-eaters would leave soon for South Africa, only to return in April. They didn't stress about the decision to migrate, they just did it. I concentrated on the moon that was now so bright it outshone the stars. I didn't know it then, but a full moon would become a reassuring touchstone to me over the next few years.

———

After South Luangwa, Gayle and I flew to Lusaka for a transfer that would take us to a camp on the Zambezi River, where we'd spend our last week together. In the tiny domestic departure lounge, with randomly placed rows of plastic seating, a few creaky ceiling fans kept the barely cooled air moving among the twenty or so passengers waiting for the small safari flights.

A slightly disheveled blonde woman about my age, wearing a yellow shift and animal-print scarf, was walking around the room trying to sell a huge bouquet of flowers. I wondered who would buy flowers before getting on a small plane to go on safari? She made her way toward me. "Shirlorgale?" she asked with a British accent. I'd never heard of that type of flower before.

"No, thanks," I answered. She moved on to Gayle, asking the same thing: "Shirlorgale?" Gayle shook her head.

Despite the third-world feel of the place, there was an internet connection—something we hadn't had for the past week. I logged on and saw several emails from the property management agency. Turned out my house was a hot property, and they'd already found someone who wanted to move in December 15 and sign a two-year lease. My stomach dropped and my mind started racing. No way.

"What do you think I should do?" I asked Gayle. She shrugged, not even looking up from her computer. She'd been listening to me whine about the same questions all week. Clearly, she was sick of hearing about my dilemma. I was usually pretty good at making decisions. Why was this one so hard?

If I traveled for a year—or two!—I wouldn't only be giving up the security of having a home (something I'd always owned in the past thirty years). I'd also be giving up my friends, my lifestyle, and even my persona. I had been a professional with a law degree, a corporate title, and a rolling five-year plan. Who would I be if I were all alone, flitting from place to place like a vagabond? I relished the idea of seeing more of the world, exploring cultures, and being free to follow a whim or recommendation, but I could still do all that the way I always had—with shorter trips and a home base. I was intrigued by the idea of being "retired" differently than most other people. But I was also scared to try it.

I'd told the company I wouldn't have internet, so I decided to ignore the email. If I lost the renter, so be it. I simply couldn't decide yet.

The woman selling flowers circled back. "Aren't you Shirl?" she said clearly. "Or are you Gale?"

Suddenly I understood. "Oh, yes, I'm Cheryl."

She pressed the flowers into my hands. "I knew it! I'm Jayne—your travel planner—and these are for you. Happy Birthday!"

I was floored. I stuttered a hello and a how and a what.

"I flew in from Portugal on my way to a company meeting here in Lusaka," Jayne explained. "I knew I had only twenty minutes to overlap with your layover, so I didn't want to tell you in advance in case it didn't work out. My local contact here got the flowers for me."

She turned to Gayle and handed her an oblong black box. "Hide this so she doesn't see it." There was no way to hide the label of an expensive French champagne.

Now it was Gayle's turn to look surprised. "Unbelievable! I asked Jayne to make sure we had champagne to celebrate your birthday, but I didn't expect a hand delivery."

The loudspeaker announced that our flight was boarding. We took a few quick photos of each other before saying good-bye to Jayne, then headed out to the plane, the large bouquet cradled like a baby in my arms. How lucky was I to have a longtime friend and an internet stranger pull off a champagne transfer in the middle of Africa? I felt overwhelmed with gratitude.

"You must come to Portugal," Jayne called out after us. "This wasn't a real visit."

"Be careful," I laughed. "I'm known for showing up."

———

There were only two other tourists on the flight that took us south from Lusaka to an airstrip beside the Zambezi River. This river, the fourth longest on the continent, formed the border between Zambia and Zimbabwe. Chris, our guide for the week, met us at the airstrip, then took us to a small motorboat to go upriver to our camp. A hundred hippo eyes and fifty noses peeked out of the water along the way. Chris gave them wide berth. After the heat of South Luangwa, being on the river felt like paradise.

The camp welcome included a cold Mosi beer and the news that there was internet. Better yet, there were also deep wicker chairs on a shaded deck overlooking a reedy channel noisy with birdsong. Three lions were visible on a small island, and directly in front of us, more than fifty elephants were feeding and splashing.

"The elephants are often in camp, day or night," Chris said. "Never try to walk past one. Always call a ranger."

"I love that there are so many," Gayle said. Elephants were among her favorites.

"We have many at the camp because we protect them. But their population in Zambia is in trouble from poaching and habitat loss." We'd already heard plenty from James about the same problem for rhinos and wild dogs.

We finished our beers, then went to our Bedouin-style tent, set under large mahogany trees. Gayle chose one of the two beds and picked up the welcome note artfully arranged with feathers on a tray.

"It's a quote by Karen Blixen, the author of *Out of Africa*. 'If there were one more thing I could do, it would be to go on safari once again.' Perfect." Gayle said.

I put on my reading glasses and picked up the note from my bed. "'A journey of a thousand miles begins with a single step.' Confucius." He was right, of course, and I knew that the single step I needed to take was responding to the property management company.

"I'm going to stop dithering," I said to Gayle. "It's time to change my life." If I left for a year or so to travel, the house and my friends would still be there when I got back. I logged into the internet and sent an email. "Will rent the house starting January 1, but only for eighteen months. Please confirm if these conditions are acceptable." The single step taken, I logged off and got ready for the evening game drive.

That night, I felt strangely calm as I fell asleep to the constant buzz of cicadas and the distant sound of hyenas whooping. If not this tenant, then another, I thought. Either way would be fine.

The affirmative answer came back the next day. Now all I had to do was make a plan for December. My mind swirled with tasks: find a storage unit, arrange movers, figure out mail and health insurance and luggage and phone and, well, a hundred other things. Oh, and decide where to go. But most importantly, I had to resist the urge to plan my next adventure while I was still in the middle of this one.

———————

"Happy Birthday-in-Africa!" Gayle said when a knock on the door at five a.m. signaled our coffee's arrival. We'd flown from Zambia to the Phinda Conservancy in South Africa for our final five days of safari. We had come there specifically to see cheetah—which I'd never seen—but so far with no luck. We only had two days left.

As we were further south than Zambia, the air was brisk at 5:45 when we left on the morning game drive, and I was glad I had the fleece jacket that had seemed so superfluous in Zambia. From the start, we saw more animals than usual. We found a white rhinoceros with a hornless baby the size of a big dog. Further along the dirt track, a pair of rare black rhinos munched on shrubs. Giraffes jumped in the air, front legs extended as they ran. Two baby giraffes cavorted with zebras as if in a children's storybook. A lone wildebeest bounded in front of the car to join the hundreds of others in the field. A family of twenty elephants strolled through a thicket of trees on their way to a water hole.

On that evening's game drive, we spent an hour watching eight fuzzy lion cubs playing and climbing over two lionesses (mom and her sister?) who had lain down in the middle of the road. None of them cared about our camera shutters clicking barely twenty yards away. We finally tore ourselves away from the family scene and were nearly back to camp when we finally saw cheetahs. A mama lying quietly in the grass with her two cubs. They never moved, but I was still thrilled.

"My birthday is truly complete," I said. But it wasn't over yet. That night at dinner, we drank a perfectly chilled bottle of champagne with a sumptuous seafood medley.

"To good friends and exciting journeys," I said, holding up a flute of bubbles and clinking glasses with Gayle.

If this day—and everything that had happened during the entire safari—presaged even a hint of the as-yet-unplanned adventures of the next eighteen months, I'd made the right decision to become a full-time world traveler.

CHAPTER 2

USA

DECEMBER 2014

"Do you have a copy of your visa?" the Virgin Australia agent asked, when I tried to check in for my flight from LAX to Melbourne, Australia. "It's usually linked to the reservation, but I can't find one."

Visa? No, I didn't remember getting a visa. Oh jeez, how stupid could I be? Some world traveler I was. I forgot to get the damn visa. Now what? After a month of nonstop work to get ready for this trip, how long would I have to wait in Los Angeles before the visa came through? I felt sick. And embarrassed.

It was December 31, and I was at the counter with a twenty-six-inch suitcase to check, and a daypack and leather tote to carry on. My Portland home was rented and what belongings I hadn't given away or sold resided in a 10' x 15' storage unit. I was officially a homeless bag lady, the age-old fear transformed into an adventure. I was supposed to fly to Melbourne to spend a week with longtime Australian friend Jenny and her husband, then move on to New Zealand for six weeks. Because I wasn't quite ready to be a full-time traveler, I planned to return to the United States in late February to ski and figure out what was next.

The month of December had been a whirlwind of packing and planning. I updated my will and flew to Pennsylvania to visit my elderly mother, just in case. I gave away furniture, clothes, and housewares, shedding relentlessly. I even started to shed my old environmental career persona, updating my LinkedIn profile to say I was now a writer and traveler. I had "farewell" lunches, dinners, and drinks with friends. I packed my car with skis and winter gear, drove five hundred miles to my brother's house in Idaho, where I would store the car, then flew back to Portland.

Because it was December, I'd often take a break at night to watch a sappy Hallmark Christmas movie. But during the day, I made lists. Packing and moving details. Addresses to change (my brother would get my mail). Things to keep at the front of the storage unit. I wrote each list on large flip-chart pages and pasted them on the walls of my den, like I used to do when facilitating meetings in the corporate world. As soon as I'd cross something off, I'd add three more things. I lived by the lists.

As I stood at the check-in counter at LAX, I realized I had never added "get a visa" to any list. So it didn't get done. The check-in agent's brow knitted as he tapped furiously on the keyboard.

"I forgot to get one," I finally said. "What happens now?" I braced for the worst.

"It's not a problem," the agent said, looking relieved that it wasn't his error. "You can get a visa online in just a few minutes. You have plenty of time." He gave me the web address and airport wifi passcode and told me if I applied online I'd have it within ten minutes. I could only hope he was right.

I put on my reading glasses, easily accessible as a critical piece of my travel wardrobe, and tried to do the application on my iPhone, but the forms didn't show well on the little screen and my fingers were shaking. I lambasted myself for my lack of organization and my cockiness about traveling. Doing the application on the phone would never work. Finally, in frustration, I pulled my laptop from my carry-on and logged in, sweating with anxiety. I also pulled out a magazine and fanned myself. You can do this, I told myself. Buck up.

The laptop was easier to manage than the phone and, as the agent had predicted, I had the confirmed visa in less than ten minutes. I couldn't believe I had made that mistake, even though I had flown over a million miles in my life and had been to Australia three times before. Back at the counter, I watched my checked bag disappear into the bowels of the airport, got my boarding pass, and officially began my adventure as a solo traveler.

———————

In my early teens I had a bulletin board in my girly, powder-blue bedroom. I remember pinning up a *National Geographic* cover photo of a climber nearing the summit of Mount Everest. He was silhouetted against a bright white snowfield, with the most amazing indigo, almost black, sky above, about as different as possible from the Crayola pastel "Sky Blue" of Pennsylvania. Then, my dream wasn't focused enough to be about travel, climbing, or seeing Mount Everest; I simply wanted one day to look up and see a sky the color of the one in the photo.

My roots are in a small coal-mining town in eastern Pennsylvania, where the women worked in the garment factories, the men worked in the mines, and the grandfathers died young from black lung disease. Money was always tight, and family vacations were something only people in the movies did. Travel consisted of a day trip to a baseball game each summer to see the Phillies (my team) or the Yankees (my brother's).

Though I had not yet started to dream of literal traveling, I did understand that, to escape the bleak future of that small coal town, I needed to go to college. After a miserable start at a small liberal arts school in Philadelphia, I got the nerve to spread my wings and transfer to the University of Utah. At nineteen years old, never having been west of Pittsburgh, student loans in hand, I got on an airplane for the first time and landed in what was, to me, an exotic place: Salt Lake City. I'd chosen the large university with its plethora of offerings as a contrast to the narrow choices of the small college, and I'd chosen the location so I could ski on what I thought of as real mountains.

Exploring Utah and nearby Colorado and Wyoming in the mid-1970s, I quickly fell in love with the granite peaks, basalt cliffs, and red rock desert vistas. The grand scale of the landscape made my soul happy in a way the hills, farmland, and dense woods of Pennsylvania never had. There was so much to see, I didn't even think about international travel until after law school, several years later.

By 2014, when I was contemplating travel as a way of life, I'd already incorporated travel as a necessity in my life. I'd ridden the Trans-Siberian Railway in the vastness of eastern Russia and drunk wine in the small towns of Italy, France, and Austria. I had marveled at the unique ecosystems of Australia, watched condors fly in the Andes, and gaped at the giant Moai heads on Easter Island. I'd explored wilderness areas and cities in forty-five of the fifty United States. And, in the last decade, I had discovered the magic of safari in South Africa, Namibia, Botswana, and Zimbabwe. When I traveled, I read about my destinations in advance and carried Berlitz pocket language books if I didn't speak the language. I was always prepared, always time constrained, and almost always with someone else.

But now I'd be a full-time solo female traveler, an expanded version of the intrepid adventurer I liked to think I already was. I would avoid places I thought of as overtouristed as well as those I deemed unsafe, and I'd seek out unique or quirky ways of experiencing the world. I hoped to travel more spontaneously than I had in the past, stay longer in a place I liked or leave earlier anyplace I didn't. I also knew I could stop at any time if I decided I didn't like it, I just wouldn't have a house to go home to.

I was a little bit scared of going it alone, but I had a habit of moving forward, not looking back. And I really did expect to have the time of my life. So, with equal parts trepidation and eagerness, I got on the plane to Melbourne.

CHAPTER 3

AUSTRALIA AND NEW ZEALAND

JANUARY–FEBRUARY 2015

"I feel like I should have a focus for my trip," I said to my friend Jenny a few days after I'd arrived. "You know, the way people search for artisanal textiles or take pilgrimage hikes."

"Didn't you say yesterday that your intention was to be spontaneous? To *not* have a purpose?"

"Well, yes, but isn't that lame? I've been thinking about a photo-of-the-day project as a sort of documentary." I was a neophyte with photography, but I had invested in a new 35mm SLR camera, regular and telephoto lenses, and six memory cards.

"For a year and a half, that would be almost five hundred photos," Jenny pointed out. "Don't you think there might be some days you don't want to carry the camera with you?"

"I think it might force me to pay attention to what I'm seeing and learn how to use my camera, too." I fiddled with the lenses while we talked.

"I think you need to relax and pay attention without the camera," Jenny said, motioning to the view.

Here in the postcard-perfect town of Sorrento, on the Mornington Peninsula south of Melbourne, the coastline stretched forever, the ocean waves lapping at sandy beaches and rocky peninsulas, seabirds circling above. Jenny was right, of course. I was completely missing the point by focusing on goals and projects instead of what was right in front of me, what I had come to see. I had a lot to learn about this new way of life.

After a week of fresh mussels from the sea and sage advice from Jenny, I left the haven of Sorrento and flew to the small town of Nelson, New Zealand, on the northwest corner of the South Island. There I was to meet Suzanne, a Swedish woman I'd agreed to travel with after my sister introduced us (virtually) because we were both planning to be in New Zealand alone during the same time. Via email, Suzanne had offered to plot an itinerary and make reservations for us, which came as a welcome relief during my crazy December. I also liked the idea of sharing quarters—and costs—since I was still apprehensive about how to afford full-time travel.

When I landed in Nelson, I was greeted by replicas of *Lord of the Rings* characters hanging from the airport ceiling and kiosks selling film location tours. Even though it had been at least fifteen years since the movies had been filmed there, the country was clearly still proud. Too bad I wasn't a fan. Suzanne had arrived earlier that day and gone on to the B&B she had booked for us. Because she said she wasn't comfortable driving on the left side of the road, I picked up the rental car she had reserved for us at the airport.

"Here are the keys," a perky young man said. "It's a Nissan." The paperwork showed the car category as "Cheap and Cheerful Budget Model with High Kilometers." Not quite what I was used to after years of renting cars on business travel.

In the first row of the parking lot, I found the ancient, dingy grey car, with the ironic model name of Sunny. The car had deep scratches on the door as if it had been keyed, roll-down windows, and a trunk with a sticky latch. The radio didn't work, but thankfully the air conditioning did. We were planning to cover a lot of miles, and I wondered if Sunny had it in her to go the distance.

I found Suzanne reading in the garden of the B&B. She looked stereotypically Scandinavian: statuesque, tall, with long blonde hair and a crooked smile. Over tea she told me she had moved to D.C. thirty years before when she had married an American, had two children in college, had recently lost her job, and had time on her hands, which was why she was on this trip. She said she loved discussing politics, adamantly supported increased gun control, and considered herself a Communist. I thought her strong Swedish accent made her sound exotic.

I told Suzanne I was single and happy about that for now, had recently retired from the corporate world, and had published my first novel the year before. I said I loved skiing, was hedonistically planning to travel for a year and a half, found politics somewhat boring, and considered myself an environmentalist with a practical bent. I was afraid my American accent made me sound unrefined.

During our first few days in Nelson, we discovered we did not have similar tastes in food, wine, or lifestyles. And I wondered if it was a mistake to have agreed to share lodging since I was already missing my private time. But Suzanne had planned an itinerary that I had bought into for the next five weeks, and we did both look forward to the scenery and adventure that New Zealand offered, so I figured things would work out.

From Nelson, we drove to Abel Tasman National Park, where we hiked over headlands thick with ferns and along sandy beaches lapped by deep-turquoise waves. We marveled at the clarity of the water at Te Waikoropupū Springs, the largest freshwater springs in the Southern Hemisphere, where I barely held back from scolding the tourist who put his hand in the water despite all the signs strictly forbidding it. I drove Sunny the Car on the famously steep and winding Queen Charlotte Sound Drive, wondering if the engine would make it on the way up and the brakes would hold on the way down.

After about two weeks, Suzanne and I left the north and east coasts to head inland over high passes and into the heart of the mountains, with snow-covered peaks towering above turquoise glacial lakes. At the base of Mount Cook, the highest peak in New Zealand, I posed beside the statute of Sir Edmund Hillary, who trained in these ice-covered mountains for his epic Everest climb. We hiked to raging waterfalls and hilltops with breathtaking panoramic views. I saw a million unfamiliar stars in the dark sky of Lake Tekapo.

The scenery was so spectacular, I couldn't believe that I had started to feel annoyed—by the unimaginative food, the polite reserve of the people, Suzanne's stories about her children, and just about everything else. Was stopping at the must-see places and moving on every day or two too much like the kind of guidebook-driven vacation travel I had often done, but now wanted to avoid? Or was the problem that I wasn't actually traveling solo like the intrepid world-traveler image I'd been playing with? Whatever the cause, I felt it was arrogant to be annoyed so early into my life-as-travel experiment.

I decided my inner introvert was craving time alone, so I convinced Suzanne she could drive on the left side and suggested she take Sunny south without me once we got to Queenstown in a few days. I'd stay in the mountains to try to rekindle my enthusiasm, testing out the unplanned vagabond adventure way of travel. We'd meet up again two weeks later for the four-day rails-to-trails bike trip (my contribution to her planning) that we'd committed to before we left the States. She seemed as happy with the new itinerary as I was.

———

Before parting ways, Suzanne and I spent a night in Queenstown, a resort town on a beautiful lake with scores of restaurants, busloads of tourists, and the added frenzy of trying to be the adventure capital of the world. Adrenaline was the key word in the offerings for bungee jumping, canyon swinging, zip-lining, skydiving, hang gliding, white-water rafting, jet-boating, parasailing, river surfing, rock climbing, abseiling, mountaineering, or even plain old hiking.

One night was enough for me. Suzanne kept Sunny, and I picked up a newer rental car with working amenities like a radio and automatic windows. I'd found a room at Lake Wanaka, a slow-paced family getaway town an hour north of Queenstown. At my cute B&B, run by a friendly couple about my age, I sat on my little balcony, poured myself a glass of wine, and watched the sun drop in the sky. Alone at last.

I had been diligently photographing New Zealand in all its wide-angle and telephoto splendor, so I fiddled with deleting or editing shots for my Photo-a-Day project. The photography had been frustrating, and despite all my efforts—including a twelve-hour National Geographic internet class—I still hadn't mastered f-stops and ISOs. Usually my not-very-artful shot-of-the-day was the one taken on the Intelligent Auto setting and, even with cropping, was not particularly interesting. I poured a second glass of wine. I didn't enjoy the project, so why keep doing it? I'd already abandoned the plan to travel to the south with Suzanne, so why not abandon the photography project too? Who needed a goal anyway? I put the camera away and felt like maybe, just maybe, I was feeling lighter and happier.

By my second day at Lake Wanaka, I knew I liked it there and decided to stay for the rest of the week, enjoying the freedom of changing plans on a whim. *This* was the kind of travel I'd imagined. I settled in, walking quiet neighborhoods in the morning, chatting with people trimming roses in their yards, and listening to shopkeepers complain about the drought and the terrible growing Chinese influence on New Zealand.

Afternoons, I went wine tasting in the nearby Central Otago region, where I met people who had worked in Oregon (reverse wine seasons) and even knew people I knew. I was treated like royalty, passed from one personal tour to the next. Although I'd always buy a bottle or two, I was often given a free one too because of the shared Oregon experience, and soon I had a full case of wine in the trunk.

One thing I hadn't done yet was fly-fish. A mecca for hard-core fly-fishers, New Zealand was renowned for its big brown trout and pristine streams. I wasn't hard core, but I'd fished for years. I decided to ask my B&B host about finding a guide.

"I know just the man for the job. My friend Bruce is the best guide there is. He's based in Queenstown but knows this country like the back of his hand. Been guiding for years, including the rich guys who want the best. The only problem is, on such short notice he probably won't be available. But here's his number."

My karma was good that day. Bruce told me he'd just had a cancellation and was free for three days, then had a one-day gig but was free for another three days after that. I told him I had a budget and could afford two days of his time plus a hotel room at high-season rates in Queensland, or three days of his time if we were fishing somewhere further out with cheaper lodging costs.

"No worries," he said, in a thick Kiwi accent. "We'll do three days. Look, we won't know where the fish are biting, so we don't want to commit to lodging ahead of time. We might stay at some cabins I know or, if you are up for it, we might camp out—I have all the gear, so you don't need anything, including a rental car. I'll meet you at noon in Queenstown day after tomorrow and we'll go from there."

"Should I make a reservation in Queenstown for that night to be sure I have a place?"

"Naaahhh," he said, his accent broad. "We can always find you something." I pictured a run-down hostel, especially since I'd made a point about the budget and Bruce knew nothing much else about me. "And I've got two guest rooms at my house if we can't. No worries," he said again. "We'll work it out."

I was nervous about this laissez-faire attitude but decided Bruce was a professional guide and I needed to trust him. I wished I didn't even have to think about whether it was safe to go off for a few days with a man I didn't know, guide or not. I decided to see how it went once we met and adjust accordingly.

Bruce was waiting for me when I got to the rental car drop-off in Queenstown. He opened the tailgate of his SUV and tossed my luggage inside. When he loaded the case of wine I had accumulated during my tastings, he laughed and said something about my knowing how to travel well.

Bruce was about my age, fit, and only slightly taller than I am, which most people would call short at five foot three. He had a pleasant, hangdog kind of smile and an easy manner. After the first few minutes, I felt completely comfortable with him and my decision to hire him for a few days. It would be okay.

"We'll head to my house to pick up the boat and go out on Lake Wakatipu this afternoon," Bruce said. "We can get the gear sorted, then try some rivers tomorrow." I suspected his plan was to see if I knew how to cast a fly rod.

"You can have a look-see at the guest rooms when we get to the house," he said as he drove up a steep road high above Queenstown. "If you feel comfortable there, it'll make things easier for planning and getting going in the morning. But if you want a hotel, it's no worries. I'll just come and get you." He was so casual, I assumed he lived with his family and a client/houseguest was a regular occurrence.

But no, when we arrived it was clear he lived alone, on a hill with an incredible view of the lake with mountains behind, in a nice house that was not fancy or ostentatious, as an American home might be with a view like that. Bruce showed me the house and guest rooms, then told me to think about whether I wanted to stay there while he got the gear ready. I imagined a horror movie about a stupid American woman getting into an awkward-at-best and dangerous-at-worst situation, with the audience thinking, "Don't stay—nobody knows you are there— what about scissors and a shower curtain?"

While he was outside, I poked around. One guest room was on the main floor, next to a private bathroom. Bruce's space was at the end of the hall, at the back of the house. The other room was a loft above the living room, with a pull-down ladder for access. If things turned weird, I thought, I could pull up the ladder at night. Not that I had any indication they would. But as a solo female traveler, I had to be prepared. Also, though, I had to learn to go with my gut feel. I picked the loft and told Bruce I'd stay.

———————

After a sunny afternoon on the lake and a few big fish, it was late when we headed back to the house, so Bruce suggested we eat at home. He cooked pasta with red sauce and made a big salad (a welcome change from restaurant food), and I contributed a bottle of wine. I must have passed the casting test, so for the next two days, Bruce and I drove down washboard dirt roads, opened and closed gates, and climbed over fences. We fished some of the most pristine and private waters I'd ever seen. But there was a dark side. Cows.

New Zealand, famous for its sheep, had less than half as many as it used to but a lot more cows. The demand for milk solids in Asia had exploded, and corporations bought out small sheep farmers to create large dairy operations. Grass was needed to feed the cows, so nitrates were used as fertilizer, subsequently getting into both surface and ground water. Animal waste, its disposal not well regulated, polluted the rivers. And the increased demand for water had even caused some streams to dry up.

"We have to work hard to find the good fishing because a lot of my regular places are gone or are too polluted," Bruce explained. "I rent helicopters for the clients with money, to fish the headwaters in the mountains."

The second night we ate in again, tired after a long day of fishing. Bruce grilled chicken and I contributed more wine. We had one more day of fishing and I had one more night at his house. After that, I had a few empty days before meeting Suzanne again. I asked Bruce for suggestions.

"If you like it here," he said, "you should stay all week. I have that commitment for day after tomorrow, but then we can go into the interior and see if we can catch some old boys in the deep holes. The day you're supposed to check into your B&B for the bike trip, we'll fish a good spot nearby, then I'll drop you off."

It was the ideal solution for me—it meant I didn't need to get a rental car or move from this comfortable house—but, uncharacteristically, I hadn't even asked how much it would cost me for the two nights I stayed at his house. I had no idea whether I could afford to stay longer, but there was no question I couldn't afford more guiding. I told Bruce as much, but with my thanks for the offer.

"No worries," he laughed. "I'm really enjoying the company—and your wine—and I never intended to charge you to stay here. It's my house! Let's say you pay for the first three days of guiding. After that, we're just two friends fishing together."

I protested, but he would hear nothing different. My gut feeling had been correct; everything was safe, professional, and fun. We did fish as friends for the next few days, with Bruce going off to catch his own fish, not always hovering nearby to help me. At one stream, he harvested and boiled yabbies (a type of crayfish) for lunch and served them in half an avocado with salt and a cold beer. A perfect meal.

On our final fishing day, far in the interior away from any towns or other people, I hunted a huge brown trout. I watched my dry fly drift in the current, patiently giving the fish a chance to see it. I let the silence of the empty landscape wash over me, concentrating on nothing else in the world except that fly. It didn't matter whether I caught that fish; my soul was nourished.

I realized my ennui was gone. And I didn't know it then, but I had started learning how a great guide, especially one who became a friend, could make a huge difference in how I experienced a place.

———————

"Be prepared for extremely hot temperatures, wear sunscreen, and beware of dehydration." Thus warned the website for the 152-kilometer, four-day, point-to-point Central Otago Rail-to-Trail bike ride from Clyde to Middlemarch. Ten thousand people a year rode all four days, as I was planning to. Suzanne was riding the shorter middle two days, shuttling Sunny the rest of the time.

The first three days of riding were pleasant because the air was cool, and unpleasant because the wind kept increasing—and was, more often than not, a headwind. The trail wound through grassy fields, across deep gorges, and into tunnels through the rocky hills. I'd expected lots of riders, but I'd only seen six the first day, four the second, and two the third, when a cold front had moved in. Suzanne and I were both chilled to the bone by the time we got to our guesthouse in a mostly abandoned railroad depot town. As with our other accommodations, we were the only guests; the proprietors lived elsewhere. That night, a howling wind made the whole building creak and groan, making sleep difficult. I was glad Suzanne was there or I would have been spooked.

I was looking forward to the final day, the longest mileage but almost all downhill. I woke up at dawn to rain pelting the window and fresh snow on the nearby peaks. The thermometer on the porch, where the wind had blown all the furniture into a corner, read 40°F. Purple clouds hung over the mountains, and it didn't look like anything would change soon. Nobody in their right mind would ride in that unseasonable weather if they didn't have to. Especially on a trail with no cell coverage. And only two road intersections. And no people. But I remembered a T-shirt a friend had given me with the slogan "Because I Said I Would." I decided to ride.

I put on my bike shorts, tights, and rain pants, plus five layers of clothing on top—pretty much everything I had brought with me for the summer climate. I dug into my luggage for a pair of souvenir sheepskin gloves I had bought weeks before in the artsy town of Geraldine.

Suzanne would drive the car along a scenic route and meet me that afternoon at the country tavern that served as the end point. In telling her what time to meet me, I added two hours to the predicted time to account for the weather.

I wish I could say that bike ride was fun. But it was the most miserable day of riding I'd ever had. Gale force headwinds blew me over twice and made me keep the bike in climbing gear the entire time, even though the trail was supposedly downhill. The rain came in squalls, once turning to a hail that forced me to stop and tuck my face into my hood. When the rain stopped, I ate an energy bar and pulled out my camera to capture the stunning beauty of golden hills, angry-dark storm clouds, and snow-dusted purple peaks in the distance. There wasn't a single other rider; they must have read the weather reports—or looked out the window. I tried to appreciate the solitude but felt like I was in a five-hour spin class from hell, barely able to get the pedals to do a single rotation. I cursed the hubris that had made me want to complete the trail by riding this fourth day—even though nobody but me gave a damn.

When I finally saw Sunny parked outside the tavern, it was an hour past the time I'd given Suzanne. My fingers were frozen to the handlebars and my feet were numb. But I was exhilarated. I laughed at the warnings from the website about heat, sun, and dehydration and decided the only one I had to worry about was the last. Dammit, it was summer in New Zealand, so I ordered a cold beer—to drink when I finished my hot cup of tea.

———————

My final weeks in New Zealand, I was back on my own. I had several revelations. First, I realized that driving around looking at scenery from a car window had been part of my earlier problem. I preferred experiencing nature, not merely looking at it. That's why the fishing and biking were so much more satisfying than the sightseeing.

Second, for me travel was enriched by interaction with locals or other travelers. And that seemed to be easier when I was by myself. During a few days in the Marlborough wine region on the North Island, I met three local women who invited me to lunch. I got a private tour of the kitchen of a trendy restaurant when I complimented the chef. I heard more worries from bartenders, waiters, and shopkeepers about the increasing presence of China in New Zealand. And two nights in a row, I stayed up late drinking wine with people from Austria I met at my B&B.

After those two nights I realized travel was indeed becoming my life, not just a temporary status. If I were on vacation, I might eat that croissant, give up that day of exercise, have another glass of wine, or stay up late for two nights in a row. But I wasn't on vacation, and bad choices took their toll. I still needed to eat right, exercise, watch how much I drank, and get a good night's sleep, just like at home. Well, with the occasional splurge, of course. After all, one of my favorite sayings had always been Oscar Wilde's "Moderation in all things, including moderation."

Finally, I accepted that if a traveling life was my new "normal" life, every day wouldn't be like a vacation day, packed with activity or filled with some extraordinary experience. Some days would be, for lack of a better term, boring. Mundane. Some places too. There would always be the day-to-day grind to find food and lodging, to organize the next leg of travel, to pay the bills. My romanticized view of being a full-time traveler was just that … romanticized. I hoped I'd remember the many lessons of New Zealand when I was back in the States, trying to figure out what to do for the next sixteen months.

CHAPTER 4

USA

FEBRUARY–APRIL 2015

It was snowing hard when I arrived in Idaho, where my car, fully loaded with ski gear, awaited me at my brother Victor's house. Good thing I'd stopped in Portland at my storage unit to stash the sundresses and pick up a down jacket, gloves, and boots.

"What are your plans now?" my brother asked over dinner.

"I'm going to chase the storms looking for deep powder and be a real ski bum," I said, knowing full well I had substantially more financial means than any mere bum. Yet I was still wary of this new way of life fitting in my budget, so I'd bought a multi-area ski pass that allowed me to ski cheaply around the West. Plus, I had invitations to visit friends in Colorado, Wyoming, Idaho, Oregon, and California, which would save significant money on lodging.

It was a good plan, except for the chase-the-storms part. A high-pressure system settled over the entire West a week after I arrived, which meant clear skies and no snow. If it did snow somewhere, the distances between ski areas were too far for me to get there in time to ski fresh powder. Instead, I spent sunny afternoons making turns on warm corn snow and drinking beer après-ski.

When I wasn't with friends, I reveled in my solitary freedom on the open road of the western United States. During long drives between states, I saw deer, elk, moose, coyotes, bald eagles, trumpeter swans, mountain bluebirds, and red-tailed hawks. I sang along to the radio's never-ending supply of country-and-western songs. And I even stopped to take pictures of the sun-splashed red sandstone formations, black-as-night basalt columns, and gray granite peaks, but never once considered reviving my ill-fated photography project. I had a car full of "stuff" and gloried in having more than two pairs of pants to choose from, and my favorite pillow to sleep on.

I spent a lot of that solo driving time thinking about how to approach the upcoming year. I wanted to do the physical things that might become difficult as I got older, stay within my budget, be safe, and explore places I'd never been. I wanted to mix up the travel experience, sometimes staying in a place for a week or a month and sometimes moving through. Geography and scenery were important, but not all-encompassing, as I had learned in New Zealand. And I wanted what I did to be a bit quirky, not standard tourist fare. With these parameters in mind, where to go?

I'd never been to the Middle East, but that area struck me as too much of a tinderbox, and I didn't relish supporting cultures so oppressive to women. A grand tour of European capitals seemed to be a different extreme—too tame, too urban, and easily done when I was older. I thought about taking buses from Mexico to the tip of Argentina, but that backpacker travel method, especially traveling alone, seemed like too much hassle and not enough comfort for a woman my age. I had never been to Asia, so maybe that was an idea. I'd just been to Africa, but that continent offered plenty more to explore, as long as I felt safe. Cruises were out of the question for three reasons: I got seasick if I so much as watched an ocean movie, I was sure I'd feel claustrophobic on a ship, and from my work I knew the big ships were often an environmental and cultural disaster for the port cities. My apologies to cruisers, but it was not for me.

I scoured travel and tour websites, looking for both trips and ideas. I read about active adventures cycling in Vietnam, hiking in Patagonia, or paddleboarding in China. There were articles about the top ten restaurants or bars in every imaginable place. I could be an "impactful" traveler, volunteer-to-do-good traveler, sustainable traveler, or authentic traveler, whatever that meant. I could rent vacation homes, house-sit for professors on sabbatical, climb mountains, or take epic train rides. I needed advice, so I called my friend James.

James had spent twenty years with a large international adventure travel company before exchanging the stress of corporate life for that of owning a Salmon River rafting company in Idaho, Middle Fork River Expeditions. "I've got two ideas for you," he said, after I described my indecision. "My friend John runs small custom river trips around the world. Go with him to the Balkans this summer for a peek into the interior instead of the popular coast."

His second recommendation, which he called a must-do, was to trek to the little-visited Mustang area of Nepal, where many Tibetans had fled when the Chinese invaded. His friend Stan, who authored some of the first guidebooks about trekking in Nepal and Bhutan, had been running trips there for decades. I'd never heard of the region, which was pronounced "Moostang," but just the sound of it was exotic and going there seemed to be the kind of off-the-beaten-track travel I wanted to do.

"Do the Mustang trip now," James told me. "The Chinese are going to build a road soon, and that will change the place. You'll start from Pokhara, where Stan lives. Afterwards you can volunteer for a few weeks at the school for Tibetan refugee children that Stan supports. I took my kids there last year and they loved it."

I wasn't so sure about the school volunteering part since I'd never had kids nor been around them, but the rest of it sounded good. Within a few weeks, I had signed up for the June river rafting trip in the Balkans, the August trek to Mustang, and, keeping my fingers crossed that it would be fun, two weeks of volunteering at the school after the trek. And since I really wanted to go to Bhutan, I asked Stan to organize a trip there after my volunteer stint.

Now I felt anchored and started adding other plans to the calendar. I decided to start by living in Krakow and studying Polish for six weeks before going to Croatia. My heritage on my mother's side was Polish, and I always liked trying to learn new languages, despite not being good at retaining vocabulary. After the Balkans river trip, my friend Kathleen from Portland would meet me to travel through Bulgaria and eastern Romania. We'd end our time together in Transylvania, so I signed up for a week-long group hiking trip in the mountains that would start the day after she left.

Even though I now had plans through October with only a few short gaps and wasn't really being an unfettered vagabond, my sense of spontaneity persisted, partly because I didn't have all the details nailed down, and partly because I didn't know where I'd go after Bhutan. Stan told me I had to have a ticket to leave Bhutan before I could get into the country, so I booked a flight back to Kathmandu, where there would be plenty of international destinations to choose from later.

Ski season was ending, and my departure date of April 30 was coming up fast. Maybe because I was starting off on my own, this time felt like the real start of my adventure. Facing the daunting task of how to pack for six months of spring, summer, and fall in both European cities and the Himalayan mountains, I went to Portland and visited my storage unit. I could have filled a suitcase with shoes alone but finally whittled the pile down to fit into the same luggage I had taken for my six weeks in New Zealand: a twenty-six-inch checked roller-bag, a small backpack, and a tote. I was quite proud of my restraint, even though I also sent a small package of what I considered to be "city clothes" to the apartment I'd rented in Poland.

My final act before getting on the plane—one that felt almost more final than the day I moved out of my house—was to sell my 1998 Volvo station wagon. Obviously I'm not a car aficionado, or I would have owned one that was less than seventeen years old, but that car had been one of the most reliable things in my life over the past two decades. I sent a message to people I knew in Portland and quickly learned that my trusty Volvo would have a good home; a close friend bought it for her daughter to use at college.

The day before I left, I was at my storage unit checking for last-minute things I might need. As I moved a small backpack out of the way, I realized it held my old travel journals. I pulled out a few volumes and read random entries. Some events I barely remembered, while others were still fresh in my mind.

I laughed when I read an entry from my first overseas trip to the Philippines almost thirty-five years earlier: "I'm convinced that traveling alone is only fun if you are going where English is spoken." I hoped I had become a different person than that young woman as I set off alone to visit a bunch of countries where English was definitely not prevalent. Happily, by this stage of my life I had perfected the art of using smiles and hand gestures.

CHAPTER 5

ROME, ITALY

MAY 2015

The Rome airport arrivals area teemed with well-dressed men who held up signs bearing the names of arriving passengers. As my flight to Krakow included a long layover in Rome, I'd extended my stay for a couple of days since I'd never been to the Eternal City. I'd arranged for a driver from my hotel to meet me, a habit I'd acquired years before to ease transition into a new place after a long international flight.

I walked back and forth several times, searching the three-deep crowd for my name. No luck. My flight had arrived half an hour early, but my experience was that drivers always knew if flights were early or late. I decided to call the hotel to check.

I tried four times before I realized I didn't have cell service. I had canceled my U.S. service, intending to get a cheaper SIM card for each country I visited, even though I'd never used that option before. I found an Information desk and asked the chic young Italian woman working there to call the hotel for me.

"We aren't allowed to make phone calls outside of the airport," she told me, in her perfect English and her perfect eye makeup. "You can buy a SIM card over there." She pointed to a kiosk. For some reason, I thought buying and installing a SIM card at the airport would be an expensive mistake and a big hassle, and I wasn't sure I wanted one for only four days anyway.

I was too warm in the stuffy airport: I'd been in the same clothes for more than twenty-two hours, my hair was flat, and rivulets of sweat ran down my back. The outdoorsy green backpack I was wearing didn't help, besides making me feel very unchic. I asked Ms. Perfect how much a cab to the city would cost. She rattled off a number three times what I'd already prepaid for my nonexistent ride, then looked behind me to help the next person in line. She was done with bedraggled me.

As I moved aside, I told myself this was part of traveling (and why some people hate it) and I should just go with the flow, take a cab, and not worry about the money. Although it was morning in Rome, my body clock thought it was midnight, and I was tired. I must have been nuts to think I wanted to travel alone. I wanted somebody to discuss options with, or help me decide what to do, or even sit with the luggage so I could look for the driver unencumbered. The forty-three pounds of my bags, which had seemed so light when I left Portland, suddenly weighed me down. I hadn't even brought an Italian phrase book to help me get by. Buck up and manage, I told myself.

I walked the greeter line one more time. Damn. Still no placard with my name on it—and a lot fewer people overall. I rummaged in my tote to find the address of the hotel, huffed a huff as only a disgruntled American can, and started toward the door to get a taxi. And saw my name. A short, round fellow haphazardly held his sign as he came through the revolving door. Magic, pure luck, or good karma—I didn't care which and was relieved I'd seen the sign at all. The driver was startled when I stopped him.

"How are you here already?" he said. "Your flight is only landing now." Thank goodness he spoke English.

"It came early," I said. "I've been here for a while."

"I am so sorry," he said, quickly taking my suitcase and backpack from me. "We usually get a notice when a flight is early. I did not get one. I am so sorry."

"No problem," I lied.

He led me to a clean car in the parking garage. I settled into the back seat with a welcome bottle of cold water and stared out the window as he drove to the hotel. For a Friday morning, there was little traffic, and most storefronts were shuttered in that European way of rolling down a graffiti-covered garage door in front of the shop.

"Why no traffic? And closed shops? Is something going on?" I asked the driver.

"It's May 1. Labor Day. Big holiday, so everything is closed. Most of the tourist places should be open, though."

I laughed at myself and my amateurish mistakes. Some world traveler I was. I arrived on a national holiday I hadn't paid attention to (although I knew it was celebrated throughout Europe), without even a cheat sheet of Italian phrases, and no way to make a phone call. I realized how dependent I had become on having ready access to information on my phone, and when it—and the internet—didn't work, I had no backup. I had either gotten sloppy or less compulsive, or both. I didn't know if either of those options were a good thing.

But one thing I did know: if this was the worst thing that happened during my travels, then I would be very lucky indeed.

———————

"The Colosseum is easy to find," the desk clerk said as he marked the way with a yellow highlighter. "It's only twenty minutes away."

A walk was what I needed to de-fuzz my brain and de-kink my body. I left the tiny side street of my hotel on the Capitoline Hill and joined the crowds on the main street. I went around the traffic circle at Piazza Venezia, with its huge statue in the center—somebody famous, I thought, before seeing on my map that it was Victor Emmanuel II. I still didn't know who that was, even though I thought I should. I made a detour down an appealing street, thinking I'd simply go around the block and then get back on track.

But there was no such thing as "around the block" in Rome. The streets meandered like a stream, changing both direction and name every hundred meters, sometimes spinning back to a major arterial and other times leading to dumpsters in an alley. I'd never had a good sense of direction and relied heavily on GPS. Which I didn't have without a SIM card.

I was lost but not worried, so I pulled out my map. Despite my reading glasses, I couldn't decipher the small print matching the teeny side streets. I decided to retrace my steps, but everything looked the same and I had no idea if I was even going in the right direction. It was early afternoon, so I kept walking, happy for the exercise and assuming I'd eventually run across a landmark I could find in big print on my map. Two smartly dressed couples stopped me and asked, in Italian, for directions to the Colosseum. Could they possibly think I looked like a local who knew where I was going? I answered in English that I had no idea, but I felt better not being the only one who couldn't find it.

I'm pretty sure I walked up and down each of the seven hills of Rome before I finally saw a sign pointing to the Colosseum. I'd been walking for an hour and half when I turned a corner and the massive ruin jumped up in front of me as if to say, "You silly thing, walking all around me for hours and not seeing me." Perhaps it was right, but I *had* seen a lot of the Roman neighborhoods. I went inside.

The Colosseum, in its day, could hold over fifty thousand people to watch the gladiator games. It seemed like thirty thousand were there on this day, and twenty thousand of them had selfie sticks, which were sold on the street for five Euros (or five dollars), alongside postcards and sunglasses. It was tough to get in close enough to read the information panels without fear of getting poked in the eye with a stick. I wondered if the spectators back then complained about the crowds.

My irritation was soon overshadowed by my disgust at the magnitude of death perpetrated in the arena. Besides the routine games, the info panels informed me, the emperor Nero ordered—for a single day-long event—ten thousand gladiators to fight to the death against eleven thousand wild animals, including hippos, leopards, lions, wolves, and elephants. Magnificent animals I traveled far and wide to see, mostly endangered now. My stomach turned as I imagined the spectacle of blood and guts pouring out of dead men and animals. I found an exit and escaped. As I stood on the sidewalk, tourists streamed around me. I needed something to brush away that residue of death by sport. I needed to have a glass of wine. And breathe.

I followed the crowded pedestrian boulevard away from the Colosseum, passing through the artists spray-painting pictures, the musicians dressed in American Indian buckskin pants and full headdresses, the sunglass and selfie-stick sellers, the swami sitting in midair without support, and the muscled young men in gladiator costumes who would pose with you for a fee. A few blocks away from the crush of the tourists, I found an inviting corner café with only a few midafternoon customers. The sun-dappled outdoor table was perfect, and when the waiter showed up I ordered a glass of crisp rosé.

The sun warmed my skin, and the dry pink wine had the distant taste of cherries. I hadn't expected to be knocked off balance by ancient history, but I was happy to be right there, right then, on a corner in Rome.

The next day, I was determined to be a good tourist, despite my Colosseum experience and my general dislike of doing touristy things. Since I only had one day, I dutifully sought out the Roman Forum's tall columns, the Spanish Steps, and the Trevi Fountain, which, it turned out, was closed for repairs, but no one had removed the thousands of coins lying on the dry bottom. Suddenly, the day was gone, and it was my final night in Rome. I found my way to a nearby restaurant recommended by the receptionist at the hotel. I drank Tuscan wine, ate boiled rabbit and spring vegetable pasta, and remembered why I always liked traveling to Italy.

I was walking back to the hotel along a pedestrian mall when I heard music. A crowd of people of all ages surrounded a small stage. The band was playing classic rock-and-roll. I stopped to listen. Between songs, an emcee solicited donations for the Rome Emergency Services. Fire dancers appeared and twirled in front of the stage. The moon, one day shy of being full, rose over the centuries-old buildings and illuminated the Italian night sky, filling me with a sense that everything was going to work out just fine.

I blended into the crowd and danced with the Romans, singing in English along with everyone else to familiar oldies, certain I'd never forget that night, even though now I don't remember which songs they played.

CHAPTER 6

POLAND

MAY–JUNE 2015

"Hello, my name is Cheryl," I said to a grey-templed man seated at the end of the U-shaped table in the bright and cheery corner classroom. I had arrived early for the first day of Polish language school in Krakow, only to find six students already seated quietly in the room. I had decided to break the ice and introduce myself.

"Stuart," he said with a British accent and a handshake. I asked him where he was from.

"I'm from London, but I spent most of my life in Norway, and now my girlfriend and I have moved here." I was relieved to have another student my age in the class.

A few seats down, I extended my hand to a pretty, blond teenager. "Hi, I'm Cheryl."

"Anna," she answered.

"Nice to meet you. Where are you from?" I asked. Anna looked nervously around the room.

A young Asian woman sitting next to Anna spoke to her in Russian. Although I had studied Russian in college forty years earlier, I obviously didn't remember much since I didn't have a clue what they said to each other. The Asian woman extended her hand to shake mine and said, "I am Jin Kyung, from South Korea. Anna does not speak English." Jeesh, it had not occurred to me that the other students might not be English speakers. I simply smiled and decided not to embarrass myself any further by trying to say a few words in Russian. It was going to be hard enough to deal with the Polish language.

I was shaking hands with Jin Kyung when a twenty-something man bustled into the room, arms full of papers and cards. He put his finger to his lips and said, "Shhh." He motioned to me and said something in Polish, which I obviously didn't understand. He repeated in English, "Please sit down and no English. We will speak only Polish in the classroom." He went to the front of the room and arranged his things.

Chastised, I sat and folded my hands like the other students and waited for class to begin.

I had arrived the day before, on a Sunday, and checked into a lovely European-style apartment I'd rented for my six weeks in Krakow. The flat was in one of three buildings in a complex, with a security guard at the entrance. The twelve-foot ceilings and six-foot windows made the space seem airy and spacious even though it consisted of only a great room, bedroom, and bathroom. Because it was owned by an American couple from Minnesota, I found all the things an American would expect: fully stocked kitchen, dining table for six, comfortable couch, good pillows and linens, and a cable TV and internet connection. I could hear a pianist in a neighboring apartment expertly practicing Chopin. Oh, how Polish, I thought as I unpacked my overstuffed luggage, set up my computer, and arranged the notebook and pens I'd brought for school on the dining room table. Everything was perfect. I felt right at home.

Both because I was worried about the weight of my luggage and because I was planning to travel in a different way than in the past, I didn't bring any guidebooks with me. But luckily, the owners had left some brochures and tourist maps, so I plotted my path to the Stare Miasto—the old town—to explore my new hometown and take advantage of the gorgeous warm and sunny spring day. The medieval square in the Stare Miasto was an easy ten-minute walk from my apartment. I passed through a narrow park into a huge cobblestoned pedestrian space, lined with crowded outdoor cafés on all four sides.

Anchoring two opposite corners of the square, I saw a large, imposing church and a smaller, copper-domed church. My tourist map identified these as the 700-year-old St Mary's Basilica and a tenth-century Catholic church. I also saw notations on the map for several statues of Pope John Paul II, who had studied in an underground seminary in Krakow after Hitler virtually banned religion in 1940 and had lived in Krakow for almost forty years. I was happy the reverence for religion didn't require the restaurants to close on Sundays, even though most stores were not open.

I found an empty table at one of the cafes and was relieved to discover the menu was in both Polish and English, since the only phrase of Polish I knew—at least until I started class the next day—was what my driver from the airport had taught me: *dziękuję ci* (thank you). I ordered a glass of rosé with a sausage-and-cheese plate for lunch.

I took off my jacket since the temperature was about 70°F. I looked out at the hive of activity in the square, including street musicians, break-dancers, flower vendors, older folks dressed in Sunday finery, young hipsters with earbuds and smartphones, and families with strollers. I wondered if it would be fun to hire one of the decorated horse-drawn carriages for a trot around the square. The overall vibe was lively and pulsing with energy, while at the same time relaxing and mellow. Listening to the conversations in animated Polish around me, I started falling in love with the city.

Of the twelve students in my Polish class, only three others were native English speakers: the Brit, a young Canadian woman from Calgary, and a teenager from Johannesburg. Besides Jin Kyung from South Korea, there was a Romanian woman, two young Russians, a mother and daughter (Anna) from Ukraine, and a Salvadoran woman. Our ages ranged from seventeen to sixty—with the Brit and me at the top end.

Such a motley crew had many reasons for studying Polish, mostly work assignments or immigration to Poland. For me, learning this language was a way to live in a foreign place and also explore my maternal heritage. My grandparents had emigrated from Poland in the wave before WWI. I never knew my grandfather, who died before I was born, but I remembered my grandmother, who died when I was twelve, as a wiry old woman with thin gray hair. Babka, we called her. When I knew her, she would have been in her early sixties—about the age I was now—but she had sailed to America when she was sixteen. Once in the United States, Babka met and married a man from her same village who had come over a few years earlier. I had always felt an affinity with my grandmother, who was loving and fun, but she never talked about the old country except to say there was nothing left there—including relatives.

In class, I realized that having listened to my grandmother speak Polish helped me "hear" the language better. Which at least was some advantage because it turned out that Polish was very difficult to learn. So my most-used word after thanks was *przepraszam*, which means "excuse me" or "I'm sorry."

Although my weekdays quickly became routine (class until one, coffee or lunch with other students, homework, exercise at the gym I'd joined, and dinner), the weekend became my time to explore. Kelsey, my Canadian classmate, and I rode bikes along the river to an ancient monastery, took a walking tour of the city, and attended the weekend festivals in the Stare Miasto, eating Polish delicacies like the ones I'd grown up with: pierogies, nut rolls, and kielbasa.

Near Krakow were two "must-do" sites: Auschwitz and the Wieliczka salt mine. "Fun stuff, this Polish tourist fare," I said to Kelsey when she suggested we go. "I'm okay with a salt mine, but I don't know if I want to go to Auschwitz. It makes me sick to my stomach to even think about it."

"I know it will be tough, but I feel like we should go," she said.

"I'll think about it." I said. I felt like I should go, but my gut said *no!*

Why did I feel so strongly? I'd read many books about the Nazis, including all three volumes of *The Rise and Fall of the Third Reich*, and had a good sense of the history of WWII, so it wasn't like I wouldn't know what to expect. Or maybe I knew too much about what to expect. I remembered my experience at the Colosseum and wondered if my revulsion there was coloring my view. It was uncharacteristic of me to shy away from difficult situations, but couldn't I remember and honor the Holocaust victims without seeing Auschwitz?

To help me work through my hesitancy, I went alone to Kazimierz, the old Jewish quarter of Krakow, and wandered the streets, reading historical markers and looking at photos from the past. Kazimierz was now an artsy, shabby-chic district, and it was easy to imagine the bustling area as it had been in the early 1940s. But I could *not* imagine how the residents had been forced into a crowded ghetto across the river, or how that ghetto was eventually decimated when most people were sent to a death camp.

I made my way back to my apartment, emotionally gutted, and knew I couldn't go to Auschwitz. I feared the place might steal my soul and haunt my memories forever. Even if I'd feel guilty later, I absolutely couldn't go. I felt like a failure.

————————

My final week in Krakow, I had two objectives: cover the gray in my reddish-brown hair and visit my grandparents' hometown. Coloring my gray needed to be done about every six to eight weeks, but I'd been observing the women of Krakow and had seen a lot of orange hair, so I was wary. I went to a small two-chair beauty shop across the street from my apartment carrying a card on which I'd written the words "No orange, please. Only reddish highlights." When she read it, the hairdresser, who spoke no English, laughed. Apprehensive as I was, when I left the shop two hours later, the color was perfect.

For the other task, I had my grandmother's birth certificate but needed a driver to take me to the small town of Paszyn, about an hour southeast of Krakow. I found Andrew, an English-speaking Pole who had lived in Chicago most of his adult life. He recommended a Sunday visit for finding relatives since people would be home and not working, even though I told him I didn't expect to find relatives and just wanted to see the area. On the way to Paszyn, I told him the family story that Babka's mother had died giving birth to Babka. When Babka was sixteen, her only brother, John, gave her the small inheritance he had been entrusted with when their mother died. She could use it for a dowry, or to buy a farm of her own, or to go to America. She got on a boat to America and never looked back.

As we neared Paszyn, the back roads meandered through rolling hillsides covered with small farms and occasional patches of forest. The terrain was strikingly similar to where I grew up in Pennsylvania, and I suspected that had something to do with why my grandparents had settled there. Once in town, we drove past a church and up a hill until we saw an older couple enjoying a Sunday picnic under a shady tree in their yard.

"Excuse me, but do you know anyone in town named Jasinska or Kruslicky?" Andrew asked. My grandmother's maiden name was Jasinska; my grandfather's surname was Kruslicky.

"Well, yes," the man said. "Our neighbor is a Kruslicky. They are at church now but should be home soon." Well, imagine that!

We drove back down the hill and heard the church bells ringing. People streamed from a white structure that looked too new to be the church my grandmother had attended.

"Let's go," Andrew said, watching the crowd dissipate. "Now we can visit the rectory and talk to the priest. We'll go up to the Kruslicky place after."

"But we don't have an appointment," I said, uncomfortable with knocking on the door on a Sunday afternoon. I had attended mass at my mother's Roman Catholic church when I was a child, but never went to the rectory.

"The priests are there to serve the flock," Andrew said.

He was already halfway up the stairs to the door.

It seemed like a long time before a white-haired priest in a black cassock opened the door. Andrew explained our mission. I could hear dishes clattering and people chattering, probably over Sunday dinner. The priest didn't seem inclined to minister to an errant American member of the flock and parked us in a side room to wait. Soon a chubby younger priest appeared, and I wondered what penance he was serving that he had to miss the meal to meet with us.

He led us downstairs to a small windowless room lined with floor-to-ceiling cupboards. The priest sat behind a wooden desk, listened to my story (as translated by Andrew), and looked at my copy of Babka's birth certificate. He got up and opened one of the tall cupboard doors. Inside I could see hundreds of tall, skinny, leather-bound ledgers, each with a Latin word and a date written on the spine. He pulled out a volume labeled 1898, the year Babka was born. With quick movements, he sat back at the desk and opened the book, scanning with his finger down the first page. Reading upside down, I could see the ledger of names had notations written in Latin beside each one.

The entry at the very bottom of the first page read "Anna Jasinska."

My heart leapt at this tangible proof I was in the same place my grandmother had lived. I asked if I could take a picture of the page and understood the answer by the priest's look: Absolutely not. No photos of anything. Chastised, I removed my hand from my tote, where I had been reaching for the camera.

The priest got up and pulled another book from the cabinet, scanning again. Then another and another, saying little. Andrew gave me a sign to sit quietly and let the man work—without questions. Over the course of the next thirty minutes, the complete story of my family emerged. And it was nothing like the version Babka had told.

Babka's mother died when Babka was nine years old, not in childbirth. The older brother, John, did exist, but he couldn't have given her money because he died when he was eighteen months old. After John, a baby named Adam was born, but he died at five months. A third boy, Martin, lived a long life in the village, as did the next two children, Sophia and Marie. The youngest child was Anna, my grandmother, who grew up in a household with a mother, father, and three siblings—all of whom she pretended did not exist as soon as she got on a ship and left Poland.

The priest, who never cracked a smile during the entire process, said the village had always been distrustful of outsiders, and leaving was frowned upon. He suspected my grandmother might have been fleeing an arranged marriage. I preferred to think she was an adventurous soul longing for something better—and that perhaps her spirit was in my DNA.

I left a generous contribution to the church on the priest's desk, as Andrew instructed me to do. Reeling from the revelations, I was glad to escape the windowless room and drive back to the top of the hill, where the potential relatives on my grandfather's side would now be home from church.

When we arrived, I saw several middle-aged men drinking beer around a picnic table in the backyard. A few women were pushing children on a swing set, while others bustled around a separate food table. A man pointed to our car as we drove in, and an old woman came around from the side of the house to greet us.

When Andrew explained our mission, she cheerfully introduced herself as Margaret Kruslicky. She was three inches shorter than me, at about five feet tall, and carried an extra fifty pounds. Her white hair was pulled back from her round face, and she wore a long blue skirt with a red T-shirt. She told us she had married into the family, but her husband was dead. Instead of introducing me to the other people in the yard, Margaret offered to take us to the cemetery. We gladly accepted.

Once at the cemetery, Margaret scrambled across the weedy terraces until we came to a cluster of Kruslicky graves, including her husband's, who was a brother of my grandfather. Margaret crossed herself and said a short prayer, then turned to Andrew and began to decipher the relationships of the names on the tombstones. I'd had no idea there were so many relatives on my maternal grandfather's side of the family.

We got back in the car to visit the old family homestead, where my grandfather's sister had lived until her death. We drove up a hill and along a ridge, then turned down a dirt road. A tumbledown building stood in a grove of thick trees, plaster falling from the corners and roof beams exposed to the elements. The weeds and bushes around the house grew waist high. The property had been abandoned, Margaret explained.

"The children all went off to the cities and wanted nothing to do with it," she said. "I don't understand why at least one of them doesn't came back." Having abandoned my own hometown, *I* understood why. "Let's go around front."

Margaret led us through the brush and pushed aside a vine hanging from a tree to reveal a spectacular view. In a meadow in front of the house, wildflowers bloomed yellow, white, and blue. Oak and walnut trees, heavy with summer leaves, shaded the porch and framed the slope as it dropped off below the house. Cultivated hillsides undulated into the hazy distance, where the tall peaks of the Tatra Mountains were faintly visible.

Andrew and Margaret were deep in conversation, so I lingered to take photographs. I fleetingly thought of asking the kids to sell me this property. I could build a stylish modern home to maximize the view and live comfortably, spending Polish zlotys instead of dollars. I'd become fluent in Polish and discover more about the many second, third, and fourth cousins I'd surely have. It would be a sort of homecoming.

I felt a shiver in my spine, despite the warm day, and felt Babka's spirit. It was not my destiny to be there, just as it wasn't hers. I had the distinct feeling Babka didn't want me digging around in the past she had so successfully buried. I would leave Paszyn and Krakow in a few days and move on to face new challenges, as she had so many years before.

THE BALKANS: CROATIA, BOSNIA AND HERZEGOVINA, SERBIA, AND MONTENEGRO

JUNE 2015

Zagreb, Croatia was deserted when I arrived on Saturday afternoon. I'd gotten a SIM card at the airport (easy and inexpensive, it turned out), so I had a cell phone map when I set out for a walk after checking into my hotel. The front desk clerk told me the stores all closed at two on Saturdays so the shopkeepers could enjoy the weekend. How civilized! And, as in Krakow, stores would not be open on Sunday either.

I walked the empty city and peeked into a few churches but generally detected no life or energy. The sidewalks practically sizzled in the summer heat, and I lost steam in less than an hour. Closing everything might have made Zagreb civilized but also made it uninteresting. At least I hadn't gotten lost, like in Rome. I headed back to the sweetness of the hotel air conditioning, reviving myself with a drink at the bar, along with a few other bedraggled tourists nursing cold beers.

The bartender suggested a nearby sidewalk café for dinner, so I eventually made my way there. The restaurant was filled with couples, a few families, and a group of five chic women celebrating some event with gifts, champagne, and lots of laughter. I wished that I were with friends, or even that those women would invite me to join them, but I resigned myself to being a single American woman eating alone. I already missed Krakow and hoped it was the heat that was making me feel cranky and lonely.

The next day, Sunday, was no cooler, so I decided to go to a park across the street from the hotel and read under the shade of the trees. To my surprise, the central gravel walkway was lined with white canopy tents, and the entire park was teeming with people young and old. I made my way into the row of vendor booths and realized they were all selling food. A banner announced "National Day," and each booth represented the different nationalities found in Croatia: Hungarian, Czech, Polish, Serb, Bosnian, Russian, German, Ukrainian, and a few more I didn't recognize.

My mouth watered at the sight of pierogies, sausages, breads, cheeses, cakes, and cookies. And beer and wine. Clearly, I'd found my lunch spot. I went to the Polish booth and, trying out my new Polish language skills, ordered pierogies and a beer, then tried to pay the full-bellied man on the other side of the counter. "*Nie, nie*," the man laughed. I thought he was telling me how bad my Polish was. But no, he gestured until I understood everything at the festival was free, including the alcohol. So much for my six weeks of language study.

I made my way along the booths tasting a little of everything, especially the cold beer. I shared a bench with an elderly couple to watch ethnic dancers in embroidered outfits perform on a stage in a large gazebo. When I got back to the hotel, I realized there hadn't been a single word of English spoken all day. I didn't feel cranky or lonely anymore and thought maybe I was getting the hang of traveling without being a tourist.

———————

I was in Croatia to join the two-week organized rafting tour my friend James had recommended months before. That Sunday night, I met the rest of the small group: Cindy, who came alone; and Steve and David, friends from college fifty years before who had done several previous trips with John, the trip leader recommended by James. Cindy was not quite my age, but all three of the men were several years older than me. Rounding out the group was our Croatian guide, Brani. The youngest of us by thirty years, he was fit and handsome, with a winsome smile. Without meaning to be ageist or sexist, I felt better knowing there would be youthful muscles along in case of emergency.

The next day we drove in a van to the put-in spot on the Mreznica River. Despite the warm summer temperatures, we donned full neoprene wetsuits, heeding Brani's warning that we *would* get wet and cold that day. From what I could see through the dense foliage on the banks, the water was calm, sea-foam green riffles barely knee deep. At least the start would be slow and easy.

"The water lever is low right now," Brani said. "So we've swapped out the rafts for inflatable double kayaks." I didn't really like that idea since even though I'd done a lot of rafting, I didn't kayak and, in fact, didn't really like whitewater. For me, the joy of being on the river was the slow drifting, watching birds and nature. Brani told us the person in back would steer and provide instruction to the person in the front. Because I was inexperienced with kayaks, I was sure I'd be going with Brani or John.

"I'll take Cheryl in front," David, a wiry septuagenarian, piped up. He had a hand-rolled cigarette dangling from his lips.

"I've never paddled inflatable kayaks before," I told him. "I should probably go with one of the guides."

"It's easy. We'll do fine," he said, handing me a paddle. I looked at John, sure he would tactfully get me out of the situation.

"David has a lot of paddling experience," John said. "So that's a good idea. Steve will go with me, and Brani can take Cindy."

Oh great. I not only had to get in a kayak, I had to go with somebody I didn't know and certainly didn't trust with my life. I knew I should never have signed up for any whitewater activity. What had I been thinking? The kayaks sat in a small eddy pool among thick trees that concealed a view downriver. David settled into the back seat of one, and I stepped gingerly into the front. Brani had waded into the shallow river to direct us. We paddled upstream out of the eddy, then Brani turned our boat downstream, holding us still from the back. On the right, a pretty ten-foot waterfall ended in a quiet mint-green pool. On the left was a shallow channel and I figured that Brani was there to help us get over to it.

"Point it straight at the arrow of water going over the falls," Brani shouted to David as he let go. "Then you'll be fine."

I wish I could say I wasn't panicked, but I could taste bile in my throat. Rapids were one thing, but were these people crazy taking tourists over a waterfall? Was I crazy for being there? Maybe I had unknowingly overstated my rafting experience and was on an experts-only trip.

By the time these thoughts went through my brain, it was too late. We hit the edge of the falls and my instincts took over. I closed my eyes and screamed bloody hell as the boat glided slowly over the drop and into the pool below. I barely got wet. Holy shit.

That night, at the rural guesthouse where we had also stayed the night before, I wandered onto the porch for what I thought was a well-deserved glass of wine after my stressful paddling day. It turned out there had been several more waterfalls that day and I had survived, maybe even enjoyed, the experience. The evening breeze was lovely and carried the light fragrance of flowering shrubs. Marija, the proprietress who had cooked dinner the night before and breakfast that morning, sank gratefully into the chair beside me when I asked her to join me.

"Do you run the guesthouse by yourself?" I asked.

"Yes, unless my grown son and daughter come to visit; then they help out," she said in accented but perfect English. "And my mother helps with the cooking and washing the dishes." I had seen an older woman sitting in the kitchen, knitting.

"That must be very difficult—and exhausting," I said. "I own a house by myself, and sometimes that seems like a lot of work—and I'm not having guests every night or cooking for them."

"Well, there's not really a choice. My husband died in the war, and I wanted my two children to go to college. So I had to earn money." She stared at her wineglass and continued flatly. "Many of us women have fended for ourselves over the last twenty-five years since our husbands, fathers, and sons were killed."

"I'm so sorry," I said feebly.

"It was a long time ago, and I survived," Marija said. "I do hope we will never see a war again. I was very scared for our lives during the war—and scared in a different way after my husband died and I had to make a life for myself and my children."

My river fears seemed petty as we sipped our wine. What did I know of fear?

I also felt bad that I remembered little about the wars that had raged from 1991 to 1995 in this part of the world. I had been living in Idaho then, with an hour commute to work each day, during which I heard regular coverage of the conflict on the radio. I remember being confused by the terms Yugoslavian, Serbian, Croatian, and Bosnian, especially when combined with the Christian and Muslim designations. I couldn't tell who was fighting whom and about what, no matter how hard I concentrated. And usually it was easier not to concentrate but to tune it out and let my mind wander. A Balkan tinderbox, what a shame. Is that a deer beside the road? Is a Bosnian Serb like a Mexican American? I hope that project at work gets back on budget. Another massacre? I need to schedule a haircut soon. I wished I had paid more attention.

The next day we drove to the Bosnia-Croatia border to run the Una River with two young local guides. My heart sank when we parked at the put-in and I spied a spectacular sixty-foot waterfall. Surely we wouldn't be expected to do that! Luckily the answer was no—there was a path to the bottom of the falls, where we'd start; better yet, we'd be in a paddle raft instead of kayaks. We walked and slid our way down to the bottom, but instead of carrying the boat down, the two guides stayed on top. From below, we watched them walk the raft through the slow-moving water above the falls into the middle of the wide river—never more than knee deep. At the precipice, they pushed the boat over the edge and Brani, who had swum out to a small rock outcrop, captured it in the eddy below. Then, to my horror and delight, both men jumped off the waterfall, the wiser of the two cupping his genitals on the way down.

We did drop over smaller waterfalls that day (by now I wasn't screaming) and floated miles of impossibly clear aquamarine water. During the slow-flowing stretches, I talked to the local guides, who told me they were Bosnian Muslims who had studied tourism in college. They lamented the state of the economy and lack of opportunities in Bosnia. It was hot, and I'd been guzzling my water but noticed that they never drank any. At lunch, they avoided the sandwiches and fruit and stretched out on the lawn instead.

Back in the boat, I naively asked them about dehydration, scolding as only a woman old enough to be their mother could do. But it was the first day of Ramadan, they told me, and although they had dispensation to drink water because of their work, neither felt the need. How ignorant of me not to know that it was the first day of the holiest month of the year in Islamic culture. I wanted to crawl into a hole. Some citizen of the world I was turning out to be.

———

The next few days we were back in Croatia, floating the Zrmanja and Cetina rivers. The landscape was beautiful, the rivers fun and not scary. Our little group had gelled well, and I was having a good time. We covered a lot of miles in the van that week, through many empty towns of buildings with bombed-out roofs or bullet-ridden walls. I gave up any pretense of being knowledgeable about what had happened and asked questions. Brani filled in the details.

"The towns were usually abandoned because the citizens were pushed out," Brani said. "Sometimes ethnic differences ripped apart families: if a Serb was married to a Croat, then they had to choose sides. A Bosnian might have had to abandon a business he ran with a Serb partner. In Croatia, loyalists to Yugoslavia might be in the same family as those who wanted independence. Before the war, Muslims and Christians mostly accepted each other, but that changed fast."

"I'm still confused by who was fighting for what," I said.

"It isn't easy," he said. "I'm sure you know that after WWII, Yugoslavia was established as a country of six republics with borders based on ethnic and historical lines: Slovenia, Croatia, Bosnia and Herzegovina, Serbia, Montenegro, and Macedonia."

I didn't know that, but I nodded my head. "Go on."

"In 1991, Slovenia and Croatia declared independence, which the Yugoslavian army (mostly Serbs) tried to prevent. Ethnic hate-speech got bad, and there was a lot of nationalist talk. But we had all been Yugoslavia for decades, so Serbs lived in Croatia, Bosnians lived in Serbia, Croatians lived in Bosnia. You get my drift." It was making more sense and I nodded again. He continued. "Then in 1992, Bosnia and Herzegovina also declared independence."

I wanted to ask why they couldn't decide on just one name but decided it wouldn't be polite.

"The Croats joined with the army of Bosnia and Herzegovina to fight against the Yugoslav army, which was essentially Serbs, but it was a loose alliance. Then, the Bosnian Croats who were Catholic fought with the

Bosnian Muslims (called Bosniaks), and things got ugly, with lots of massacres and war crimes based on both ethnic and religious grounds."

"I know there were plenty of war crime tribunals," I said. "Did most of it get sorted out there?"

"Some, but not all. I'll admit that the Croats made mistakes and committed war crimes, but the Bosnians and the Serbs were definitely the bad guys." From what little I knew, I agreed with him, but I also expected his opinion to be biased.

The time spent on the blue-green rivers was an especially peaceful respite from the stories about complicated wars and politics. But I was plunged back into the history when we got to Sarajevo, a city that, at one time, had been a model for interethnic relations, containing a mix of Ottoman, Austro-Hungarian, Slavic, Muslim, Orthodox, Catholic, and Jewish cultures. We saw where Austrian Archduke Franz Ferdinand was assassinated in 1914 by a group of five Serbians and a Bosniak, the small act that ignited a chain of events leading to World War I. We heard how some of the 1984 Olympic venues, of which the city was so proud, were now cemeteries.

As I walked through the city, life seemed normal and, but for the bullet holes everywhere, it could have been easy to ignore the fact Sarajevo withstood the longest siege of a capital city in the history of modern warfare—1,425 days, a year longer than the historic siege of Leningrad in WWII. Started by the Yugoslavian army, the siege was continued, along with other atrocities, by a group of Bosnian Serbs who wanted the city for their newly declared Republic of Srpska, under the direction of Bosnian Serb leader Radovan Karadžić. I worked hard to keep it all straight.

During our free time in the city, John suggested I visit a photography exhibit about the Srebrenica massacre that he had seen the year before.

I asked him to join me, but he declined. "Once was enough," he said, "but once was worth it." By now I knew that Srebrenica was one of the many massacres by the Bosnian Serbs, this one with the goal of killing "every able-bodied male" in the town and systematically exterminating the Bosnian Muslim community. I paused at the entrance, thinking about how I hadn't gone to Auschwitz. But I reminded myself that this was just a photo gallery, not a death camp, so I went in.

The gallery was empty, which made me feel almost haunted by the long room's hundreds of photographs documenting the genocide of 8,372 people. A film loop ran at the far end of the room, offering first-hand accounts and footage of the hours surrounding the 1995 horror. This was clearly not "just a photo gallery." The event seemed even more sickening to me when I thought about the fact that it had happened merely twenty years before. And I knew there were other places in the world where genocide still happened. I felt a guilty relief that I had never had to experience such horror.

When I left the gallery, I saw a church across the street, so I went in, looking maybe for solace or maybe a place to pull myself together. I sat in a pew at the back and studied the graceful arches with terra cotta stripes that felt Moorish, the stained-glass windows depicting Christ on the cross, and the opulence of the gold altar. I wondered how people could believe in a God, or an Allah, or a Yahweh, who would allow, or even by some accounts command, a Srebrenica to happen? Or an Auschwitz? Or a 9/11? Or the ongoing atrocities regularly committed in the name of religion or power or ethnic pride?

I wondered whether believing in any God made it easier for a person to commit atrocities—or to live through them. The longer I sat there, the angrier I became at religion (and men and weapons and ego and intolerance) and the part it plays in conflicts and death around the world. I held the simplistic view that believing in a greater force or higher power should result in more love and compassion, not hate and killing.

I left the church and wandered the streets, feeling numb and questioning my own role in the world, my own beliefs. Maybe the value of visiting a death camp or gallery documenting genocide was to make people examine their lives and values. Would I be willing to fight or die for my beliefs, political or religious—either to impose them or defend them? Did I have a moral obligation to speak up in whatever way possible when genocide was happening somewhere far away or to go to war to stop it? I honestly didn't know.

Silence characterized our ride to the Tara River that afternoon. Everyone seemed either lost in their thoughts or tired of talking. I snagged a seat in the back of the van, thankful for the lack of conversation. We'd be on the river for three days with plenty of slow, easy river time. Time when I might get back to believing things were right with the world, not all wrong.

The clear, emerald Tara ran through a beautiful, forested canyon, but the shoreline was a junky mess of plastic bags, water bottles, old shoes, and garbage. We stayed in rough fishing camps run by the scruffy men who lived there. The last night on the river, two Serb camp owners seemed keen to share their view of politics and the past. With great vehemence, they declared that Bosnian and Serbian war crimes were exaggerated and those of the Croats were much worse. I knew the Croats had committed their fair share; even Brani had admitted it. But when the men brought up Srebrenica and insisted it was a total fabrication of an event that never happened, my head and my heart hurt, and I retired early. I felt like I would never understand how people could be so stubbornly blind to facts.

Our group trip ended in Dubrovnik, a city where the massive walls were built straight into the rocky coastline lapped by cobalt-blue waves. We had a final group dinner in the old town, so I went early to explore for a while on my own. At one of the entrance gates in the wall, I stared at a large map of the city that was covered with different-colored dots. I assumed they signified restaurants, shops, and cultural sights, but on closer inspection, I saw they denoted areas affected by Serb shelling of the city. One color for buildings that had lost their roofs, another for damaged walls, and a third for pedestrians hit with shells while walking in their city. Those sixteenth-century ramparts were no match for modern weapons that came from the sky.

I went inside the walls and merged into the tourist crowd on the limestone streets. The beautifully ornate architecture caught my eye and my interest, but I soon realized the shops were selling a disappointing mishmash of tacky made-in-China Croatian souvenirs, fancy cruise-ship clothing or cheap T-shirts, and expensive jewelry instead of Croatian artisanal items that might support a local economy. I wandered aimlessly, sad for such a beautiful, historic place to be, in my opinion, ruined by obvious overtourism.

Before joining the rest of the group for dinner, I met our guide John and a local friend of his, Marco, for a drink at a small bar on a relatively quiet side street.

"So, what do you think of Croatia?" Marco asked.

"It's been wonderful. But I am surprised by how much the war has permeated my experience. Travel articles wax poetic about the pristine beaches and islands, but they rarely mention the history."

"Most people don't want to remember the past," Marco said. "They want to bask in the sun and drink good, inexpensive wine and eat fresh seafood when they are on vacation. War is not good for our new tourist economy. And neither is talking about it. We used to be quick to fight, but now we work hard at peace."

I told Marco that the Balkans trip had made me think more than I ever had about the general ethics of my travel. Should I spend my money in countries that had committed war crimes and massacres? Did it matter whether it was "old" history or "new" history? And how much time had to pass for it to count as "old"? On the other hand, were my travel dollars a way of bringing positive change and fostering an exchange of ideas? Or was I a privileged American taking advantage of a ruined economy to have a budget travel experience? I asked John and Marco what they thought.

"You are privileged to be able to even ask those questions, of course," John said.

"It's noble to support all of the Balkan economies as they emerge from the history and the war," Marco said. "We are all trying for something better."

"And it's always good for us Americans to get out of our bubble and see the way the rest of the world runs its affairs—both good and bad," John said.

I decided he was right. The people I had met were all working hard for a better future for themselves and their families. I didn't sense anybody wanted to be at war again. There was a judicial process to bring the criminals to trial, so why should the shopkeepers, hoteliers, restaurateurs, and regular folks be punished for the actions of their previous governments? But how was a traveler like me supposed to know whether everyday citizens had supported the atrocities? Was it my business to know? There wasn't a simple answer.

As John and Marco caught up with each other's lives, I retreated into my thoughts. Tomorrow the cruisers would sail north to scenic coastal towns like Split, Hvar, and Zadar, while other tourists flocked to the Croatian islands of the tourist brochures. I wondered if my travels in the interior of Croatia and through Serbia, Bosnia and Herzegovina, and Montenegro had shown me a different face of the Balkans, one of suffering and rebuilding, than that seen through nice wine and sunny beaches. This trip had made me thankful for my comparatively boring life, a life without bombing and sieges and slaughter. I knew I was lucky to live in America.

After saying good-bye to Marco, John and I made our way to the restaurant outside the city walls to join our group. Located practically on the docks, the restaurant served fresh fish and seafood caught by local fishermen. Now that was more like it. We ordered a few bottles of local wine and I felt even better. Cindy, Steve, David, and John had proven to be fun, smart, and entertaining traveling companions and I reluctantly said good-bye. They were each returning to the States, while I would fly to Bulgaria to begin yet another adventure.

CHAPTER 8

BULGARIA

JULY 2015

My Portland friend Kathleen was flying to Sofia from Scandinavia, where she had been traveling, to meet me for a few weeks of exploring Bulgaria and Romania. This was the kind of experience I had hoped for when I left the States—longtime friends meeting me as I traveled solo around the world. I'd met Kathleen, a gifted writer, about ten years earlier when we worked for the same company, but our friendship had survived long past both of our departures from that common employer. I was looking forward to spending time with her.

I had arrived at the shiny new, but small, airport terminal in Sofia several hours before Kathleen was due and was heading to the hotel to wait for her. I was relieved to see that the airport signs were not only in the Bulgarian Cyrillic alphabet, which I was able to sound out thanks to my Russian language background, but also in English. This feature not only made things easier for me, but I knew it would help Kathleen to navigate more easily.

Bulgaria was not exactly on the tourist track, but Kathleen and I had chosen it as a place neither of us would be comfortable traveling to solo, so why not go together? I was interested in the country because of a potential family connection. I'd always been told my surname, Koshuta, was Slovak, but the little research I'd done indicated it was more likely Rusyn—from a nomadic ethnic group that straddled Bulgaria, Romania, and Slovakia. Although I wasn't planning to look for ancestors and had no leads anyway, maybe I'd get lucky, as I had in Poland, and find some unexpected connections. Kathleen, on the other hand, had Norse heritage and no reason to join me in Bulgaria besides her natural curiosity and sense of adventure. Which were reason enough to go anywhere, in my opinion.

I knew very little about Bulgaria, but to plan our time there, I had looked at a map. Otherwise, I'd have had no idea the country was bordered on the west by Serbia and Macedonia (now North Macedonia), on the north by Romania, and on the south by Greece and Turkey. To the east lay the Black Sea, where the beaches were a holiday mecca for rich Russians. I had thought of Bulgaria merely as a Russian stronghold with lots of bureaucracy and vodka drinking, not yet aware that the country's history melded Greek, Slavic, Ottoman, and Persian cultures.

Within five minutes of landing in Sofia, I had my bag and easily spotted the driver my hotel had sent since, unlike in Rome, there were only three waiting greeters. The short, dour man holding a sign with my name written in English on it offered no hint of welcome. Then again, nobody in the airport was smiling. He did take my luggage, though, then led me through the parking lot to his small, beat-up Russian-made sedan, with roll-down windows that barely worked and a deteriorating dashboard that had seen too much sun or cold or age, or all of the above. I thought of Sunny, the car in New Zealand, and crossed my fingers.

The narrow, potholed road that led out of the airport was lined with decaying, graffiti-covered industrial buildings surrounded by weedy fields full of trash and tires. The sky was dark with heavy clouds, and the wind blew empty plastic bags across the fields to be snagged by decrepit wire fences. There was not a single "Welcome to Sofia" sign in sight—in English or Cyrillic. The driver spoke halting English, so we didn't have much conversation, except for his occasional comments about how awful Communism was and how difficult it was to make a living in Bulgaria. After five minutes, we turned onto a major arterial lined with mind-numbingly ugly high-rise block buildings, their peeling concrete walls dirty with diesel soot and each tiny balcony festooned with laundry and a satellite dish.

When we reached the city center, the streets suddenly became wide, tree lined and beautifully maintained. Startled by the contrast to the other road, we passed massive, stark but clean government buildings on either side. Men in business suits and women in dark skirts and heels ducked into modern-looking cafés and restaurants, presumably for lunch since it was just after noon, but still nobody seemed to be smiling. Perhaps it was the impending storm, but everything felt dark and oppressive.

I checked into our hotel and took a tiny elevator to my fourth-floor room, which was large but furnished with beat-up furniture from the 1960s. I unpacked a few things, then went back down to the reception desk in the small, marble-floored lobby.

"Where can I buy some wine and cheese?"

"In the next building along this street," the desk clerk said. "You cannot miss it; it is close, but perhaps you should take an umbrella." He motioned outside to the ominous clouds and pointed at a stand near the door filled with black umbrellas. I took a chance and left without one.

I stopped at the Bancomat (ATM) outside the hotel and withdrew a few Levs, the local currency, then continued to the small market, which carried basic food items, soft drinks, cleaning supplies, and a large selection of wine, liquor, and beer. The Italian, Greek, Romanian, and Bulgarian wines were no more expensive than about $7 US. I picked a Bulgarian one for $2, then found a package of crackers and two chunks of cheese. I paid with my Levs and a smile but got a scowl in return. I ducked into the hotel lobby just as the skies opened and it poured rain.

I hadn't seen Kathleen, a beautiful, petite blond who always looked serene no matter how much stress she was under, since I had left Portland in April. When she arrived midafternoon looking fresh despite having traveled all day, I wasn't surprised. We celebrated the launch of our Eastern European adventure with a glass of the not-bad Bulgarian wine and a bite of cheese, then decided to visit the St. Alexander Nevsky Cathedral before finding a place for dinner. Kathleen had brought a guidebook that told us the cathedral was reputed to hold 5,000 people and had been built to commemorate the 200,000 Russian soldiers who died during the 1877–78 Russo-Turkish War. That conflict liberated Bulgaria from the five hundred years of Ottoman rule called the "Turkish Yoke."

Well, throwing off that Turkish yoke led to a hundred years of nationalism that resulted in the persecution of many ethnic groups, especially Turks. By the 1980s, Bulgaria had conducted massive sweeps to move Turks back to Turkey and forced almost a million remaining Turks to change their names to sound more Bulgarian. I was struck by how similar those events were to the Turks' treatment of ethnic minorities in their own country over the centuries, including the Armenian genocide during WWI. The concept of someone who is your friend or neighbor one day becoming your enemy the next was no easier for me to understand than when I was in the Balkans.

I was curious to see how the imposing and impressive gold-domed cathedral had survived that complicated history and the change in Bulgarian-Russian relations now that Bulgaria was part of NATO and the European Union. The exterior of the building, covered with meticulous mosaics of saints, looked well cared for. But inside, the cavernous space with no pews or chairs (in traditional Orthodox church set-up) appeared dark and dingy despite the walls and pillars of Italian marble, Brazilian onyx, and alabaster. The icons and murals were smudged with smoke from candles. I couldn't tell whether the atmosphere inside of the cathedral was intentionally oppressive or the result of neglect.

After a short while I was happy to head outside, where thankfully the rain had let up. Kathleen and I went to the park across the street from the cathedral, where vendors played games on their cell phones under plastic tarps while selling religious icons that looked like those in the Byzantine Catholic church in Pennsylvania I had attended with my father. Although I'd abandoned both my father's Byzantine and my mother's Roman Catholicism when I was a teen, the tchotchkes made this strange place feel familiar.

We found our way to the street where I'd seen the office workers lunching earlier, hoping to find something decent for dinner. I didn't have high hopes for Bulgarian cuisine, expecting overcooked root vegetables and meat dishes made with animal parts I didn't want to eat. We spotted a restaurant called Bodega that looked inviting with imported hams hanging in the window. It was packed with earnest businessmen and more casually dressed younger patrons, who took turns going outside to smoke. After the darkness of the afternoon, Kathleen and I felt re-energized by the lighthearted vibe of tasty tapas, cheap wine, and a guitarist playing Spanish folk songs.

After dinner, we caught a cab back to the hotel with a driver who spoke excellent English. He told us about working two jobs to make ends meet. "Communism ruined Bulgaria," he said. "The people in the countryside, they miss it, the never-having-to-think-for-yourself life, the guaranteed salary that you could barely live on. There was no reason to become a doctor because you would get paid the same as the flower-seller. Now we have joined the EU and are learning to be capitalists, but still the Communists try to control everything. We are now free to travel to other European countries; I'd go if I could afford it. Oh, look ahead"—he pointed through the windshield— "and you can see our famous statue of Sofia. It was put up in 2000 after we tore down the statue of Lenin."

A seventy-foot-high bronze of a woman stood in the middle of the traffic circle. Her flowing dark brown gown was blown back as if in a wind, revealing the shape of her legs and waist; her voluptuous figure was further emphasized by a plunging neckline.

"It was supposed to be Saint Sofia," the driver continued, "but when it was finished everyone said it was too sexy to be a saint, so now it is just called Sofia."

"Well, aren't you happy that it isn't Lenin anymore?" I asked.

"Ha!" He practically spat the answer. "Nothing has changed. The face on the statue is that of the mistress of the Communist party boss."

———————

I can't remember whether it was Kathleen or I who found the website for Wild Thyme, an unlikely eco-retreat in the middle of the Bulgarian countryside, but we both thought driving a rental car several hours east of Sofia and spending a few days there would be a good way to see how people lived in Bulgaria. From there, we'd continue north to the Bulgarian border town of Ruse to drop off the rental car and meet a Romanian driver in the opposite border town of Giurgiu. That driver would then take us a few hours east to Tulcea, where we had hired a guide for a Danube Delta tour.

Viktor, the owner of the Sofia rental car company and a fluent English speaker, brought the car directly to our hotel. In the lobby, while we completed the paperwork, Viktor drew a crude map of where he would meet us in Ruse to pick up the car before we crossed into Romania.

"How will you get across the border?" he asked.

"Can't we just walk and meet our taxi on the other side?" Kathleen asked.

"No. You cannot do that." Viktor was firm. "The border station is a few kilometers before the bridge, and it is the same on the other side. The bridge across the Danube is more than two kilometers long."

I kicked myself for not having researched the border crossing more thoroughly or even thinking about how difficult it might be moving about in Eastern Europe. Viktor, seeing the look of dismay on my face, quickly added that he could help.

"I will arrange for a taxi to take you across the bridge to the border station in Romania. Only certain licensed drivers can cross regularly, and they can't take you anywhere else except over or back."

I wanted to hug him. There was no way we would have figured that out. Viktor took a yellow marker from his pocket and, unfolding a roadmap for Bulgaria, drew a line along our route to Wild Thyme. He said we could follow him out of the city to the freeway.

We settled into our (thankfully) relatively new car, and after fifteen minutes of circuitous one-way streets and numerous turns, we were finally on our own on the motorway, headed for our designated lunch stop in the ancient capital of Bulgaria, Veliko Tarnovo, about two and a half hours away. I asked Kathleen to find it on the map Viktor had given us so we could follow the towns along the way and make sure we were on track.

"I can't do that, Cheryl," she said, peering intently at the map spread across her lap, clearly suppressing a laugh.

"Why not?"

"Everything is in Cyrillic!"

———————

The national motorway was new and smooth, dotted with signs announcing that EU funding had paid for the road and bridges. We drove with the lights always on, as Viktor had alerted us to that requirement. As Americans, we liked the freedom of traveling by car, although the U.S. State Department had warned that "driving in Bulgaria is dangerous" due to "aggressive driving habits" such as swerving into oncoming traffic at high speeds and going the wrong way on divided highways. As an additional hazard, the numerous horse- and oxen-drawn carts on the road moved at very slow speeds and lacked headlights . . . or taillights.

About an hour outside of Sofia, I heard a rasping sound beneath the car, as if we were dragging a branch. I sped up, hoping to lose it, and the noise stopped. But when I slowed down, the sound came back. I stopped to look under the car, but saw nothing there. The car seemed to be running fine, so we kept going until the next exit, where we got off in search of a service station and, with any luck, a mechanic who could take a look.

A few kilometers after exiting, we came to a small gas station at the edge of town. I was relieved to see a service bay with a car up on a lift, and a man working beneath it. I parked the car near the open garage door and got out. The mechanic, a big, burly man, wiped his hands on his gray overalls and came out to meet me. When I asked him if he spoke English, he looked at me and shrugged. Thank goodness I had brushed up on my Russian on the plane, suspecting it might come in handy. I pointed underneath the car and said, in Russian, that there was a problem. He nodded, then simply lay down on the ground and slid his head underneath the car, stopping only because there wasn't enough clearance for his chest and belly. In the meantime, Kathleen was on her cell phone, calling Viktor.

The mechanic tinkered for a while, then came out from under the car, speaking fast and furious, arms gesturing. I didn't understand a word, but it didn't sound good. I thanked my lucky stars that Kathleen was with me. She had reached Viktor and handed the phone to the mechanic.

He listened for a minute, then shouted at Viktor; I did several times understand the word "bad." After a few minutes, he handed the phone back to Kathleen, motioned for us to stay put, and went into his shop.

"Okay, okay," I heard Kathleen saying to Viktor. "Are you sure? Then why was the mechanic so concerned?" She listened to the reply. "Okay. Thank you. Okay."

"That didn't sound good," I said, imagining having to wait there for a few hours while Viktor came from Sofia to rescue us.

"Apparently the oil pan wasn't put on properly when they changed the oil just before giving us the car. So the mechanic will take it off and put it in the trunk. The car is okay to drive without it."

"So why was this guy upset?"

"He was mad at the lousy work the mechanics in Sofia did. Most of their conversation was this guy telling Viktor how bad the work was and that he should find better workers like the ones here in this village. Oh, and Viktor said we aren't to pay him—he arranged that already."

Sure enough, the mechanic returned with a large black plastic garbage bag, got under the car, removed the oil pan, wrapped it in the bag, and put it in the trunk. I tried to tip him, but he backed away with his hands in the air, saying in Russian and Bulgarian, "No, unnecessary, thank you, good-bye." At least I think that's what he said. In any case, it was clear he wanted nothing to do with our money.

The car worked perfectly fine without the oil pan, so we stopped in Veliko Tarnovo for a quick walk and lunch before continuing to the tiny village of Palamartsa where Wild Thyme was located. For miles and miles, we drove through fields of commercially grown sunflowers stretching as far as the eye could see on the rolling hills. In full bloom and following the arc of the sun, the thousands of tall flowers created a yellow sea. With the cloudless sky and fresh air, there was nothing oppressive about this golden countryside.

When we arrived at Wild Thyme, we were met by Chris and Claire, a middle-aged British couple who had wanted to get back to the land. Unable to afford anything in Britain or Western Europe, they had chosen Bulgaria. They lived in a nineteenth-century farmhouse that they had renovated using traditional materials and techniques, but we would stay in a cottage next door that had a bathroom in a separate building with a composting toilet and solar hot water shower. The outside of the cottage was painted a colorful mix of terra cotta, white, and bright blue; the inside was cozy with a big wooden farm table and old stuffed furniture. Claire also showed us her organic garden and the goats they used to supply cheese and milk. The welcome basket of just-picked vegetables and goat cheese made a nice addition to the provisions we'd picked up at a grocery store in Veliko Tarnovo. We settled in for a relaxing stay.

Daily life in Palamartsa ran on a strict timetable. Each morning at nine a.m., we joined Chris to walk his three goats down the lane to an intersection where the shepherd added them to the large flock he was taking to pasture. Two women who lived in houses nearby brought their goats too. If you weren't there on time, the shepherd would move on without your kids, just like a school bus. We returned at four p.m. sharp to pick up the goats.

Chris told us about the growing expat community in Palamartsa—up to fifty people from all over Europe, but mostly older Brits. Houses were cheap because of massive migration to Sofia when the collective farms of the Soviet Era were liquidated and became big corporate enterprises, employing fewer local people. I suspected that being a young Bulgarian in one of these villages wasn't much different from life in the coal-mining town where I grew up: the best option for making money and a better life was in the cities.

Chris was an archaeologist with a keen interest in the nearby caves of Ivanovo, a World Heritage site since 1979, and one afternoon he took us to see them. We drove to a wide gorge pockmarked with caves. Monks had inhabited the caves from the 1200s to the 1700s and developed an entire cave community, including forty cave churches, many painted with frescoes in the thirteenth century. We climbed a narrow path along the cliff face to see the best specimen, a two-room cave where the paintings had been completely shielded from weather and held their vibrant color. I was surprised to see the landscapes, nudes, and village scenes reflecting an originality beyond the traditional icons of saints and biblical stories I usually saw in churches. One particularly striking depiction was of the Last Supper—eerily similar to Leonardo da Vinci's masterpiece, but painted a hundred years earlier. I couldn't help wondering how this creative concept had made its way to Milan—and who was the real genius.

Our last night at Wild Thyme, Claire had arranged for Maria, a local woman who had grown up in Palamartsa, to come to our cottage and teach us how to make a traditional Bulgarian meal of *banista* (eggs in pastry), *sarmi* (stuffed cabbage), and *shopska salata* (green salad). Maria arrived carrying a huge bowl filled with fresh yellow peppers, cabbage, onions, garlic, rice, tomatoes, yoghurt, homemade dough wrapped in plastic, sunflower seed oil (of course!), cheese, mushrooms, and eggs. Claire joined us to translate and brought a British pudding for dessert. Kathleen and I contributed several bottles of wine to the cause. We held a running conversation in a mix of Bulgarian, Russian, French, and English, our fluency increasing with each glass of wine.

We learned that Maria was in her mid-sixties and had lived through interesting—and hard—times in Bulgaria. Because her family had farm animals to provide milk, she was not stooped over from the osteoporosis that affected so many other women her age. She told us about the difficulties for women when their husbands died from work-related accidents, which were common, or alcohol-related diseases, which were even more common. Maria said it was easy for women to find work, but despite the equality promised by Communism, it was difficult to get paid a man's wage to support your family.

"Why are two American women traveling without their husbands to Bulgaria?" Maria asked, her question translated by Claire. Plenty of British and French people stayed with Chris and Claire, but rarely Americans.

"We want to see how people live in different parts of the world," I said. Maria looked skeptical.

"Where are your husbands?"

"Kathleen's husband is working, and I am not married," I said. At that Maria's eyes lit up.

"Then you should stay here in Palamartsa and be my friend," she said. "The shepherd's girlfriend left him a few months ago. He owns many cows and goats. He would be a good catch for you."

Well, maybe I'd find love on this trip after all. "Is he the shepherd who takes your goats, Claire?" I asked, thinking with horror of the skinny man with a bushy mustache and only a few teeth.

"No, a different one," she translated for Maria.

"I want a man with teeth," I said, just to be sure.

Claire could barely translate for laughing. She and Maria went back and forth, trying to get it right. Finally Claire said, "She doesn't think the shepherd she knows will work out after all because he, too, has no teeth. But if you stay, she will try to come up with other options."

That night I thought about what it took for foreigners to move to a place like Palamartsa, far from any trendy little town or tourist hot spot, with a difficult language barrier and no young people. And what it would take for me to do something like that. I saw the allure of the clearly friendly people, pastoral lifestyle and low cost of living. But I simply wasn't drawn to Bulgaria's culture, landscape, or post-Communist lifestyle. Even Maria's offer of an eligible bachelor with teeth wasn't enough to tempt me to stay.

ROMANIA

JULY–AUGUST 2015

Kathleen and I easily crossed the border from Ruse, Bulgaria, to Giurgiu, Romania, thanks to Viktor's help; once we got there, we could see it would have been a nightmare otherwise. We were headed to Tulcea, the gateway city on the edge of the unique ecosystem of the Danube Delta, where we would start a four-day boat trip into the 1,600 square miles of marshes, floating reed islands, channels, streams, and lakes that fall mostly within Romania, with only the northern corner in Ukraine.

I was hoping to spot a few life-lister birds in the over 320 species that spent the summer in the Delta, especially migrants from Mongolia, the Arctic, and Siberia. Kathleen and I had chosen a small tour company with a long history on the Delta and an assurance via email that they knew the local flora and fauna.

Cyprian, our guide, was young, moon faced, pudgy, and fluent in English. He met us at our hotel and led us to the nearby dock, strutting in front of us and not even offering to help with our luggage. We boarded a small, motorized boat with a tiny, one-seat closed control cabin. The deck in the stern was barely six feet wide, with padded benches on either side and two folding chairs in front of an outboard motor. A tarp was rigged over the deck for shade. It was more rustic than I had expected for a private tourist boat.

"Do you have the bird field guide we emailed about?" I asked.

"No," Cyprian said. "I think it's on my father's boat."

"Well, let's get it before we go," I said. For me, having a field guide was an important amenity.

Cyprian looked annoyed and called to a man about my age on the adjacent boat, who came over with a book he handed to Cyprian. "Please enjoy your trip," Cyprian's father said with a French accent. We exchanged pleasantries before he left and we backed out of the Tulcea dock and started downriver. Kathleen and I settled into the chairs in the back of the boat under the canopy.

"I'm thirty-two," Cyprian said in answer to our request to tell us about himself once we were safely out of the harbor. "I'm married with two children, and I'm a computer programmer. I took a leave of absence from my programming job for the summer to help my father. I might decide to change careers, take over the business, and become a professional tour guide."

"So you'll decide after the summer?" Kathleen asked.

"Maybe. They didn't really appreciate my skills at that other job anyway, and I'm enjoying doing the tours." I wondered if this boastful young man really had a job to go back to. "You know, my father only speaks Romanian and French, so you're lucky to have me as your guide instead of him." I suspected Kathleen had the same thought I did: the charming, experienced owner of the company would have been a far better option than Cyprian.

We motored downstream on calm water in a broad channel for a couple of hours. Cyprian sat in the cabin, keeping the throttle at full blast despite talking or texting on his cell phone. Kathleen and I alternated between the chairs and the bench in the stern, the wind blowing through our hair, our stomachs luckily as calm as the water. Eventually, Cyprian slowed the boat and we entered the channeled wetlands of the Delta, reeds towering over our heads as we wended our way through small passages that opened and closed randomly. When Cyprian cut the motor to drift among the reeds, we were engulfed with a powerful silence and stifling mid-July humidity. Little birds flitted teasingly in and out of the cattails and sedges while water birds floated lazily along.

"Can you help me identify these birds?" I asked Cyprian.

"Those are ducks," he said, handing me the birding guide.

"What kind?" I said, flipping through the book.

"Just ducks," he said. I grimaced and tried to hold my tongue. My birding aspirations were doomed. Cyprian was useless. I would have to paw through the book and hope to identify each bird myself.

Kathleen, ever tactful, jumped in before I could say anything. "Tell us about your name. It's Greek, isn't it?"

"Cyprian is a common Romanian name. It has no connection with Greece and isn't a Greek name. I don't know why you would think that."

She tried again. "Tell us about your children."

"My boy is seven and my girl is four. I want to have a third child, but my wife doesn't."

"Well, you'll have to work that out," Kathleen said.

"Nothing to work out," Cyprian said. "I am the man, so I will decide and tell her what to do."

"And she'll do it?" Kathleen asked skeptically.

"Of course. Otherwise, she would not be my wife." He ignored our raised eyebrows.

By midafternoon we arrived at the small village where we would stay. Cyprian complained about the size and heaviness of our luggage as he reluctantly took it (after first waiting to see if we would) from the rickety boat ramp to the hotel. Kathleen and I were happy to ditch him for the rest of the day and, after a walk around town, eat dinner in the air-conditioned dining room with a bottle of cold wine. We still had three days to go and vowed to try not to be annoyed with him, despite his chauvinism. The natural beauty of the Delta would make up for his shortcomings.

The next morning, Cyprian was scheduled to meet us at 10 a.m. at the hotel. Packed and ready to go, we could see the boat moored at the dock, but there was no sign of Cyprian. We could have waited inside in the air conditioning but, certain he'd be there shortly, we'd hauled our luggage outside and sat at a table near the dock, getting crankier by the minute as the stifling air and biting mosquitos sapped our energy. Around 10:30, Cyprian strolled up to us with a big smile on his face and a hearty good morning.

"We were supposed to meet at ten," I said sternly.

"I sent you a text this morning changing it to 10:30. Didn't you get it?"

"No. I told you last night I didn't have cell service here."

He had conveniently forgotten that but could tell we were not happy. We got on the boat and felt the welcome relief of the breeze as we motored away. Cyprian was quiet until we turned into one of the side channels.

"Look at that flower." Cyprian pointed at a water lily. It was a delicate white flower with yellow pistils; the flexible stem looked like long beads strung together in alternating red and white. "It's endangered. You have to know where to find it."

"It's beautiful," I said. I could tell he was trying to be nice.

"I know you like the environmental stuff," he said, looking at me. "It's hard to find these, so I hope I'll get a tip when the trip ends and you won't be mad about this morning."

I rolled my eyes as I raised my binoculars to watch a pair of storks fly overhead. Kathleen pored over the book to identify them. Cyprian leaned off the other side of the boat.

"My present to you," he said, coming up from the water and handing each of us a necklace, the red and white stem as the chain and the delicate endangered lily hanging like a pendant from it.

"But these are endangered, Cyprian. You shouldn't have picked them."

"I know," he said almost proudly. "You can wear them, unless another boat comes by; in that case take off the necklace and stow it in the seat. Especially if it is a police boat."

I wasn't sure whether to laugh or cry but put the creation around my neck. Later, I noticed that the wet flower had dyed a yellow stain on my only white shirt. When Cyprian told me we had cell signal and wanted me to check my texts (to prove he had sent me one that morning), I saw a text that said, "Meet at 10:30. And get me a sandwich from the hotel for lunch." I decided I didn't want to laugh or cry; I wanted to punch him.

By afternoon, we made it to the Black Sea, where I took a swim at a beach with more cows than people. On the way back into the main shipping channel, the tilted bridge tower of a sunken ship stuck out of the water near the Ukrainian border, bright red words in English visible slightly above the water line: Safety First. "Ukraine has nothing to do with Romania," Cyprian announced. "They have always been a separate country with no influence here."

Over the course of the day, Cyprian contradicted most things we said about how the rest of the world worked, including America, although he had never left Romania. He also didn't seem to know or acknowledge Romania's past. Maybe it was simply a sign of youth, but he clearly thought he knew everything and was going to tell us about it.

That evening, Cyprian suggested motoring out to watch the sunset over the Black Sea. Kathleen and I bought a bottle of cheap sparkling wine from the bar, took three glasses, and headed out. The mosquitos were in full force at the dock, but once we got into the channels, a nice breeze kept them away. We stopped at a spot with miles of low sedges and reeds poking out of the water to the west, where the tangerine sun was slowly dropping. As we poured the bubbly into the glasses, a cacophony of frogs started up. A few clouds hung low on the horizon, first pastel pink, then purple, then bright orange. The frogs got louder.

We poured a second glass. The frogs got louder still. There must have been thousands. It sounded like tens of thousands. We literally could barely hear each other. Kathleen and I looked to Cyprian for an explanation, but he said he'd never heard them before. The sun crept closer and closer to the horizon. The frogs bellowed with an otherworldly, manic sound. As the final sliver of sun dropped out of sight, the clouds turned red.

And the frogs stopped.

Instantly.

All at once.

Not a gradual slowing, not a few stragglers croaking once the mass had finished, but all of them, all at once. Completely. Stopped.

Like when the orchestra plays the final notes of a rousing piece and the conductor closes his hands and there is complete silence. Like when the fire alarm that's been blaring for five minutes during the annual test suddenly stops. Except this was nature, not an on-off switch controlled by people. Somehow the frogs knew to stop simultaneously.

Kathleen and I looked at each other, saying nothing except "wow." I filled our glasses. "Now that deserves a toast," I said. "I have never, ever, in all my years of being in nature, seen or heard anything like that."

At that point, I didn't care about Cyprian and his Romanian machismo, the heat and humidity, or the oppressiveness of post-Communist states. That kind of experience in nature is something you can't plan for, but if you are in the right place at the right time, you might get lucky. In my life, I'd experienced many unforgettable moments that grabbed my soul, and I'd add this one to the list. I was happy Kathleen was there to confirm that the event had even happened.

We lodged that night in a small village along the river, at a guesthouse run by a young woman. She explained that the charming trim designs on the eaves, the colorful paint, and the many people with light hair and green eyes were a function of the area's Ukrainian heritage. Cyprian pretended not to hear.

Later that night, Kathleen and I dissected Cyprian's attitude and Romanian culture over a cold beer.

"It bothers me that I'm bothered by him," I said. "I should be more understanding. He's just reflecting his culture."

"Maybe, but he has a lot to learn if he wants to be in the tourism business. Being exposed to us independent American women will be good for him," Kathleen said. "But he is a jerk."

I had to agree. Just as a good guide like Bruce or Brani could make a trip special, a Cyprian could leave a bad taste in your mouth. But even he couldn't ruin my memory of those frogs. On the other hand, I *cannot* remember whether we tipped him.

A six-hour taxi ride took us from Tulcea to the center of Romania and Brasov, a city of 300,000 people in a valley of the Carpathian Mountains, otherwise known as Transylvania. I was happy to be back in the mountains after the flatness and heat of the Delta. Bram Stoker, a Brit, based his novel *Dracula* on the vampire myths of this region, and now Brasov has a big tourist business, starting in the well-preserved medieval city center, where pedestrian-only streets branch out from a central square with a large church. Beside the city, a tram runs up a hill to a café and a sign mimicking the famous Hollywood one—a tall white series of letters announcing BRASOV. What is billed as Dracula's castle, a few miles outside of Brasov, was really the home of Queen Marie (1875–1938). Seized by the Communist party in 1948, the building was repatriated to the family after the fall of Communism, then opened for tourism in 2009.

Kathleen's partner, Richard, flew over from the United States for the weekend to join us; she would return to the States with him. An international businessman, he was used to making two-to-three-day trips overseas, so this one didn't even faze him. We spent our time hanging out in the city, drinking coffee in the morning, cava in the afternoon, and wine at night. We sat at the outdoor cafés and ate little bites. We toured Queen Marie's castle and, intrigued to learn she had spent time in Oregon in the early 1900s, I bought a copy of her autobiography. We took the tram to the hilltop café at the Brasov sign and hiked down to the city through the forest on a rocky path. The first night there, we found an Italian restaurant off a side street that was so good, we went back again the next two nights. It was a great way to travel—not feeling like we had to do anything except hang out and watch the world go by.

I was sorry to see Richard and Kathleen go, since we'd been having such a good time together. Once they left, I joined the week-long group hiking trip I had signed up for to explore the mountains on foot. Every day, three other American women— friends who did a yearly trip together—and I hiked steep uphill tracks to scenic viewpoints, descending to charming medieval villages to spend the night.

Transylvania offered much more than just the Dracula theme, but the region didn't interest me enough to spend any more time there. I had the next two weeks free (part of the "plan to be spontaneous") before I had to be in Vienna to catch a flight to Kathmandu and decided to see more of Romania.

"I need to keep hiking every day to get ready for trekking in Nepal," I said to the guide when I asked for advice. "I'd like to stay in one place with well-marked trails that I can do on my own. I don't need tourist distractions, just a comfortable getaway. Any ideas?"

He knew the perfect place in the far northeastern corner: a lodge he said was his favorite place to stay in all of Romania. There were miles of marked walking trails, and the area was known for the unique cluster of churches painted centuries ago with icons—both inside and out. He called and booked me a room for ten days, after which I would fly to Vienna.

I flew from Bucharest to Iasi, the second largest city in Romania (although I had never heard of it), then drove a rental car for three hours to the region called Bucovina. In this part of Romania, they had forgotten to turn the calendar page about a century ago. The hillsides were dotted with villagers in colorful embroidered garb, cutting hay with scythes and piling it by hand into haystacks. I carefully navigated the road filled with slow-moving wooden horse-drawn carts carrying hay, milk jugs, and, if the driver was Roma, copper stills or colorful skirts to sell.

My guesthouse was a three-story traditional alpine A-frame, on a hill above a small village. My room on the top floor was a large suite with a little balcony, but I quickly realized it was essentially the attic, where the midsummer heat became trapped in the vaulted ceilings. The next day, I asked Elena, one of the owners, if I might get a fan.

"Of course," said Elena said, clearly struggling to speak English. "I will find it and bring it to you."

"Thank you. Can you show me where to hike?" I asked.

"Straight here." Elena pointed to the road going up the hill past the inn. "Then follow the marks on trees—white square with blue cross. Back to bottom of road here." She pointed in a big circle. "Easy."

I set off, water bottle in hand, the blue crosses easy to follow as I made my way through a lovely forest. But as the path became steeper, I started having trouble finding the blue crosses. When I came out of the woods and onto an open hillside where sheep were grazing, I found the crosses had been painted onto rocks placed along a well-worn trail. The path went above a cluster of small wooden buildings, where three huge dogs lunged at the ends of their chains, barking at me as if I were the only meal they'd get that week. About a half a mile later, I reached an unsigned fork in the trail. I tried the left and then the right but couldn't find any blue markers. Although Elena had said it was a loop trail (at least I thought that's what she'd said), I was smart enough to know it was stupid to proceed without markers. I had to go back the way I had come.

When I got to the guesthouse, nobody was in sight. I had slipped on my way down the steep section of trail and jammed my finger badly, so I went into the kitchen and found some ice cubes (a treasured commodity, I later learned) for my finger. Hot and sweaty from the hike, I was disappointed to find no fan in my room. That night at dinner, I asked again.

"Yes, we have a fan," Elena said. "I will ask my husband to find it. Perhaps tomorrow."

It was muggy in the dining room, so I sat near the door onto the deck and opened it to get some air. When the waitress came by, she'd close it, and after three times, I gave up. Instead of complaining, I ordered a bottle of wine and noticed that the nearly full dining room was surprisingly quiet. The Romanian diners were speaking very softly, if at all, usually with a hand shielding their mouths so the next table couldn't hear or see. I wondered if that habit was a vestige from the days when neighbors informed on neighbors and it was best to keep one's business to oneself. There wasn't much laughing or smiling, despite open wine bottles on every table. It was an oddly unsettling ambience.

The next afternoon I looked for Elena to ask again about the fan. I found her in a windowless room behind the kitchen, ironing pillowcases, sweat dripping from her brow. I didn't even need to ask before she said, "My husband is getting a fan." Sure, sure, I thought, and realized that if they had one, she would surely have been using it in that cramped space. Later that day she told me he had found one at the electronics store, but it was too small. So he was still looking.

Dinner that night was chicken in a dark brown gravy, with a green vegetable cooked beyond recognition. I drank more wine. After dinner, I went outside to the wide deck overlooking the village and sat in the still, hot night air, avoiding going up to my stuffy room. At the top of the hill directly opposite, a faint glow soon became a bright, golden full moon that silhouetted individual trees on the ridge as it rose. I had forgotten there would be a blue moon—a second full moon that month, a rare treat. So what if the food wasn't great and the hiking paths were difficult to follow? I was in Romania, and if I was seeking an "authentic" experience, then that's what I was getting. I calmed my inner critic and let the moonlight wash over me.

When I returned to my room, I found a beautiful white four-foot-high oscillating fan, blowing away the heat and bad thoughts of the day. It wasn't until much later that I learned of the Romanian belief that being in a draft (from a fan or an open door) will almost always cause a cold or cough, sometimes a toothache, and, in serious circumstances, even disease, paralysis, or death. Sometimes you just don't know when people are trying to save your life.

———————

Before traveling full-time, I had maintained a regular yoga practice, and my body was feeling the negative effects of a few months without it. My attic room had ample space, but the wood floor was slippery, and I needed a yoga mat. When I asked Elena if there was anywhere to buy one, she told me the nearest store was an hour's drive away in Suceava—at the mall. I set off to see what a Romanian mall was like.

Now it might seem simple to say "I set off," but anytime I had to navigate by myself presented a challenge. Even though I always made sure to get a GPS when I rented a car (no, you can't rely on having a cell signal everywhere for using your phone), I had a love-hate relationship with it. Having little sense of direction, I'd be completely befuddled when I was supposed to "go south" at an unmarked intersection. Without a full-sized map to see the whole region, I found long-distance trips even more stressful than getting lost in a town. I might drive fifty miles the wrong way before I figured it out. But what was I to do? Get in the car and hope for the best.

Luckily, the drive was uneventful, the highlight being a suburb where the Roma lived in huge red houses adorned with silver ornaments hung like year-round Christmas decorations. Most houses had shiny cars parked in front, but many also had the wooden carts I'd seen so often on the road. The Roma have been discriminated against for centuries, plying their trades of coppering, tending horses, and telling fortunes. But here in Romania, the normally nomadic people had settled down and put their own stamp of individuality on the town. Their colorful community offered a sharp contrast to the drabness of the countryside.

When I arrived at the mall, its parking lot packed with cars, I could have been anywhere in the developed world. Inside, the air-conditioned halls were lined with European chain stores. The sporting goods store on the second floor had small sections for basketball, tennis, and running, and a large section for soccer. And yes, they had yoga mats! I bought a cobalt blue one with a black nylon carrying case, and when I arrived at the guesthouse without getting lost, I celebrated with a long yoga session in front of my fancy fan.

———————

After my first hiking debacle, I'd done several shorter hikes, but I felt uncomfortable out in these woods by myself. I rarely saw other people, and when I did, they were gruff-looking men, maybe innocently out for a walk, but still. So I gave up on hiking and concentrated on yoga to keep me in shape for Nepal. With my free time, I decided to visit the eight famous painted monasteries of Bucovina.

I read that these Byzantine art masterpieces were famed for their elaborate fifteenth- and sixteenth-century frescoes covering the exterior walls of the churches, telling Biblical stories via picture panels as in a comic book. Except there was nothing comical about these paintings. I'd been in a lot of churches, since they always seemed to be part of the tourist experience in Europe, so I was used to the gruesome depictions of hell, with pitchforks and fire, the bloody crucifixion statues and paintings, and even the head of St. John the Baptist on a tray. But I soon noticed these paintings went far beyond.

Battle scenes with great gore and guts abounded, the villains generally depicted as Turks and Muslims, perhaps reflecting the Ottoman Empire threat of the time. Lots of scourging, and bloody backs streaked dark red with blood. At one monastery, the devil was a woman. From the ladder to heaven, sinners fell to terrible, violent death and dismemberment. But worst were the many, many paintings of beheadings—in step-by-step gory detail.

After visiting four monasteries, I decided I'd had enough of religious violence. I skipped the other four and spent my remaining days doing yoga, reading and writing, and drinking wine. I realized I had chosen my location badly. I thought I wanted solitude and easy hiking, but this remote hotel had neither character nor inviting characters to talk to. What I should have asked for was a vibrant small town, with a variety of restaurants, some foreign tourist traffic, well-marked walking trails, and maybe scenic mountains thrown in—more like Brasov with its good-time vibe.

My final day in Romania, I finished reading the short autobiography of Queen Marie I'd picked up in Brasov. Born into a British royal family, she married Romanian King Frederic and ruled with him in the early part of the twentieth century. Her observation from the early 1920s rang true to me almost one hundred years later:

> From the beginning of time Romania was a land subject to invasions. One tyrannical master after another laid heavy hands upon its people… [and] the result is that the Romanian folk are not gay. Their songs are sad, their dances slow,… [and] rarely are their voices loud; the tunes they play on their flutes wail out endlessly their longing and desire that appear to remain eternally unsatisfied, to contain no hope, no fulfillment.

Although Queen Marie loved Romania to the end, I felt eager to find a more jovial atmosphere.

CHAPTER 10

VIENNA, AUSTRIA

AUGUST 2015

"I'll have the Käsespatzle and a glass of white wine, please," I said to my lunch waiter at the outdoor café in Vienna. "And the apfelstrudel for dessert." He nodded solemnly and scurried off. A chubby pack of T-shirted American tourists walked by, leading me to wonder if I should have passed on the dessert.

Vienna was exactly what I needed. A touch of luxury after Romania and Bulgaria and before Nepal. I was well under budget (Eastern Europe had been a bargain), so I splurged on a nice hotel in the center of the city, near the Albertina Museum. I booked four nights in a modern suite with down pillows and comforter, a big flat-screen TV, dimmer lights, a fancy three-headed shower (that I couldn't figure out how to work), and lots of huge, fluffy towels. I didn't really miss those things when I didn't have them (except maybe the pillows), but I sure appreciated them now that I did.

I had never been to Vienna and, as had become a new pattern, hadn't done any advance research. Upon arrival, I unpacked my bag and followed another pattern—setting off on foot to get lost with a small-print tourist map and no reading glasses.

I reveled in the modern urban feel of Vienna after the past couple months of Soviet-era drabness, architectural nightmares, and the carcasses of towns devastated by war or economics. This city felt prosperous and alive, with beautifully maintained old buildings, museums, monuments, and parks. I didn't even get lost. In busy sidewalk cafés, people speaking German, Italian, French, and English seemed happy and carefree, enjoying the music capital of the world.

Back in my hotel room after the apfelstrudel, I looked up the history of Vienna and learned it is a marvel of reconstruction and resilience. The city's location on the Danube (far from the Delta) has always been strategic; it served as capital of the Holy Roman Empire in the 1400s, the last defense against the European invasion of the Ottoman Turks in the 1600s (after they took both Bulgaria and Hungary), the capital of the Austro-Hungarian Empire in the 1800s, and just another city in Hitler's Germany when he declared that Austria ceased to exist. During WWII, fifty-two bombing attacks destroyed twenty percent of the city's houses. Historians estimate that barely forty civilian vehicles survived the raids; over three thousand bomb craters pockmarked the landscape. It wasn't until 1955 that the country regained its sovereignty and Vienna could begin yet another rebirth.

I reconnected with the Austrians I had met in New Zealand at the B&B and was treated to a home-cooked meal one night and a special wine region dinner the next. I shopped for a sweatshirt and pants to take to Nepal. I ate a lot of pastries and enjoyed wandering the city. But my top priority was to get my hair colored. I hadn't had it done since my "no orange" experience in Krakow, so I asked the woman at hotel reception for help with an appointment on short notice. She made a few calls while I waited, then told me I was in luck. "I got you into the best salon in town, tomorrow at 11:30."

At the appointed time, I arrived at a very chic salon, the kind you almost feel too dowdy to enter no matter what you look like. I checked in with the Goth receptionist, who then handed me over to a young woman with spiky pink hair, who escorted me to a chair where the stylist, Tomas, came to talk to me. He was as flamboyant as a young, hip gay man could be, dressed in a tight pair of jeans rolled up to exactly the right length above his sockless ankles and loafers, and a loose tank top showing off his new chest tattoo, which complemented the ones on his arms. He spoke English, although I had looked up how to say "no orange" in German just in case, so I told him I needed a trim of my hair and bangs ("fringe," he called them).

Tomas went to fix the color while another young girl brought me a glass of wine and massaged my temples with an aromatherapy oil. She offered a manicure while I waited, but for my upcoming trekking in Nepal the last thing I needed was nail polish. While putting the dye on my hair, Tomas told me he had grown up in Krakow. I asked him why he would ever leave such a beautiful city.

"Oh, darling," he said, "you have no idea what it was like being gay in that ultra-Catholic city. Just horrible. I couldn't wait to finish school and get out of there."

I hadn't thought of that.

After Tomas finished and the color had set for half an hour, another young girl, this one dressed in a Japanese-style anime outfit, took me to the sink to wash my hair and give me a ten-minute scalp massage. I was liking this place. When I went back to Tomas's chair, yet another woman combed out my hair. What was she, number four? Or five? Tomas returned and picked up the scissors.

"Remember, I'm growing it out, so don't cut much. But the fringe can be a tad shorter since it will be another two months before I can get it cut again."

Tomas trimmed the edges of my hair, telling me a story with great animation as the scissors swung around wildly. He combed out my bangs and picked up a piece. Before I knew it, he had cut off half the length so it hung only to the middle of my forehead.

"Too short," I squealed, but too late.

"Oh, I thought you said you wanted it short for your hike. If I were hiking, I would want everything short, but of course I wouldn't be hiking." He laughed at himself and picked up another piece. "It will look fine. Don't worry. You'll like it."

What could I do? He finished the bangs with a straight cut across the front—very much the style for a chic twenty-something with no lines in her forehead and thick lips that could handle a bright red lipstick to go with the look. But I looked more like someone from the 1950s, maybe myself at age eight with a pixie bowl haircut. Or, put more positively, like Audrey Hepburn in *Roman Holiday*. That was it. They were my Audrey Hepburn bangs. And at least my hair wasn't orange.

I thanked Tomas (although under my breath I cursed him) and went to reception to check out. A young woman with purple hair took my credit card to pay for what turned out to be the most expensive visit I'd ever had to a hairdresser—more than twice what I usually paid in the States. I guess it cost a lot to support all those girls running around.

My last night at the hotel, I curled up in crisp white sheets with a glass of Austrian red wine, looking out the window at the sculptural detail of the green copper dome on the neighboring building, feeling the romance of the muted lights of the city, and admiring the huge statue of a horse and rider on a pedestal high above the pedestrians. I had gotten my fix of urban culture and indulged in a good dose of creature comforts. Now I was re-energized for more exotic adventures.

CHAPTER 11

MUSTANG, NEPAL

AUGUST 2015

"*Bistari, bistari*," my Sherpa guide said as I placed one foot in front of the other, plodding up the steep, rocky path. He repeated it in English: "Slowly, slowly." Above 13,000 feet in the Himalaya, the thin air made it hard to breathe. Despite the cool temperature (in the fifties), a steady stream of sweat dripped off my nose. I didn't wipe it. For each six steps, I silently chanted the Buddhist mantra Om Mani Padme Hum, holding the hum for three steps to let it resonate. Saying the mantra helped keep me moving.

I was a few days into a three-week trek into the remote Mustang region of Nepal. I'd gotten used to hearing the name as "Moostang," a pronunciation that seemed to emphasize its foreignness. I was completely in awe of the rocky, dry landscape with snow-capped mountains rising so far into the sky I could hardly believe it. Using the mantra, I kept my pace steady: I walked within my breath and not ahead of it. Around the next bend, I saw a huge pile of stones with a pole rising from the middle, secured by ropes strung out on three sides like a tent. Scores of frayed prayer flags tied to the ropes flapped in the wind. I'd made it to the top of the Gyu La Pass.

I picked up a small stone and added it to the pile, following the tradition of the people who had passed this way over the centuries, always on foot or on horseback. A short path on the right led onto a promontory, below which the world dropped off thousands of feet into the river chasm. I took off my daypack and walked to the edge. A few ravens flew below me, and the wind nudged me to sit down. I was suddenly overcome with an emotion I could only describe as happiness. My mind shouted a question over the wind: "Why did it take me so long to come here?"

———————

But I'm ahead of myself—I wasn't magically transported from a café in Vienna to a remote mountain pass in northwestern Nepal. First I flew to Kathmandu, where Durga, a smiling representative from the trekking company, met me outside the international terminal.

"Welcome to Nepal," Durga said, after introducing himself and placing around my neck a white *kata*, the ceremonial silk scarf given at the arrival or departure of guests. "It is good of you to come. So many tourists have canceled their trips because of the earthquake."

Four months earlier, a major earthquake had devastated large parts of Nepal, including Kathmandu. Almost half of all flights into the country had been eliminated as tourists canceled trips, even to unaffected areas or for trips that were months away. It had never occurred to me to cancel.

Durga shepherded me across a parking lot to the tiny domestic terminal with only four airline counters: Yeti Airlines, Goma Air, Tara Air, and Buddha Air. I was booked on Goma, though I thought Buddha Air might have been more auspicious. Skipping the line, Durga handed my bag to a man behind the counter and got a boarding pass.

"Your flight leaves in twenty minutes," Durga said. "You must go through security now." He pointed at the single X-ray machine, where I put my backpack and tote bag. "You go to the right to the women's side. Big Dawa will be at the airport in Pokhara to meet you. I will see you when you return after the trek." He pressed his palms together and said, "Namaste."

I went through a small, draped area for a private, quick pat-down out of sight of men. Beyond was a cramped dingy area filled with waiting passengers. My flight was already being called for boarding.

On the twenty-five-minute flight west to Pokhara, I saw my first view of the Himalayan mountains, stretching seemingly forever east and west. The twelve-seater plane's cruising altitude was 12,000 feet, yet many peaks were well over 20,000 feet high. I was glued to the window; I was going trekking in the Himalaya!

At the tiny Pokhara airport, Big Dawa, a chubby, middle-aged man, was waiting for me in the staggering humidity. We rode in an open jeep to the guesthouse owned by Stan, the friend of my friend James (who'd told me about this trip). Big Dawa told me Stan had been in the hospital, having become dehydrated during the Mustang trek two weeks before. He had only been home for a day, so I might not meet him until the next day. That didn't matter to me, since I'd been flying all day and wanted nothing more than a shower, a cold drink, and maybe a nap.

We drove to a three-story building in a residential neighborhood. The main floor seemed to be a lobby, but without any furniture. Big Dawa took me directly to the third-floor dining area, with a long wooden table and chairs, and offered me a cold drink from a rusty refrigerator. Ragged curtains hung in front of aluminum windows; thick black mold covered the sills. I don't know what I expected for lodging in Pokhara, but it wasn't this house that looked like it hadn't been cleaned for a year. The bedrooms were on the second floor, but not in much better shape. The bathroom fixtures were rusted from the damp climate, and on the bed sat one sad pillow atop a faded coverlet. I was hopeful when I saw a ceiling fan, but Big Dawa said the electricity was rationed.

"Sometimes we have power for a few hours during the day, but always between nine and ten at night. You can use the fan then. And make sure to charge your camera and phone batteries."

The situation was a far cry from the luxuries of Vienna. I realized I had expected primitive conditions on the trek, but not while still in town.

Over the next few days, my soon-to-be trekking companions filtered in. The first to arrive were Martin, an Australian who had done the Mustang trip before, and Duane, an American climber who often traveled in Nepal and knew Stan well. I asked them for advice about things I should buy in Pokhara that I might need on the trek.

"There are lots of things," Duane said. "Let's go shopping." The three of us walked to the tourist street, full of cheap brand-name knockoffs. I bought a $2 neoprene water bottle (which cracked the second day; I was lucky to find a replacement in a small mountain village en route—for $22!), a $5 pair of adjustable hiking poles (which broke after three days and had to be duct-taped together), an ugly purple wicking-fabric shirt, and an extra pair of wool socks.

"For three weeks of sleeping in a tent," Martin said, "a pillow is a nice luxury." I couldn't have agreed more.

We walked a few blocks to a non-tourist shopping area, where I bought a pillow and a patterned lime-green pillowcase.

"Did you bring a sleeping bag and travel sheet?" Duane asked.

"No, Stan is providing a sleeping bag," I said.

"You probably should buy the matching sheet set too," Duane said. "Stan's standards aren't always up to snuff." Yes, I had noticed.

Back at the guesthouse that evening, Stan was feeling well enough to join me and Duane on the veranda before dinner. Although pale and weak from his hospital stay, Stan filled his glass with a generous portion of gin and a small splash of tonic. The men traded news of mutual friends. I was grateful Stan didn't ask me what I thought of his guesthouse. When Duane told him about my purchases, Stan laughed, clearly oblivious to my reason for buying the sheets.

———

The rest of the group arrived the next day. Gretchen, Sara, and Justin were expats living in Bangkok, while Nima and Sherene lived in Nepal and knew Stan but not each other.

Before dinner, I went to the rooftop deck, where a slight breeze gave some relief from the heat. Nima was already there, and Sherene and Duane joined us a few minutes later. Nima told us he was a Sherpa from the Khumbu, the Everest region of Nepal. He had met and married an American woman, then lived in Seattle with her for twenty years. After a divorce, he had returned to the family land in the Khumbu and now ran a guesthouse. Sherene told us she grew up in Malaysia (her father's country), had spent time in China (her mother's country), and now lived in Kathmandu. She was a thick-set woman who had shaved her head so she wouldn't have to deal with her hair on the trek. I wasn't willing to go that far, but maybe my short Audrey Hepburn bangs were a blessing in disguise.

When Duane and I said we were from the States, Sherene jumped in. "Americans have no concept of the poverty in Nepal. Climbers and trekkers spend thousands of dollars to come here, while most of the people have nothing."

"Our tourist dollars help the economy," Duane said. I stayed silent, surprised by the venom in Sherene's voice, although I agreed with Duane, so I nodded. My philosophy was that travel was a way of connecting with people, not a means to exploit them, and I tried to "buy local" when I could. Many countries' economies were very tourist dependent, and I was happy to support them.

Sherene looked at me and said, "Yeah, spend your tourist dollars pampering yourselves. Really, who takes sheets and pillows on a trek?"

Martin must have told her about our excursion. I shrugged and laughed to break the tension. "Guilty. I like to be comfortable when I sleep."

Sherene smirked and abruptly stood up. I thought about defending myself by pointing out I was thirty years older than her but stayed quiet.

I was happy she didn't know I had also asked for a double sleeping pad. As she huffed away, I resolved to stay out of her way.

The next morning, we flew in a prop plane from Pokhara to the town of Jomson, our starting point, at an elevation of around 9,000 feet. We would be trekking for seven days into the heart of the Forbidden Kingdom of Mustang, which borders Tibet. Travel to the area had been closed to Westerners until 1993, and even now the number of visitors was tightly controlled. It wasn't until 2008 that the country became a district of Nepal. I was elated to be traveling in such a remote place.

Our destination was the annual Yartung Horse Festival, in the ancient city of Lo Manthang, where we'd stay for four days, then turn around and walk back. Before we left Jomson, Duane and I stocked up on small bottles of Khukri Rum (the local liquor), even though Martin told us we could replenish the supply in the small villages we'd pass through. Liquor was another luxury I preferred not to forsake if I didn't have to.

For our small group of eight trekkers, we had quite a large support group. A young man called Little Dawa oversaw three other Sherpa guides, two cooks, four kitchen boys, a local man whose job was unclear, two pony men for the eight horses guests could choose to ride, two mule men to manage the eight beasts who carried the tents, sleeping pads, luggage (mine complete with pillow, sheets, and yoga mat), food, and the mess tent, including a table and chairs for ten.

The first few days of hiking were relatively short and easy, designed to help us acclimate to the higher altitude. The temperatures were cool in the morning, warming to tee-shirt weather by afternoon. I felt strong and fit, despite my worries that I wouldn't be in shape. We followed a path along the wide, graveled Kali Gandaki River, through a beautiful, deep red rock canyon. After a few days, we crossed the river on a sturdy metal bridge and headed up into the mountains. As we gained elevation, the occasional cloud break revealed the snow-capped peaks of the Annapurna range in the distance. Absolutely, stunningly beautiful.

The group quickly settled into a routine. Each morning at 5:30 a.m., the kitchen staff delivered coffee or tea to the tents. (Everyone had their own tent.) Promptly at 6:00 a.m., a basin of hot wash water arrived. By 6:30, we were dressed, duffels packed, and ready for breakfast, which we ate while the staff rolled up the sleeping pads, took down the tents, and loaded the gear on the mules. Little Dawa would then brief us about what to expect that day, always telling us how many hours we'd be walking, never how many miles. It struck me as odd that we had a precise morning schedule, here in a place where time meant nothing other than sunrise and sunset.

I walked alone for a few hours every day, but also often walked with Gretchen and Sarah. They were both Americans, but neither had lived in the States for the past twenty years. Gretchen published lifestyle magazines for several Asian cities, and Sarah was a freelance journalist and author. We talked about books, careers, aging, and men. We shared stories about travel, sights to see, and foods to eat. We discussed religion and art and the politics of Asia. I was fascinated with their foreign perspectives on the world, including on America.

Each afternoon, when we arrived at our campsite, the tents had been set up in a row or semicircle, our sleeping gear and luggage already placed inside. Camps were usually near a teahouse with running water, and I'd read, do yoga if there was a flat spot (ignoring Sherene's look when I rolled out the yoga mat), or simply sit in the camp chair looking at the mountains. I sipped and savored a tot of my Khukri Rum each night.

The day after we crossed the Gyu La, we had a rest day, camping in the schoolyard of the small elementary school that served the region. When the kids arrived in the morning, they were bashfully curious, fixedly watching us brush our teeth or drink coffee until they had to go inside to class. I wondered what they thought about us strange foreigners camping in their schoolyard. That afternoon, when the teachers brought all fifteen of the children to the courtyard to perform a song, Martin filmed them with his iPad, then showed them the video. He seemed so at ease with the kids while they clambered over him, while I was uncertain as to what to do, even as a spectator. What had I been thinking to volunteer at a school when I had no experience? I was definitely going to be in over my head. Maybe I could talk the principal into letting me do photocopying or clean the toilets.

———————

We'd been on the trek for a week and were close to Lo Manthang when I realized something had shifted. The days passed simultaneously slowly and quickly. Nothing about my life seemed familiar anymore. I was hiking in a pair of baggy flowered pants I'd bought in Vienna (possibly the only piece of flowered clothing I'd ever owned), and when I looked in the rare mirror, I saw those crazy bangs. My past felt irrelevant, as if it were a collection of stories about somebody else. Instead of talking much, I found myself sitting back and listening more. I could have sworn that my heartbeat had slowed to half its normal rate, despite the altitude. I felt an inexplicable calmness.

The total lack of input from the outside world—no cell phone, TV, or internet access—surely contributed to the way I felt. But so did talking with Nima, a Buddhist and daily meditator who had given up an urban American lifestyle to return to the mountains. I'd read quite a bit about Buddhism, but Nima's teaching brought it alive. He emphasized the importance of patience and compassion. He encouraged me to be more deliberate about my sporadic meditation. He was a model of the calmness I wished I could keep forever.

I thought about times I'd been distracted in my life by inconsequential things, pointlessly annoyed by minor inconveniences or events totally beyond my control. Nima told me the path to enlightenment included insight into one's true nature and compassion for all beings. He pointed out that some Buddhists pray to meet difficult and uncooperative people because they want to practice patience, and I wondered if Sherene, who continued to insult or contradict me whenever she could, was another teacher in a way.

I was also feeling an unexpectedly intense emotion about the landscape. Nature and mountains had always made me happy. But when I caught a glimpse of the towering glacier-covered peaks or peered into a deep river chasm, an almost overwhelming joy rose from the pit of my stomach.

I'd been turning the ubiquitous prayer wheels whenever I passed them and putting stones on the cairns at the passes. I continued to chant Om Mani Padme Hum as I walked. To show compassion for all life, I moved nuisance earwigs out of my tent instead of crushing them. But whenever I congratulated myself for adopting the Buddhist attitude to live without desire for creature comforts and material things, I had to acknowledge that I was grateful for my pillow and longed for a hot shower, clean hair, and a bed.

Whether it was the scenery, the solitude, or simply the altitude, I felt like I had unearthed a deep part of my soul that had been buried beneath busyness, expectations, or lack of awareness. I had often declared that I wasn't traveling to "find myself," but there I was, finding a hidden part of me despite not looking.

———————

Lo Manthang, at an elevation of 12,600 feet, was a remote town of only a few hundred people that dated from 1380. Only twelve miles from the Chinese-Tibetan border pass, this ancient walled capital city of the province of Mustang sat in a wide swath of rolling hills and meadows.

"The Chinese want a road from Tibet to this area," Little Dawa said. "We are nervous about giving the Chinese access, since we could never fight them if they took this territory like they did Tibet. A road will change the character of Lo Manthang and Mustang forever."

Our camp was on the edge of town, in a small grassy field directly across from a two-story hotel. In late afternoon there was already a chill to the air.

"The hotel has rooms available if anyone wants to rent one instead of staying in the tents," Little Dawa told us. "They each have a bathroom with a shower, but you can also buy a shower next door if you stay in the tents." The room cost about $3; to take a shower without the room was fifty cents.

I'd backpacked and camped a lot in my day and was no stranger to sleeping on the ground in a tent, but it had been a few decades since I'd done it for several nights in a row, and my back and right hip were feeling it. "I'll take a room," I said, knowing it would feed Sherene's stereotype of me. I was happy that Sara, Justin, and Nima also chose the hotel.

I was pleasantly surprised to find that the room and the bathroom were meticulously clean. I put my matching sheet and pillowcase on the bed and fluffed up the extra pillow. The bathroom was narrow and spare, a toilet at one end, sink at the other, and showerhead coming out of the wall in the middle. I took a glorious, steamy shower and washed my hair, not caring that the entire room got wet. I washed most of my clothes and hung them around the bedroom to dry. I was ready to explore Lo Manthang.

I followed the main street to a small square in town, past two-story shops of ochre or white adobe, with colorfully painted doors framed by prayer flags. The women I saw wore traditional long, wrapped skirts, silk shirts, woolen vests, and woven belts. The men were more modern, in jeans, T-shirts, and fleece jackets. At the far end of town, the monastery school hummed with maroon-and-orange-clad young monks sweeping or playing in the courtyard. I saw a few German and British tourists, but the town was mostly empty. Because of the earthquake, Little Dawa said, only forty trekking permits had been issued this year, instead of the usual three hundred.

Shopkeepers stood in the doorways, smiling and inviting me in to see woven rugs, Tibetan turquoise and coral jewelry, bowls and boxes, Buddhist paintings, or handmade woolen scarves and gloves. To my surprise, most vendors spoke enough English to carry on a conversation. They all had the same story: they were hungry for business and cash, worried about surviving the season without the meager tourist money they usually earned.

"We can't eat our goods," an old woman told me.

I bought a pair of earrings from her. Then another pair from the delightful man who showed me rugs I couldn't carry. And a third and fourth pair from women with babies on their hips. I was earring rich and felt like I'd done my part.

———————

I had no idea what to expect from the three-day Yartung Horse Festival, which officially began the next afternoon. I thought it might be like a county fair with games and food. I was wrong. The first day featured a short opening parade before the participants moved to a large field about a mile outside town.

Gretchen and I walked up to the field, expecting some festivities. We saw six large three-sided canvas tents painted with Tibetan symbols and designs, but nothing much was happening. Men lounged in the tents, being served food and drinks by the women, who then gathered separately to chat around the cooking fires. Horses fed in the lush pasture. We took photos but felt like interlopers, so we went back to town.

It turned out that the main events of the festival were the nightly horse races on the dirt street outside of the town walls. Gretchen and I found a spot amid the crowd where we could easily see the racers fly by, most dressed in loose pants, embroidered tunics, and bright gold khatas around their necks. Their tiny Himalayan ponies had colorful blankets under their saddles, and some had scarves tied around their necks too.

I never did find out what the rules were, or even whether there were any. Sometimes two riders raced each other. Other times, a single galloping rider tried to perform a feat such as knocking a bottle off a wall with a rock or picking up a scarf from the ground. The third night, the local monks got onto and fell off the horses, holding onto the reins for dear life in their bright orange robes and maroon sneakers. The crowd cheered and laughed, and I felt privileged to be part of this ancient festival in this hidden corner of the world.

Our final night in Lo Manthang, I took a long, hot shower and snuggled into my bed. The next day we would tackle the highest pass of the trip, at 14,500 feet. A cold front had moved in, and temperatures had dropped into the thirties. I knew the hiking wouldn't be easy, but I was ready to walk again.

———————

We got an early start for the hike out of Lo Manthang, moving gradually uphill past the field where the big tents were being taken down. It was a lousy, foggy day. Within an hour, the rain started and spat on us our entire way to the top of the pass. I wore most of my layers but was still chilled, despite the effort of going uphill. At the top, I tied prayer flags I'd bought in town onto the many strings already there, hoping for the fog to lift for a view from the high point of the trip, but no luck. I guess my karma wasn't good enough. We started down the steep back side of the pass and soon stopped for lunch at what Little Dawa said was the oldest monastery in Nepal.

The place seemed creepy and deserted, and although Little Dawa said eight or nine monks lived there, we never saw any. We ate lunch in a small unheated room and tried unsuccessfully to warm up. I might have imagined it, or it might have been the weather, but everyone seemed on edge.

After lunch, we went into the main temple building. We took our shoes off, as always, and padded in with stockinged feet. The walls were covered in paintings, as was typical for the monasteries, but these were different and more menacing. Demons and monsters with lurid grins squished people and animals under their taloned feet. Some had crowns made of skulls; others had snakes wrapped around them.

"The paintings depict what you will see when you die," Little Dawa said. "Knowing what to expect helps you pass through that phase of death more easily. The gods and goddesses must be worshiped, but it's the Protectors who will make sure the demons don't get you." He pointed to a wall painting several centuries old. But the Protector was dancing on crushed bodies just like the demons and, worse yet, wore a necklace of severed heads. The pictures reminded me of the gruesome church paintings in Romania. Historically important they might be, but I'd had enough and went back outside.

Dark clouds continued to hang over us, and the wind had picked up. I shivered as if the spirits didn't want us there. As I sat alone in the courtyard, Little Dawa appeared. He told me that Sherene wanted to make camp at the monastery, but the weather was getting worse, and he thought we should go to the originally intended lower camp. The thought of spending the night at the monastery filled me with an inexplicable dread.

"We definitely should not stay here," I said firmly. "We are not meant to be here right now."

As if all he needed was an affirmation, he nodded and gave word to the porters to leave for the lower camp. When the rest of the group joined us, we started downhill, my feeling of unease slowly dissipating. Within an hour, the skies were clear, and the wind had died completely. Our campsite provided the most beautiful and spectacular location of the whole trip: a lush green meadow with a few grazing horses, in front of stunning red rock cliffs with ancient cave dwellings high above the ground. Before dinner, I had a big swallow of Khukri Rum and wondered if my insistence on leaving had somehow pleased the Protectors.

———————

Our final week of trekking was as satisfying as the first. I'd managed to avoid confrontations with Sherene and had become friends with Nima and Gretchen. Nima had invited me to come to his guesthouse and hike in the Everest region (the Khumbu) for the next few weeks. I had been snobbishly spurning the popular Everest Base Camp route, but his invitation was tempting.

"I can easily arrange for a guide for you," Nima said. "You could stay at my place for a night or two, then trek for a couple of weeks before the prime tourist season starts. That is, if there will be any tourists this year, given the earthquake."

"I'd love to do it, Nima, but I've made a commitment to volunteer at Stan's school, and I don't want to let them down on short notice," I said sadly. I'd always had a thing about following through on commitments, probably why I'd been given the "Because I Said I Would" T-shirt.

"Think about it and talk to Stan when we get back. I'm sure he'd understand. It won't take long to organize if you decide to come."

After almost three weeks, we reached the last day of the trek. My skin was desert dry, but my feet were thankfully blister-free as I walked alone back into Jomson late in the afternoon, lagging behind to stretch out that final day as long as I could. We'd spend the night there and catch the first flight to Pokhara in the morning.

The hotel lobby had an internet connection, so when I walked in, I saw my companions' heads bowed over devices that had been dark and silent for the past few weeks. But I was still in the Himalaya and didn't want to trade a minute of it for looking at a phone or computer. Instead,

I ordered mint tea and sat at the window, watching the evening sun light up the face of a snow-covered peak right behind the airstrip.

"Don't you want to know if your family is okay?" Duane asked, when I explained that I would not check emails or news until I got to Pokhara. "Aren't you curious about what's happened in the world?"

I did fervently hope all was well with my family and friends. But if something bad had happened, what could I do until I got to Pokhara? Nothing. The same was true for news of the world. I had been happy for the past several weeks not knowing, so why change that?

The next morning, we flew back to the still oppressively sticky lowlands of Pokhara and Stan's dirty guesthouse. It was Thursday night, and all I could think about was how on Monday, I had to bear the humidity and go to the school for two weeks surrounded by boisterous children. My calmness was quickly evaporating.

I went to the third floor, hoping to find Stan. The moldy windows in the stuffy dining room had still not been cleaned, but Stan was out on the deck with a tall drink I assumed was gin. I decided not to beat around the bush.

"Nima has invited me to his place and to trek in the Everest region next week," I told Stan. "I'd like to go, but I'm concerned about my commitment to the school. What would you think if I made a donation instead of volunteering? Would that be a culturally insensitive thing to do? Please be honest with me."

Stan laughed. "Hell, no," he said. "Money is always better than time. Go to the Khumbu and forget the volunteering."

"But James said the volunteering was important."

"James brought his two young daughters, so having them participate at the school was important to him. If you don't want to volunteer, it won't make any difference. Sometimes it's hard for the teachers to find something for volunteers to do without distracting the kids. They need books and clothes and computers more than your time."

"Why didn't you tell me that before?" I asked with a huge sense of relief. I knew how to give money.

"Americans and Australians always want to volunteer. It makes them feel good. You asked about volunteering, so that's what I arranged."

I made a generous contribution to the school, but I knew the amount was more about me than about the kids. I wished I were a better person, but this was the truth.

CHAPTER 12

KATHMANDU, NEPAL

AUGUST–SEPTEMBER 2015

The seven-dollar bus ride took seven hours, even though Kathmandu is only 120 miles from Pokhara. And that was on the express. The neon green coach was modern and comfortable, with air conditioning and Wi-Fi, not at all like the crowded school bus I expected. For hours, the bus climbed up a long pass of nonstop hairpin turns and drop-offs without guardrails, with few passing lanes or pullouts anywhere. Both the uphill and downhill traffic slowed to the pace of the biggest, most overloaded truck. Eventually our bus crested the pass and started downhill into the twenty-square-mile, smog-filled Kathmandu valley that was home to 2.5 million people. The two-lane road merged into city streets where motorcycles, cars, trucks, and buses ignored any lane markings while pedestrians and bicyclists flitted in and out of the swarm. The city seemed dirty, chaotic, and polluted, the feeling exacerbated by random piles of earthquake rubble.

At a crowded intersection, Nima and I got off the bus. He would stay with a friend that night and fly home to the Khumbu the next morning, while I'd spend a day in Kathmandu with Gretchen before flying to Lukla to meet him again. I collected my suitcase and got into the cab that Nima had hailed.

"I'll see you in a few days," he said. "I hope you enjoy the Hotel Tibet." Gretchen had recommended the hotel to me and Durga, who had met me when I first arrived in Nepal, had made the reservation for me.

The cabbie maneuvered through the chaos of the busy streets to the Lazimpat neighborhood, where he turned onto a small, quiet side street. At the dead end, a modern Sheraton loomed to the left while a traditional wooden building with a porched entrance, the Hotel Tibet, sat serenely on the right. I went into a cool, comfortably appointed lobby that begged one to linger, and breathed a sigh of relief that I wasn't at Stan's any longer.

"The rooftop bar and restaurant are on the fifth floor," the check-in clerk told me. My clean, bright room on the third floor had twenty-four-hour air conditioning and electricity, internet, and a mini-fridge to keep my water cold. These small luxuries seemed extravagant.

The hotel had a next-day laundry service, so I changed into the one clean outfit I had left and sent everything else to be washed. I turned on my computer, logged into an internet that worked (unlike Stan's), and found weeks of emails. One of them was from Kathleen, confirming that she and Stephanie, another Portland friend, would meet me in Portugal in October after my trip to Bhutan. I bought a plane ticket from Kathmandu to Lisbon and felt lucky to have my close friend researching where to go and what to do.

I went upstairs to the large outdoor terrace for dinner and was pleased to see several deep couches and chairs, along with a few dining tables, and only a few people. I sank into one of the couches with my feet curled under me, a comfy contrast to the hard benches of the teahouses, the folding camp chairs of the trek, and the wooden chairs at Stan's. I enjoyed a vodka tonic and pasta dinner in the now cool evening air.

In the distance, on the horizon, a comfortably familiar thick, orange full moon was rising. I snapped a picture with my phone and remembered the moon in Zambia. I scanned my photos and figured out that I had photographed the full moon in clear skies nine months in a row: in Zambia, Portland, Australia, New Zealand, Idaho, Wyoming, Krakow (twice), Romania, and now here. What were the chances of that? The moon seemed to be as much of a vagabond wandering the world as I was trying to be. Surely it was a good omen.

The next day, Sunday, Gretchen, who had been to Kathmandu many times, and I met at my hotel and set out on foot. Sometimes there were skinny sidewalks, but mostly we walked in the gutter along with everybody else, many people wearing face masks because of the dense diesel fumes. The women wore brightly colored saris and carried open umbrellas to block the sun. The men sported jeans and T-shirts or loose-fitting dress shirts. Bicyclists swerved in and out of the traffic; buses passed within inches of my shoulders. I was frayed by the noise and stress and realized that what I had come to think of as my Mustang calm was completely gone. Gretchen, tall and regal, walked firmly and confidently ahead.

We went to Thamel, the usually packed and chaotic tourist area, now empty because tourists weren't coming. I resisted buying any of the cheap but tempting knockoff items, after my Pokhara experience, but did find an authentic name-brand pair of gray hiking pants to replace my Viennese flowered pair. We paged through coffee-table books in Gretchen's favorite bookstore and fingered cashmere sweaters in a fancy shop outside of Thamel.

By late afternoon, we were exhausted from walking all day in ninety-degree heat.

"How about a cold beer?" Gretchen said. "The Garden of Dreams is around the corner."

"Sounds perfect."

We passed through a gate in a high wall into a quiet space, with tables set on a grassy lawn under shady trees. Part of the space was closed because of earthquake damage, but the feeling of serenity was palpable. The beer slid down easily.

"I'm sad we have to say good-bye," I said.

"Me too," she said. "But the joy of meeting new people when traveling overshadows the sadness, doesn't it?"

I said I supposed so, but I still felt a little lonely. Gretchen had evening plans with her friends, so I went alone to the rooftop terrace, ordered a vodka tonic, and ate chicken satay for dinner. I watched the moon come up again but went to bed early. I had to be up at 4:15 a.m. to make sure I had everything packed and ready to go by 5:00, when my ride would arrive to take me to the airport for my flight to Lukla. I was ready to be done with the chaos and pollution of Kathmandu and get back to the mountains.

———

That early, quiet Monday morning, we drove fifteen minutes through town to the airport. We saw a few bicyclists and pedestrians, and a few unexpected joggers, but hardly any cars. The streets were dark, and I realized there were no streetlights. At the airport, the parking lot was also dark, except for a lone streetlight in the distance. A woman with three large thermoses sat on the curb by the terminal entrance, selling cups of tea.

Durga had coordinated details with Nima for this part of the trip and was waiting for me when the driver dropped me off with the small duffel bag I'd bought the day before. (I had left unneeded things in my suitcase at the hotel.) Durga had a larger duffel with him that contained supplies Nima had asked him to send along with me. I hoped I wouldn't get asked that security question about whether I had packed my own luggage.

Durga led me through the dark construction zone at the old domestic terminal I'd flown to Pokhara from when I'd first arrived in the country. "I'll see you again in two weeks," he said as I went through the women's side of the security checkpoint. In the small departure lounge, there was no indication that anyone was boarding or even queueing, even though my Goma Air flight was scheduled to leave in fifteen minutes. I surveyed the room I had breezed through so quickly a few weeks before and saw metallic benches, ceiling fans barely moving stale air, a coffee and pastry counter, and an unmanned tourist information kiosk. The room resembled a dreary bus terminal, and certainly not a place where you'd want to spend a lot of time.

I found a seat in the crowded room and waited patiently. The Goma Air gate featured no electronic boards with flight information or helpful personnel, but around 6:30, a woman showed up and made a fuzzy announcement over the loudspeakers. I couldn't understand a word of it so went up to ask. The woman behind the counter looked to be about fifty years old, with beautiful skin and a long black braid down her back. She wore an orange sari that matched the Goma Air logo. She told me there was no visibility at Lukla, but there would be an announcement if anything changed. "Don't leave the area," she said. "A flight can take off with no notice if a weather window opens." I found a seat along the wall where I could keep an eye on the gate.

Most of the waiting passengers were Nepali, including rumpled businessmen, women with small children, a nun wearing thick socks and Birkenstocks, and a woman in a rich red sari with gold embroidery and a Slinky's worth of gold bangles from wrist to elbow. I assumed the rest were tourists like me: white or Asian people with small backpacks and camera gear, wearing hiking boots and carrying heavy jackets, heeding the oft-repeated travel advice to wear your heaviest, bulkiest items to save room in your luggage—despite that fact that it was 90 degrees outside and probably 80 inside. I had packed my coat but wore my boots since Nima had told me there were no roads and I'd begin walking immediately. I overheard people speaking in Japanese, German, French, some Scandinavian language I couldn't discern, and British- and Australian-accented English. I didn't hear any other Americans.

As the morning wore on, flights came and went, but none to or from Lukla. When I had started out that morning, I knew of Lukla's reputation as the most dangerous airport in the world because its short, steep landing strip—with no electronic flight aides—has a mountain face at one end and a cliff at the other. At 9,334 feet, the airport often got closed due to fog or unpredictable mountain winds. Since there are no roads to Lukla, you either fly in or walk for two days from the nearest road.

As the morning wore on, passengers arriving for later-scheduled flights accumulated in the waiting area. Durga had told me I was scheduled on the six a.m. flight because priority for a seat on any flight that did take off for Lukla was based on a passenger's originally scheduled flight time. If only one flight got to Lukla, I would be on it. Whenever I heard another incomprehensible announcement over the scratchy PA system, I'd go to the counter to ask the sari-clad woman what she had said. If the announcement was about the continued delay, Durga would text me with the same update. I felt better knowing he was monitoring the situation.

A little after eleven o'clock, the woman from the Goma Air counter came over and sat beside me.

"We can only fly in the mountains in the mornings, before the weather becomes unpredictable," she said. "We usually wait until one o'clock to cancel flights, but it is so bad today, all flights are canceled now." She went back to the counter and made the same announcement. I had no idea why she had decided to tell me the news in person.

I picked up my phone to call Durga, but he had already sent a text saying I should go outside; a car would come to get me. A man carrying my two duffels mysteriously appeared and led me to the terminal entrance, where he put the bags onto a cart pulled by a five-foot-tall man wearing worn jeans and a T-shirt with "BOY" on the front. BOY shook his head no when I asked if he spoke English, then led me back through the construction site to a car parked at the curb. He put my luggage in the trunk.

"Did Durga send this car?" I asked, apprehensive because it wasn't a taxi, and I didn't even have a destination. "Where am I going?"

"Durga, yes," BOY said. "Durga, yes." I squeezed into the back seat of the tiny car and hoped my trust in Durga wasn't misplaced.

A few minutes after I got in the car, Durga called. "Your room at the Hotel Tibet is ready. You will have the same room, if that is okay." It was okay. I liked that room. But even more, I liked that I had a room. When I arrived, it was as if I had never left—the room had been cleaned, my suitcase had been placed on the luggage stand, and a bottle of cold water was in the mini-fridge. I would spend another day in Kathmandu whether I wanted to or not.

I ate lunch at the hotel, then perused a Kathmandu guidebook that had been left in the lobby. Although I had come to Nepal for the mountains, Kathmandu's ancient Hindi and Buddhist cultures intrigued me. Since I'd have a few days when I came back through on my way to Bhutan, I decided to ask Durga to organize a tour for me. I took a short walk along the busy main street, but it was too nerve wracking and clammy to go far.

I went back to the hotel's quiet dead-end street and stopped in several small shops to browse. The vendors, eager for business, engaged me in conversation, telling me about the difficulties that year with no tourists. After Lo Manthang, I had enough earrings to last a lifetime, so I reluctantly pressed my hands together at my heart, like all the Nepalis did, and said "Namaste" when I left each shop empty-handed.

That night, I ate a light dinner on the rooftop and enjoyed two vodka tonics. I went to bed early to be ready for my flight to Lukla the next day.

Tuesday morning at five a.m., a car was waiting outside my hotel. At the airport, BOY (in the same T-shirt) unloaded my luggage from the trunk, and Durga appeared.

"Durga, you didn't have to come out this early in the morning," I said. "I can check in myself."

"It is no problem," he said. I admit I felt better with him there.

Once inside the waiting area, I made a beeline for the row of seats I'd scoped out the day before, near a door that sometimes opened to the outside and let in some fresh air. Things were looking good as the rising sun revealed breaks in the cloud cover, but there were no flights. Around ten, the Goma Air woman came over to talk. She told me her name and that it meant "jasmine," but as I wasn't familiar with the name I promptly forgot it. She said she was Buddhist, and we talked for an hour about how best to live one's life. I was fascinated, both by the conversation and the fact that an airline employee would just hang out with me.

After she went back to work, I struck up conversations with some of the tourists I recognized from the day before. Most were getting anxious and talked about their limited vacation time. If they lost another day, they wouldn't get to their destination—Everest Base Camp. My Khumbu trip was different; I had no reservations, and no final destination. So for me, a delay merely meant one fewer day spent in the high mountains of the Khumbu region. Nevertheless, I was disappointed when the orange-sari Goma Air woman came over at 12:30 to tell me all flights were again canceled for the day. "All things happen for a reason," she said. "It's best not to worry about it if the flight is canceled."

Back at the hotel, I took a quick nap, then decided to have a late lunch somewhere in Thamel, the tourist area of Kathmandu I'd visited with Gretchen two days before. I'd stupidly neglected to take the tourist map, even though I remembered my reading glasses. I sweated in the heat, and couldn't find the street that would take me to Thamel, so I retraced my steps toward the hotel.

At the corner of the main street and the quiet dead end was a bakery I had passed each day. I decided a pastry would be fine for lunch and went inside. To my surprise, behind the bakery, not visible from the street, was a small restaurant and wine bar. I went in and sat at the bar. There were scores of bottles along the wall, sorted by country of origin, and the wine list showed ten wines by the glass. After three weeks of beer, Khukri Rum, and vodka, I couldn't wait to get a glass of decent wine. I ordered a cold Australian chardonnay to go with a mozzarella-and-onion panini and thought I was in heaven.

Later that evening, when I returned to the rooftop bar for the third night in a row, the waiter brought me a vodka tonic before I'd even ordered it. I guess I was becoming a regular.

––––––––––

Wednesday morning, same routine. This time, though, the kitchen staff had prepared a take-away breakfast box for me, with a pastry and an apple. It was a nice touch. The night desk clerk (who had been there each morning when I'd checked out) wished me luck and told me that surely the flight would go today since the moon was out and flights were rarely canceled three days in a row. I felt optimistic.

In the departure lounge, I parked myself in the same row of hard metal seats against the wall by the door that opened. I soon learned all flights were delayed, as usual. A few people waiting with me the past two days told me they were leaving to take the bus, then walk the two days to Lukla. New passengers fretted about the delays, and I smiled, surprised at my own patience. The morning wore on, and instead of getting up when the unintelligible announcements crackled on the loudspeaker, I looked over at the Goma Air desk to see if anyone was there. If not, I went back to my reading or writing. One positive thing: I was getting a lot of that done, even if the waiting was tedious and uncomfortable.

Midmorning, the representative in the orange sari came over to chat again. Our conversation turned to the status of women in Nepal.

"There have been many gains in the past fifteen years," she said. "In the urban areas, women are educated, go into business, and even run for office. But things are not so good in the rural areas, where old customs die hard. For example, wife-beating is generally accepted, despite a government campaign to stop it."

She went on to describe the high incidence of child marriage—especially to old men—driven by poverty or religion. "As if these marriages weren't bad enough," she said, "if the man dies while the girl is still young, she becomes a 'child widow' and is considered bad luck, or perhaps even a witch. She can't remarry or look a man in the eye for the rest of her life."

She stood up to leave, straightening her orange sari. "Our culture hides these things from tourists. But female tourists like you, especially traveling alone, give us women strength to know things can be different."

Despite the clear skies, the day's flights were all canceled at exactly eleven o'clock. I had been talking with an American couple from Chicago scheduled on that morning's six o'clock flight when the woman whom I now considered my personal Goma Air representative came over to tell me the news. As she walked back to the desk to make the announcement, the man said it was ridiculous that they had to wait five hours only to discover the flight was canceled; his wife added that they were wasting their vacation sitting around in this dumpy airport all day. To make them feel better, I pointed out that it was my third day of waiting, and since they'd canceled the flights at eleven instead of one o'clock, they now had the day to explore the city. They didn't look convinced. I channeled Goma Air Lady and said, "You know, we're lucky that the planes aren't flying when it isn't safe. There is a reason the universe has delayed us; we just don't know what it is."

"Aren't you worried that you won't get to see Mount Everest?" they asked me.

"No," I said, and meant it. "If I get there, it's fine and I'll be happy. If not, I'm still in this amazing place, learning about the culture, meeting interesting people." Of course, I had come from three weeks in Mustang; this wasn't my annual vacation from a hectic work life in Chicago.

"See you tomorrow," I said to the American couple, as BOY collected my luggage on his cart and we went back through the busy construction area to the waiting car.

Back at the hotel, the now familiar staff greeted me with a "Welcome back, Miss Cheryl, your same room is ready for you."

I did a yoga session on my Romanian yoga mat, then took my own advice and, making sure I had my map and glasses, went to visit the Royal Palace, where the royal family had been slaughtered by a relative a few short years before. But when I arrived, sweaty from my walk, the palace had already closed for the day. I turned around and went back, the only good news being that I was getting used to walking on the busy street.

That night, I went back to the wine café for dinner, then stopped at the rooftop bar for a nightcap. The waiter looked surprised to see me.

"You didn't get to Lukla?" he asked, when he brought my vodka tonic. "Did you not try?"

"Still bad weather," I said. "The planes didn't fly."

"Very unusual for this time of year," he said. "You will get there tomorrow for sure."

"I hope so," I said halfheartedly, but realized I had accepted my circumstances. Seeing Mount Everest seemed less and less important.

I went to bed early that night and thought about my conversation with the couple from Chicago. Had I been delayed as a test of my patience or my understanding of the Buddhist concept of acceptance without desire? Or for a chance to learn more from the woman I now thought of as Goma Air Lady? A third option was that there was simply bad weather.

Thursday morning, I woke up before the alarm went off. Surely I would get to Lukla today. When I checked out with the night clerk, he gave me a hotel card with his personal phone number on it and told me he wanted to take me to his village to meet his mother. I smiled and said, "Perhaps." Then he told me he loved me and hoped I would get to Lukla that day.

The airport scene was unchanged. I went to my favorite seat by the open door, said hello to the passengers I recognized, and settled in to wait, since the flights were . . . delayed. The Chicago couple said their tour organizer told them they'd be bused closer to Lukla if the flight didn't leave today. I suspected most companies regularly built in a few extra days to account for delays like this.

At one point, a young British woman came over to chat. "Someone told me you've been waiting here for four days. Is it true?" She was with a group of college students on a tour to Everest Base Camp.

"Yes," I smiled, surprised at my notoriety.

"Our tour leader is arranging a helicopter to go to Lukla, but it's very expensive. Do you want to chip in and come along?" I had heard that often helicopters could land even when planes could not.

I was tempted, but it didn't feel like the right decision. As it was still early and the weather clear, I declined. An hour later, Goma Air Lady, whom I now considered a friend even though I couldn't remember her name, came over to tell me that a plane had just taken off from Lukla. If the skies stayed clear, it would pick us up and take us there. I hadn't thought much about the people who were stuck in Lukla trying to get to Kathmandu but now understood why Durga had played it safe and booked me on a flight out of Lukla four days before my Bhutan flight.

I put away my book and got ready to go. The terminal was buzzing with excitement as passengers lined up at the counter. Twenty minutes later, we boarded an old bus that drove around the small airfield to the sixteen-seater orange Goma Air plane that had landed minutes before. I felt smug about my decision not to take the helicopter as the engines revved for takeoff. But then they stopped.

What now? I could see the pilots flipping switches in the cockpit, shaking their heads. One of them turned around to the passengers, the plane so small no intercom was needed. "The cloud cover has come back in, and the Lukla airport is closed. I'm sorry, but you'll have to return to the terminal." There was a collective groan.

Back in my hard metal seat by the open door, anxious foreigners pacing around me, I was trying for one of the on-again/off-again internet connections in the departure lounge. Clearly it was off again. A baby was crying a few rows over, and a little boy kicked me and my armrest as he tried to squeeze into the seat next to me with his mother. I was fairly certain that I wouldn't get to Lukla that day. But somehow none of it bothered me.

At one o'clock, my Goma Air friend told me the flights were canceled. "I'm so sorry," she said.

"It's okay," I said. "I'm not usually so calm about these things, but I feel different somehow."

"Serenity comes when you trade expectations for acceptance," she said.

Mmhhh. Maybe that was the secret to my Mustang calm.

BOY took my bags to the waiting car, and I went back to the Hotel Tibet for what was now my fifth night. Thank goodness Durga had gotten me a good rate and I hadn't splurged on a fancy hotel. He also felt sorry for me and had hired a driver to take me to the Boudhanath Stupa, a very holy place for Buddhists in Nepal and a symbol of the city, although only fifteen percent of Kathmandu's population is Buddhist. I was glad to see some of the city without having to walk in the heat.

For the third night in a row, I went to the wine café for dinner. I was sitting at the bar, twirling a glass of cold Spanish wine, when a tall blond man came in wearing baggy shorts, a T-shirt, and sandals, looking like a scruffy tourist who had lost his way. He sat a few stools down from me and ordered without asking for a menu. He looked about ten years younger than me and spoke with an American accent. To my surprise, he didn't whip out his cell phone, like most lone diners, but looked over and asked me about the wine I was drinking.

We were soon sitting next to each other, sharing plates of food and stories. He introduced himself as Jim and said he worked for the State Department. He had come to Kathmandu to help with earthquake issues, but hadn't yet found an apartment, so lived in a suite at the Sheraton across from my hotel.

"I apologize for my clothes," he said. "Usually nobody is here on a Thursday night. I've come directly from yoga class and didn't bother to change."

We drank more wine, I told him of my travels, and he told me about his somewhat itinerant life. We shared contact info after Jim suggested we have dinner again after my Lukla trek. I liked him and thought it would be fun.

Jim walked me to my hotel, where he gave me a hug and a hesitant kiss goodnight on the porch. Inside the lobby, the night clerk was already on duty. He looked both happy to see me again and forlorn, possibly because he'd seen Jim kiss me. He told me again that he loved me and had enjoyed having me at the hotel—and that I would surely get to Lukla the next day. I told him I'd see him in the morning and got into the elevator. My phone pinged with a text. "Wondering why I didn't make that kiss last longer. Sleep tight. Jim." I wondered the same thing.

———

Day five of trying to get to Lukla. The kitchen staff had my breakfast packed in a box, the night clerk wished me luck and reminded me I had agreed to meet his mother, Durga was at the airport to see me into the terminal, and my seat in the corner was empty. Given the overcast sky and threat of rain, I was pretty sure I wasn't getting to Lukla that day and thought maybe I could see Jim again that night. I had my computer halfway out of my backpack, ready to settle in, when my Goma Air friend hustled over.

"No, today you are going," she said excitedly. I pushed the laptop back in and pulled the zipper closed. She pulled me up by the hand and took my bag over to the counter. "You must be first in line." I was the only person who had stuck it out all week. I tried not to get excited, since I'd been skunked the day before.

"Thank you," I said, not sure I'd ever see her again if the plane actually took off. "Thank you for everything."

"Namaste." She bowed slightly with her hands together at her heart. Then she made an announcement for the rest of the passengers.

The fifth time was the charm. The plane effortlessly took off at 6:15 a.m. and rose above the clouds to a clear blue sky for the barely thirty-minute flight. There were no seat assignments, so I took a seat in the second row on the left-hand side (Durga's suggestion), behind two young Israeli girls with video cameras. The view of the mountains was even more spectacular than on my flight to Pokhara a month earlier, when I'd first glimpsed the Himalaya. As the plane descended toward the most dangerous airport in the world, I could see the crazy steepness of the short runway through the cockpit despite the Israeli girls' arms and cameras held up to film the landing. When the wheels hit the runway, the pilot applied the brakes, the engines went into reverse, and the plane stopped. Very suddenly. Which was a good thing, since the mountain face rose literally straight up in front of the plane. There was no room to spare. The landing lived up to its reputation.

I remembered something Nima had told me the Buddha said. "Do not dwell in the past, do not dream of the future, concentrate the mind on the present moment."

Yep. Right now, in the present moment, I was finally in the fabled town of Lukla.

CHAPTER 13

EVEREST TREK, NEPAL

SEPTEMBER 2015

Apparently Durga had called my guide, Mingma, to tell him I was on the flight that morning. Mingma met me at the outdoor concrete slab that served as baggage claim at the tiny Lukla airport. A beefy, thirty-something Sherpa, he was Nima's brother-in-law. Many people think that the word Sherpa means a person who carries things, but it is actually the name of an ethnic group that has always lived in the high mountains. "Shar" means east, and "pa" means people, so in Tibetan they are the eastern people. The word is a common surname in the region; Nima's last name was Sherpa.

With Mingma was a tiny man who, at four foot eleven inches, couldn't have weighed more than one hundred pounds soaking wet. He introduced himself as Diraj, my porter, then hoisted the two duffels onto his shoulders as if they weighed nothing and was gone before I could put on my little daypack. Mingma and I climbed a rocky path along the airport boundary, next to a chainlink fence. The small mountain town of Lukla was just over the rise, its narrow streets filled with mountaineering shops, guesthouses, and restaurants to serve the tourists, who—I now knew—sometimes spent a few days there waiting for flights.

Ten minutes later, we were drinking tea and eating breakfast at a guesthouse. I still couldn't believe I was really in Lukla. I asked Mingma how far we would walk that day.

"It's about two hours to my village, then another hour to Nima's house," Mingma said.

"But don't you live here in Lukla?" I asked.

"No," Mingma said.

"Then how did you know I'd be on the flight today? You didn't walk here this morning, did you?"

"Yes, I did. I've walked here every morning for the past five days."

I looked at him incredulously.

"And back again?"

"Yes. But at least that was in the daylight." Mingma's broad smile let me know he was only half joking. "You'll spend the night at Nima's. Tomorrow we will start hiking and see how far we get. That will be up to the weather, your fitness, and your ability to acclimate to altitude."

"And fate," I said.

"Yes," Mingma agreed. "Mostly fate."

Our walk started on a smooth dirt trail mostly downhill, with stone steps built into some of the steep sections. The temperature was a pleasant seventy degrees, but soon clouds moved in and enveloped the area in fog. When we got to his village, Mingma pointed out tents pitched next to uninhabitable houses or even piles of rock that used to be a house.

"My wife and I lost everything in the earthquake," he said, "but no lives, so we are happy. We are living in this place temporarily while we rebuild our home and guesthouse in our village, further along the trail."

"Have you received any international aid?" I asked, having donated money to relief efforts myself.

"The Red Cross came right away and handed out tents and some food, but that's about it. We hear about more money, but the government has it tied up in Kathmandu. The only people rebuilding are the ones like me with savings or relatives who can help."

What discouraging news. In Mustang, people lost business. Here they lost that and their homes. And sometimes friends or family. I knew that traveling wasn't always about having a good time; sometimes the plight of the people you met was heartbreaking. I was glad I hadn't canceled my trip and that my tourist dollars, donations, and generous tips were likely helping in some way.

We left the village by crossing the river on a steel suspension bridge, then started uphill to Nima's house in Phakding, called The Beyul and Hermitage Farm. The word Beyul means "sacred valley" and connotes a paradise that requires enormous effort to reach; Nima's guesthouse lived up to the description. The one-story ranch-style house had large windows looking out over the valley, a flagstone patio filled with wicker furniture, and prayer flags everywhere sending messages to the heavens. Nima welcomed us on the patio with a pitcher of cold juice.

"So you finally made it," Nima said. "Have a drink and then I'll show you the house."

Nima had eclectically decorated his home with traditional Nepalese carpets, Bhutanese and Navajo weavings, and hand-made American wedding-ring quilts. The kitchen, which opened onto the large living and dining area, had a slate counter and deep ceramic farmhouse sink. The house was the polar opposite of Stan's place: clean, inviting, and beautiful.

"I had to import most of the building materials," Nima said. "Quality things aren't available here, or even in India. I wanted this guesthouse to be as comfortable as the house I owned in Seattle."

"It's all so modern and different from Mustang," I said.

"Yes, and different from most things here in the Khumbu too," he said. "Of course, everything had to be flown to Lukla and then carried on somebody's back up here to the house. Some of the heavy things took oxen, so it was difficult."

So, the solar panels that heated water for my shower, the collection of Himalaya coffee-table books, the bottles of Chilean wine, the toilet paper in the bathroom, the thick mattress on the bed, and even the tin roof all had to be carried in from somewhere by somebody. I thought of tiny Diraj effortlessly hoisting the relatively lightweight duffels onto his shoulders and how much I took roads for granted before coming to Nepal.

That night I snuggled into the comfortable bed but woke the next morning to rain. I got dressed and padded out to the living room, where I could smell freshly brewed coffee. Outside, a heavy cloud cover obscured even the slight view we'd had the day before.

"If it doesn't let up," Nima said, "I don't think you should walk today. It's two days to Namche Bazaar if it is dry. In the rain, the trail can be very slippery and dangerous. It wouldn't be fun."

"But if I don't leave today, I might not get far enough to see Mount Everest, right?"

"That will depend completely on the weather. There are several spots along the trail to see at least the top of it."

"You know, Nima, I'm wondering if maybe I wasn't meant to trek here. Remember how in Mustang I told you I thought the Everest Base Camp trail was overtouristed and I didn't want to participate in making it worse? I wonder if I have bad karma now for thinking that. Everything has conspired against me."

Nima laughed. "It's possible," he said. I wished he hadn't agreed.

Mingma arrived just then. He'd hiked up that morning from his house in half the time it had taken me the day before.

"The conditions are terrible," he said. "I think it would be best to wait a day."

I took a sip of coffee. "That's settled, then," I said. "What difference will one more day make?" Secretly, I hoped my acceptance would help my karma.

The next day brought weather good enough for hiking, but it was still solid overcast. The trek was much tougher than in Mustang, where I could see big mountains in the distance as I walked in river valleys or on plateaus. Here, I felt like I was really *in* the big mountains, despite the constant cloud cover that obscured the highest peaks. The trail would go uphill to a high point, then down to a bridge over the river, and then back up the other side.

On the second day of walking, we crossed the highest bridge on the trail, almost two hundred feet above the water. Hundreds of prayer flags festooned the narrow suspension bridge, and I could barely find room to add mine to the mix to ensure my safe passage. Below, I could see the confluence of the Bhote Koshi, flowing from the border with Tibet, and the Dudh Koshi, which comes from Mount Everest. I was in the middle of the bridge taking photos when four porters with their heads down started across at a good pace. I hurried to the other side and watched them pass, each man wearing thick rubber flip-flops and carrying five sheets of 5´ x 8´ plywood strapped to his back, going somewhere for earthquake repairs.

On the trail, there had been only a handful of other trekkers, but scores of porters were heading to the villages with huge loads of bottled water, soft drinks, ramen noodles, toilet paper, and cases of beer. A few, like the plywood porters, carried unwieldy objects like water heaters, bags of cement, or small refrigerators. Those on the way back to Lukla carried far lighter, insanely huge bundles of trash that towered over their heads. Seeing the effort needed to deal with the earthquake and simply live life in this part of the world, I felt privileged and a little embarrassed carrying only my tiny daypack.

The trail continued through a dense rhododendron forest (unfortunately not in bloom) and eventually reached a high point where we stopped for a rest.

"If it were clear," Mingma said, "we'd be able to see Mount Everest at the head of this valley."

I peered out into the dense clouds. "I'm not going to see Everest," I told him. "I've always bad-mouthed this trek as a crowded highway, but we've hardly seen anyone. Now I have bad karma, which serves me right."

Mingma laughed. "This year is different because the earthquake scared away the tourists. Plus, you're a week or two ahead of the trekking season. That's why it's only you and the porters carrying supplies. In another month, if we are lucky enough to have tourists come, your description of it as a highway will be correct."

"No," I said. "I have bad karma. But please keep telling me where I would see Everest if it were clear, just so I know."

"Maybe you can fool your karma if you call it Chomolungma, the Tibetan name for the mountain, instead of Everest. It means 'Goddess Mother of Mountain.'"

"I like that idea," I said. "It's so much more elegant and appropriate than some British surveyor's last name. Chomolungma it is."

We climbed for another ninety minutes before finally arriving at Namche Bazaar, a village known in climbing legend as the last place to stock up before setting off to base camp. Half the village had been severely damaged by the earthquake, while the half on the opposite hillside was virtually untouched. Building sites on the damaged side were teeming with workers. Namche looked much bigger and more developed than I had imagined, but, in keeping with my trail experience so far, the town seemed deserted. Many restaurants and shops weren't open, although Mingma told me that during the high season the town was crowded, the hotels booked, and the restaurants and bars full of trekkers. We walked up a steep street to our hotel on the undamaged side of town; there were no other guests. Diraj had long before placed my duffel bag on one of the two twin beds in my room.

After the long day of hiking, I craved a hot shower and a cold beer (which I'd been thinking about ever since the beer porter passed me hours before). But there was no electricity, so no hot water. Apparently, there hadn't been electricity for the past few days, because the power came from the Chinese, who were using the off-season to "clean" the hydroelectric dams. I'd never heard of such a thing, but what could I do? I sponged off with cold water and went to the hotel dining room, where Mingma and I (the only patrons) dined by candlelight on *dahl bot* (rice-and-lentil soup) cooked over a gas stove, and drank beer that was cold because it was kept outside. No electricity meant no heat in the bedroom either, so Nima's cousin—who owned the hotel—brought me two extra blankets to stay warm.

As final validation of my bad karma, Mingma told me that the weather forecast was for more of the same and I should prepare to hike in rain the next day. "But," he added, "the weather in the mountains is difficult to predict, so we might get lucky and see Chomolungma."

I had accepted that I wasn't going to see Chomolungma regardless of what I called her. The mountains I *could* see were impressive enough. I brushed my teeth by the light of my headlamp, crawled under the blankets on the thin mattress atop a wooden platform, and fell fast asleep.

———

I awoke to insistent rapping on the door.

"Wake up," I heard Mingma say. "Get dressed quickly. The mountains are visible, but the weather is changing fast. I'll meet you downstairs in five minutes." It was 5:30 and still pitch dark. I jumped out of my warm bed, threw on long underwear and pants, added my wool vest and down coat, grabbed my scarf and gloves and camera, and went downstairs. Mingma was waiting outside the door. "Hurry" was all he said as we took off through the deserted town.

Namche Bazaar is at 10,000 feet elevation, and I could feel every bit of it as we practically ran down a set of stairs and then up another, across to the "damaged" side of town. Mingma waited for me whenever there was a turn in the route but kept me moving at the fastest pace I could manage, given the altitude and the fact that I had been in a dead sleep fifteen minutes earlier. I fumbled with my jacket zipper, trying to open it to cool off. I was dressed for standing around, not running uphill.

Even in the darkness, I could see the outline of a nearby peak invisible the day before. A zillion stars dotted the clear sky, but I could also see a thick cloud layer in the valley below. Mingma led me up a steep path out of town, and although I carried no pack, no water, nothing except my camera, I was gasping for air.

Twenty minutes after leaving the hotel, we crested the hill onto a flat field that turned out to be a helipad. At the far end of the field was a bronze statue of Tenzig Norgay, the first man to summit Mount Everest when he led the New Zealander Edmund Hillary to the top on May 29, 1953, a year and half before I was born. Already five people gathered near the statue, waiting for the light of sunrise.

Mingma led me to a low wall at the edge of the plateau and pointed to the right, where a massive spire was becoming visible in the first light. "That's Ama Dablam," he said. "Follow the horizon at the end of the valley and you can see three peaks. The sharp one on the left is Lhotse, the fourth highest mountain in the world. The big one on the right is Nuptse. The triangular peak in the middle is Chomolungma. Congratulations."

I had a lump in my throat and my breath came in short jabs. I had said it didn't matter whether I saw this mountain, but wow was I wrong. I felt small, insignificant, humbled. And like the luckiest person in the world.

As the dawn light hit the south face of Everest, I briefly thought about taking photos but wanted to savor the moment in my soul, not through the lens of a camera. After a while, though, as the ridges and cirques of the mountains took shape and shadow in the light, I took pictures, despite knowing they could never capture the extreme emotion of this experience.

Images of the few other times I'd had a similar feeling flashed through my consciousness. In 1994, on the Trans-Siberian Railway, after rolling through endless forest, then emerging onto the shoreline of Lake Baikal. In 2008, when the spires of the Torres del Paine peaks in Chile slipped off their cloak of clouds to become starkly visible above a turquoise glacial lake. And most vividly in 2014, when, on a remote hilltop in Alaska at -10°F, the northern lights fell on me like colored rain. That time I had to wipe the tears away quickly so they wouldn't freeze on my face.

"Turn around," Mingma said, interrupting my thoughts and pointing to the valley where the clouds had been chasing me up the hill earlier. I could see hundreds of feet into the ravine where the river flowed. "The weather has changed," he said. "It will be clear all day today for us." I couldn't believe my eyes, or my karma.

Within an hour, more people arrived at the viewpoint, and I thanked Mingma for being such a great guide and getting me there for first light—and the relative solitude. A group of ten Australian girls were talking nonstop, more intent on posing for photos than looking at the view. Five Brits seemed as awed as I was and quietly took photos of each other. Three young men with their Sherpa guide came running up the hill and immediately started shooting videos and taking selfies. Two American couples asked me to take their photo, and I obliged. "Are you traveling alone?" they asked.

"No, I've got a Sherpa guide," I said.

"Yes, but you're not with a group. How brave."

I didn't feel brave, I felt giddy. There was nothing special about what I'd done other than to meet Nima and accept his unexpected invitation to visit.

———

After the Chomolungma morning, Mingma and I enjoyed a beautiful day of hiking to Tengboche, where Everest made a great backdrop for photos of a large red Buddhist monastery with intricately carved woodwork eaves and window frames. Along the way, the Everest massifs popped in and out of view from the trail, white fluffy clouds filled the sky, and the temperature rose enough for me to shed my jacket. I thought my cheeks would probably be sore that night from all the smiling.

From Tengboche, a half-hour downhill hike took me to Deboche, where I would spend the night before turning around. This was the farthest I could go, thanks to those five days trying to get to Lukla. The guesthouse was quite large. I accessed my upstairs room through a common area with the traditional benches around the walls and small red tables in front. An ancient monk dressed in a crimson robe and pointed hat was sitting motionless in front of a window, propped up with pillows, his feet stretched out in front of him. Prayer beads were looped through the fingers of one hand, and he held an open book in front of him with the other. To be polite, I said namaste as I walked by, but he didn't acknowledge me and never moved a muscle. I wondered if he was deaf, and perhaps blind too.

My room had a view of Everest, Nuptse, Lhotse, and Ama Dablam, but it wasn't the kind of room to sit around in. As with the night before, there were two simple twin beds on wood platforms and a bench along the wall for my duffel. The bathroom had a toilet and sink, but I had to go downstairs to use the shower. No big deal, I thought, except for having to pass through the common area again. I gathered my towel and overnight kit and again said namaste to the monk as I walked through. Again no reaction. I realized the monk had not changed his position one bit. I braved a slightly longer look and, not seeing any hint of breath or movement, realized this was a diorama, perhaps a Buddhist art display to show tourists what the monks looked like. I felt really silly having said namaste twice to a mannequin.

After a shower, I went back to my room, this time ignoring the diorama monk except to notice he still hadn't moved. Duh, of course not. I sat on the hard bed to write in my journal, hoping to capture the awe of the day. I must have nodded off because I was awakened by the sound of deep melodic chanting. I glanced out the window—wispy clouds blew over and around the mountains as the daylight faded. I stuck my head out the door and realized the sound was coming from the diorama room. When I tiptoed out, I saw ten yellow-robed monks sitting cross-legged on the benches, their books open on the low tables. The monks followed lines on the pages with their fingers as they chanted, the deep resonance entering my body like an electric current. Then I realized that, unbelievably, the diorama monk was moving his lips. He wasn't an art exhibit after all!

Later, in the dining room, I sat near the wood stove, enjoying a mushroom pizza made with a thick, rough crust, yak cheese, canned tomato sauce, and canned mushrooms (that somebody had carried up there). The owner brought me a steaming cup of tea.

"I hope the monks did not inconvenience you this afternoon with their chanting," he said. "After the earthquake damaged the monastery, they moved here until the building is fit to occupy again."

Inconvenienced? No way. Just like the elephants in the lobby in Zambia, the monks chanting next to my room in Nepal epitomized the wonders of travel that I loved.

———————

The next morning, I could see there were even fewer clouds than the day before. After breakfast, the diminutive Diraj, carrying my pack as well as a payload of garbage from the lodge, took off at a trot ahead of me and Mingma. We walked up the hill toward the Tengboche Monastery, Chomolungma at our backs. Beside the path I could see yellow buttercup flowers, some kind of ground cover with small purple blooms, and blue foxglove. I'd been so intent on watching the mountains the day before that I hadn't even noticed them. A large beetle with scarlet wings landed on a rock in front of me, then crawled away. A kaleidoscope of small golden butterflies—the color of the monks' robes—flew alongside me for a while; one lightly landed on my outstretched arm. When we got to the top of the hill, Mingma directed me down a faint side path along a ridge.

"There's a special place—very holy for the monks—about a quarter of a mile along this path, with a good view," he said. "I'm going to call Nima with an update and will wait for you here. Don't hurry."

Bushes higher than my head lined the path until I came to a small clearing. I sat on a rough-hewn bench and immediately felt the Mustang calmness flow through me like a golden stream. A lone raven floated on the breeze in front of me, then soared away, the only bird I'd seen that day. I felt the beauty of the setting in my bones, and decided to do a short meditation before enjoying my last close-up view of Chomolungma. I closed my eyes.

My heart rate and breathing slowed. I could smell the scent of the small flowers on the bushes. There was no sound except the granite boulders growing moss. I didn't move a muscle except to slowly, very slowly, open my eyes and let my gaze drift upwards to the view before me.

Iridescent white snow covered the steep sides of Chomolungma and Ama Dablam, their clear and bright silhouettes stark against the now completely cloudless sky. Suddenly my heart was racing, and a tightness in my chest rose to my throat, making my breath come in joyful gulps.

Almost fifty years after I had pinned the *National Geographic* cover to my bulletin board, I was finally seeing that unreal, incredible indigo sky.

BHUTAN

SEPTEMBER 2015

My flight to Paro, Bhutan, from Kathmandu was barely an hour long, just enough time to reflect on all that had happened since the surprise of a Chomolungma dawn and my almost mystical experience at Tengboche seeing the indigo sky of my dreams. Apparently my karma had repaired itself because the weather was clear for the rest of the trek and the flight from Lukla took off right on schedule, first try. Back in Kathmandu with four days to kill, I reconnected with Jim, who took me to city sights, restaurants, a jazz club, and bed. The night before I left, he asked me to come back to Kathmandu (and him) after Bhutan, or at least after Portugal. Our time together had seemed somewhat magical, and I was tempted. I even wondered if he might be the karmic relationship of fall 2015 that my astrologer had foretold. But I knew I was on a different path. As the plane approached the runway in Paro, I concluded that my destiny at this point was to meet interesting men, flirt with love, then move on. I was convinced that if I actually found love, I would know it and be willing to change my plans.

The Paro airport arrivals hall was quiet and almost serene. No touts, no throngs of greeters, no bustle. Sonam, the tall thirty-year-old guide I'd spend the next two and a half weeks with, placed a silk kata around my neck on top of the departure one Durga had given me. He, like the other men in the airport, was wearing the traditional Bhutanese *gho*, a cloak-like garment with long, folded-up white sleeves, worn with dark knee socks. All the women were dressed in what I learned was a *kira*, patterned cloth wrapped to form a floor-length skirt, topped with a solid-colored shirt and short silk jacket.

"Why is everyone dressed alike?" I asked Sonam.

"It is the law," Sonam said. "All citizens must wear the national dress when working. The designs date back to the sixteenth century."

On the way to the hotel, Harker, the driver who would be with us the entire trip, slowed down as we passed an imposing structure that looked like part fortress and part temple.

"This is the Paro Dzong, built in the fifteenth century," Sonam said. "A *dzong* is a monastery that also serves as the regional administrative center. We will visit it tomorrow."

My hotel, a former palace with intricately carved lintels and woodwork and a large garden complete with prayer wheels, sat across the valley from the dzong. Dinner was included at the hotel, so after Sonam saw that I was checked in, he told me he'd be back in the morning. When I explored the hotel, I found an ornately decorated altar/meditation room that had a wood floor perfect for yoga. I retrieved the blue Romanian yoga mat from my room, stretched my travel-weary back and hips, and promised myself to be more diligent in my yoga practice while I was here, especially when spaces like this were available.

I felt immersed in Bhutanese culture until I went to the dining room, in a separate, modern building. The brightly lit room had a sterile feel, with several stainless steel buffet trays over small butane burners, reminding me of the countless business conferences I had attended over the years. The buffet offered a bland selection of overcooked noodles, three pans of soggy vegetables, something that looked like chicken in cream sauce, and lots of rice. Both wine (very expensive) and beer were available, so I settled for a beer with my boring but edible meal.

On the way back to my room, I smelled jasmine in the warm night air. Across the valley, the dzong shone warmly with yellow lights. Behind the elegantly curved roofline, I could see a bright spot and realized that my old friend the full moon was rising. I thought about Jim in Kathmandu and felt very alone.

The next day, Sonam took me to the dzong, where he added a ceremonial long white sash to his gho before entering, as required by tradition as a sign of respect. Large Buddhist story murals lined the inner walls, similar to those I'd seen in Nepal, but brighter in color. Bare-armed monks in red robes did their chores amidst men conducting business, all in traditional dress, including the white sash.

A large flag flapped in the breeze above the dzong.

"Is the flag for the monastery or the government?" I asked.

"That is the Bhutanese flag," Sonam said. "You can see it has a dragon in the middle to symbolize our country. The background is half yellow, representing the authority of the King, and half orange, representing the authority of the monasteries."

"So who rules?"

"Both. Our culture blends them," he said. I guessed the arrangement worked because seventy-five percent of the population were Buddhists.

We left the dzong and drove into Paro, which, despite having an airport, was a small town of dirt streets lined with small shops. As he had at the dzong, Harker stayed with the parked car while Sonam and I walked through town. I noticed that the tourist shops all seemed to be selling identical stuff—mass-produced in either India or China, I suspected.

We went into one store with shelves filled with what looked like folded tablecloths. A young woman in a green and orange kira, an orange silk blouse, and a cream-colored jacket stood behind a long, empty counter. "This is the kira shop," Sonam said. "The Bhutanese method of weaving is unique in the world. Weavers learn from their mothers, and the talented ones will study further in the crafts school. To make the skirt, three pieces of fabric are sewn together." He pointed at the shelves behind the woman. "Which ones do you like?"

I chose a geometric pattern of purple and red threads on white silk. The clerk took the fabric from the shelf and spread it out on the counter. It was eight feet long, plus fringe on both ends, and not quite two feet wide. "This piece will be joined with two others to make the kira," Sonam said.

"It's beautiful," I said, fingering the silk and admiring the weaving technique of making the pattern without carrying the threads across the back. I thought it would make a great wall hanging.

"How do you wear it?" I asked the woman. She took a completed kira from the shelf and wrapped the unwieldy length of fabric on top of her existing skirt, adjusted the length, then folded over the top. "You wear a belt to keep it together and at the right length," she said.

As the woman and I talked, Sonam stepped back, engrossed in his cell phone. I looked at several other patterns until, finally, Sonam asked me if I wanted to buy one. I wondered if men everywhere became bored shopping with women.

"I would love to"—I gave my standard answer—"but I have no room in my luggage."

"We have very reliable post here," Sonam said. "You can leave the package in the car until you are ready to leave. Then we can mail it and anything else you buy."

"Okay. But shouldn't I wait to see if I like something else better? It's only my second day here."

"You will find the best weavers here in Paro and Thimpu," Sonam said. I didn't yet know that the patterns represented the preserved culture and would be identical everywhere.

After a breakfast of toast and eggs, we left Paro for the ninety-minute drive to Thimpu along pristine rivers and over a mountain pass, everyone in their lane, no horns honking. I felt quite safe in the back seat of the almost brand-new, comfortable minivan. Thimpu was the largest city in the country at 100,000 people. Once in the capital, we visited the national museum (antique weavings with the same patterns I'd seen in the shop) before Sonam deposited me at a bland, Western-style hotel in the middle of town.

Since this hotel clearly didn't have a tranquil altar room for yoga, I headed out for a walk. There were only two main streets, each a few blocks long, with no stop lights and not much traffic. Despite the mandate to wear traditional dress for work, the few clothing shops I passed displayed very provocative clubbing clothes. I wondered if the workers in the clubs were required to wear the kira and gho, which would have created a jarring juxtaposition.

I wandered into several tourist shops selling the same things as in Paro: woven fabric, Buddhist paintings, and wooden carvings. Although the vendors told me everything was handmade, I saw no unique variation in any item. I checked several times for "Made in India" labels but never found one.

I had high hopes for my hotel dinner that night when I saw a menu, not a buffet, but the selection was limited and the fare again bland potatoes, chicken, and beer. As Sonam had instructed for good luck, I spritzed with my fingers a touch of my drink out to the deities in the area before consuming it.

I knew that Sonam was not staying in the same hotel, but just as I finished dinner, he showed up.

"How did you know I was still here in the dining room?" I asked, puzzled by his sudden appearance.

"The hotel called me to tell me you were finishing your meal," he said, as if that were normal practice. "So I came over to make sure everything is okay."

How absurd, I thought. Did they call every guide about every guest's activity? What about my privacy? Sonam had already told me he'd pick me up at ten the next day, so why did he need to be here? "Everything is fine, thank you," I said, not asking any of those questions. "What are we doing tomorrow?"

"We will visit the national craft school, where the thirteen traditional crafts of Bhutan are taught. It's a government school, but admission is very competitive. In the school's store you can buy things made by both students and masters."

We chatted for a few more minutes. Then Sonam left as suddenly as he had appeared.

The next day, at the school, I felt like I was at one of those history theme parks where people dress as in olden times and show you how things used to be done. Except here, those things were still being done the same way—and students were taught to replicate what had been done for hundreds of years.

We visited a building for painters, one for wood carvers, and several others for calligraphy, sculpting, metal casting, gold and silver crafts, and blacksmithing.

"The students must study for many years," Sonam told me, as we entered a classroom filled with young men all painting the figure of the Buddha. "For example, the painting school takes six years. These students are about ready to graduate."

"But all of their paintings look exactly alike," I said, confused.

"Yes, of course," Sonam said with a look of surprise. "The traditional crafts retain the purity of ancient times. I understand that is rare in your Western culture. But for us, each act of creating is also an act of spirituality that reflects our sacred beliefs."

I struggled to understand. "So how are these students distinguished from the beginners or each other?"

"Oh, the beginners do not yet understand the proportions of each painting or, for example, the exact placement of Buddha's finger when doing a painting such as this." Sonam held up his index finger, emulating what everyone was currently painting. "Also, each year the students use finer brushes. After decades of experience, a master may be painting with a brush made from a single human hair."

I still didn't understand. "But do they ever get to paint anything but the Buddha stories? What about individual creativity?"

Sonam paused for a moment as if trying to figure out how to tactfully explain something to an uncouth person. "The importance of the craft lies in the craft itself," he said. "Our traditional art is part of our daily lives. We do not need to be creative."

"Is that why none of the paintings are signed?"

"Yes. The sign of a master is not a signature, but the ability to make a perfect copy."

And finally, I did understand. His words explained the monotony of the gift shop contents, at least as I saw them. The items were in fact each done by hand, to a standard as strict as a machine's. From the Bhutanese perspective, perfection was not the creation of a new *Mona Lisa* but rather the ability to precisely re-create the same thing over and over.

———————

I had scheduled my trip to Bhutan around my Nepal schedule, but luckily my timing coincided with the sacred mask festivals, called *tschechus*, held at each dzong in spring and fall. I was even luckier that the Thimpu Tschechu took place while I was in the city. "This festival is the largest in the country, with the most skilled dancers," Sonam said as Harker drove us to the Thimpu Dzong. A line of cars waited to get into the parking lot, and the atmosphere mirrored that of a big event anywhere: people carrying picnic baskets and blankets, chatting excitedly, and waving to friends. Except that here, everyone wore the gho or brightly colored kira.

Inside the dzong courtyard, Sonam guided me through the crowd to a makeshift bleacher. Because the few other white people in the bleachers were toting huge cameras, I felt almost inconspicuous with my tiny telephoto lens. Most Bhutanese spread their blankets on the hard, stone surface of the interior plaza, then ate or talked with neighbors while waiting for the action to begin. In a separate cordoned area, the elder monks in red robes sat sedately while the younger men and teens draped themselves across the staircase below. Beside them, the band was ready to play on an assortment of drums, cymbals, bells, and long alpine-looking horns.

Soon a troupe of monks dressed in multicolored gowns entered the plaza wearing large papier-mâché masks representing the heads of birds, animals, or deities. Each mask was cleverly tied to the top of a monk's head so he could see out of the mouth opening and look a menacing foot taller than he was. As if that weren't enough, the masks themselves were grotesque and scary, often incorporating small skulls around the top and expressions of anger with fanged teeth, like the paintings in the monasteries in Mustang. The dancers, circling the plaza, stepped slowly and deliberately to the dirge-like sounds of the horns and drums.

"At a tschechu, dances tell stories from Buddhist culture," Sonam explained. "This dance is called the Death Passage Dance. When you die, you must pass through many stages before reincarnation. These masks represent the demons you will encounter. The idea is that if you recognize them, you won't fear them, and your transition will be easier."

I remembered the same explanation for the murals in Mustang at the creepy monastery. Very different from Christian paintings, where depictions of demons were meant to scare you into being a good person on earth.

"It's quite scary," I said as the dancers started twirling like dervishes, their gowns flying out horizontally and long strands of "hair" from the masks swinging wildly. "Are all the dances like this?"

"No, it depends on the story being told. We will see many different dances at the other festivals we will attend. And there are also comedy performances."

"Do the dances change from year to year?" I asked.

"Oh, no. The dances were developed by the great lama Pema Lingpa in the fifteenth century. They do not change."

————————

I chose to go to Bhutan mainly because of its experiment with Gross National Happiness. In my career as a sustainability expert, I'd been reading about it for years: an entire country driving its culture toward a triple bottom line involving the economy, environment, and social equity, instead of a simple Gross Domestic Product. It seemed an admirable—if difficult—goal, and I wanted to see how it worked.

The first and most obvious indicator of this policy concerned the regulation of tourism. In 2015, all international visitors (except tourists from neighboring India) had to pay a minimum of $250 (U.S. per day (plus $40 for a single traveler like me). This fee bought a licensed tour guide, a vehicle with a driver, three-star lodging, three meals a day, admission to museums, and all the tea you could possibly drink. You could pay more to stay in limited four- or five-star hotels, but you couldn't travel any more cheaply. This policy of high value–low volume tourism specifically rejected the crowds-of-independent-backpackers tourist model (common in India and Nepal) in favor of preserving culture and nature, and building the economy. Part of the fee was a sustainable tourism royalty of $65 per day, which went toward free education, free healthcare, poverty alleviation, and building infrastructure.

Bhutan's total population, at 700,000, was smaller than that of most U.S. states (except Vermont and Wyoming), and foreigners were not allowed entry until the early 1990s. Monarchy reigned until 2008, when the king voluntarily changed the system to a democracy but kept a role. Photos of the beloved king and queen were everywhere, including on the popular campaign-like buttons many people wore.

To preserve the culture, in addition to the traditional dress requirement and the thirteen traditional crafts I'd seen at the school, all buildings displayed the Bhutanese construction style: temple-like rooflines, painted wood trim, and auspicious omens on the walls (like tigers, mandalas, or phalluses).

Whether stemming from their history of being governed by a monarchy, the Buddhist acceptance of things the way they are, or other factors too complex for me to comprehend during a short stay in the country, the people did seem pretty darn content.

We left Thimpu the day after the festival and headed for the middle and eastern parts of the country. Over the next week, as we drove through forests and inched over mountain passes on sinuous, single-lane roads with precipitous drops, I tied prayer flags at every pass to ensure safe passage, as I had learned to do in Nepal, and spun prayer wheels whenever I saw them. But I also learned about the greater importance for Bhutanese Buddhists of blessings and accumulation of merit.

As an agnostic, I believe in the power of the universe, but not a single deity or even multiple deities. Yet, as a traveler, I lit candles in churches, wore head coverings as a sign of respect, and made donations in places of worship regardless of my beliefs. I thought of these actions as insurance, in case my skepticism of organized religion was wrong. I understood the Christian and Muslim precepts that the reason to live a good or religious life was to earn a place in heaven. But for the Buddhists, I learned, the goal was a better life in reincarnation and, eventually, enlightenment. Which seemed like an even better reason to get some insurance.

Of course, insurance costs money. I gave money to the monk who presented me with a black string to wear around my neck for warding off disease. And to another who gave me blessed medicine for good health and vitality: five pebbles that looked like peppercorns, in an orange envelope. When I put money in the offering tray at a temple, the attendant monk would pour blessed saffron water into my cupped hands so I could take a sip and then splash the remainder on my head. I was worried about getting sick from the water, so I only pretended to sip, risking my chances at reincarnation.

I was apparently blessed with good luck just for seeing a pickup truck adorned with yellow scarves—a sign it was carrying a dead body to the cremation grounds. On Hindu Blessed Machinery Day (the Buddhists are accommodating in their gratitude), my driver Harker decorated our car with balloons and streamers, and we drove to a roadside blessing area, where a man in ratty jeans splashed the car with water, put red tikka dots on my forehead, tied orange string on our wrists, and gave us paper cones filled with nuts and candy.

Another day I accumulated merit by circling the interior of a dark temple three times while wearing a fifty-five-pound chain mail cloak made by the Bhutanese king/spiritual teacher Pema Lingpa in the early 1500s. What a weird workout.

But perhaps the most unusual blessing came at the temple to the Divine Madman, a Buddhist monk who arrived in Bhutan in 1499 with the belief that enlightenment could be achieved through many means, not just monastic or religious practices. Known for drinking a lot and seducing women (who supposedly sought his blessing in the form of sex), he introduced the practice of painting giant phalluses on buildings and hanging phallic figures over doorways to drive away evil spirits. Because of its power to awaken unenlightened beings, the Divine Madman's penis earned the designation "Thunderbolt of Flaming Wisdom," clearly the best name for one that I had ever heard!

At his temple, in addition to the saffron water sip/splash, I earned merit when I received the coveted tap on the head by the Madman's own bow, and a yak horn that was a symbol of his penis. Sonam insisted that I buy, as the ultimate protective talisman, a carved yak-bone phallus to wear around my neck on my blessed black string. He opened his collar and showed me an identical one he always wore under his gho.

Between the blessings, I marveled at the countryside we drove through, cloaked in rolling fog most mornings and evoking a mystical feeling when clouds parted to reveal temples and dzongs from the seventeenth century. These structures, including the famous Tiger's Nest Monastery, perched impossibly on the sides of mountains.

I stayed in alpine-style wooden guesthouses, usually without reliable electricity or internet. The food was the same everywhere: either tourist buffets for the foreign palate, or the local favorite that Sonam and Harker ate every day but proved too much for my acid stomach—spicy chili and cheese. Service in the restaurants was spotty to nonexistent; I felt like the wait staff were as confused about what to do as I was about why they weren't doing it.

Promptness and schedules did seem to be critical though. At one hotel, I was asked what time I wanted dinner and replied that 7:30 would be fine. At 7:35, a young girl came to my room to fetch me because the soup had already been put on the table and was getting cold. Playing by the rules was also important. One evening, out for a walk before dinner, I got a call from Sonam asking if I were okay. The front desk had called him because I had been gone for over half an hour and hadn't told them where I was going. I didn't even know they'd seen me leave.

––––––––––

The Bumthang District of Bhutan was both the religious heartland of the country, boasting the oldest temples and monasteries (dating from the first century), and the agricultural heartland for buckwheat, rice, and potatoes. The area was also the farthest east I would travel before turning around to loop back to Paro. My final night there, Sonam informed me that the next day was Blessed Rainy Day. That figured. It had rained at some point every day since I had arrived in the country.

"You must take a shower first thing in the morning," he said. "Then you will get good weather."

"Sure," I said, not bothering to ask how, on Blessed Rainy Day, one could expect good weather.

The next morning I was not surprised that it was raining as I braved the hotel's lukewarm water to take a shower. We drove for an hour to the top of a pass, tied prayer flags in the rain, then proceeded steeply downhill. Within fifteen minutes the rain stopped and the clouds cleared! Beneath bright blue skies, a row of stunning white peaks of the Himalaya were visible to the north—the first good view I'd had of them in Bhutan. I felt like I could see forever. My lukewarm shower was worth it.

As we drove toward our guesthouse in the Phobjikha Valley (famous as a wintering site for endangered black-necked cranes, although I was too early in the season to see them), I thought about the Gross National Happiness experiment of Bhutan. I knew I was one of a small number of people privileged enough to gain entry to this unique country filled with spectacular landscapes, calm people, and plentiful blessings, yet I was disappointed. My high hopes had been dashed by the feeling that perhaps the happiness was a bit too controlled, whether by the government, the religion, or the individual self.

When we arrived at the guesthouse, I was excited to have an internet connection, the first one in a week. My heart skipped a few beats when I saw Jim had sent an email every day—chatty, funny, and heartbroken. But there was bad news from my friends Kathleen and Stephanie, who were supposed to meet me in Portugal the next week. Both had last-minute family emergencies and could not join me.

What a setback. I was really looking forward to traveling with friends. And because I'd been leaving all the details up to them, I had virtually nothing planned in Portugal other than my first few nights in a Lisbon hotel. I'd have to wait until I got there to figure things out, since I knew I wouldn't have reliable internet for the rest of the week. I would also have to choose where to go after Portugal since I had absolutely nothing else lined up. It was only October and my house in Portland was rented out until June, so I was only halfway through my adventure. I was finally going to experience being a vagabond without a plan.

CHAPTER 15

PORTUGAL

OCTOBER 2015

"I'll have the octopus and shrimp, a green salad, the cheese plate, and a glass of red wine, please," I said to the waiter, while dining alone in Lisbon my first night there. For the past two months, I'd been working on being happy with what I had, not wanting or desiring other things. But to tell the truth, I had grown tired of rice, lentils, beer, and whiskey.

I had decided to look on the bright side and view my unexpected solitude in Portugal as another chance to be spontaneous and do whatever I wanted. When the immigration official at the Lisbon airport asked me how long I was staying in Portugal, I didn't have an answer. But without a guidebook or a plan, I felt unanchored instead of spontaneous.

For the next few days, I wandered the city and satisfied my urban cravings (although not as extravagantly as in Vienna and without an expensive haircut). I decided that traveling without a guidebook had been fine so far, but now I needed one, but there were none in English. I did find a Berlitz language book designed for Portuguese speakers to speak English, so I bought it even though I'd be without a reference for how to pronounce the Portuguese words. Using the internet, I'd calculated that Portugal was about the size of the western third of my home state of Oregon, so I could easily see the whole country if I rented a car. Maybe spend a month driving around, starting in the north and then following my whims to wherever. On a vacation rental site, I found a stone farmhouse with a lovely terrace a few hours north of Lisbon. The rate was ridiculously cheap, so I booked it for five days. That would give me plenty of time to figure out where to go next.

When I picked up a rental car, I accepted a free upgrade to a small SUV. The GPS served me well for the few hours until I left the major freeway in the town where my rental was located. After several twists and turns, I was directed to a dead end in a farmer's field. Darkness was falling, and I'd passed the appointed time for meeting the landlord, so I called her. Once I followed her directions instead of the GPS, I found the farmhouse easily, but as I pulled into the drive, the skies opened with torrential rain. I ran from the car to the open kitchen door.

"I'm sorry you got lost," said the middle-aged woman dressed in jeans and a leather jacket. "We are off the beaten path, but that is what makes it so lovely. Let's take a tour, and then you can bring in your things."

The kitchen was tiny, with an even smaller living room beside it. Up a winding stone staircase was the bedroom, larger than the downstairs rooms but very cold. So far, the place barely resembled the photos on the internet.

"Where's the terrace?" I asked. "I'm looking forward to spending some time outside once the storm passes." I remembered the photo of inviting white cushions on lounge chairs and a dining table.

"Oh, it's a rooftop terrace," she said. "I'll show it to you, but we've already put away the furniture for the season. It's too cold to be out there now." We went up another staircase and looked out the door. Chairs and tables were stacked in the corner, with no cushions in sight. We went back down to the kitchen.

"Will I need a password for the internet?" I asked, feeling more disappointed each minute.

"No password. The internet only works in the bedroom, since the stone walls block the signal everywhere else. If you stand by the window, you have your best chance of a connection."

No internet was the last straw. If I was going to plan my Portugal adventure while here, I'd need internet. This place was a bust.

"You can call me if there is anything else you need," the landlady said, before rushing through the rain to her car.

How could I have made such a big mistake? I prided myself on seeing behind the photos on those websites. Maybe the inside of the house felt less inviting because of the storm outside. I knew that things often looked different in the light of day. Maybe the internet would work, the saggy sofa would be comfortable, and the view would be spectacular. I had brought some cheese, crackers, and snacks from Lisbon, and luckily a bottle of wine, so I made "dinner" instead of venturing out into the rainy night to find a restaurant. I was certain that if I left, I'd never find my way back.

After eating, I went upstairs and crawled into bed to read for a while. When I turned out the lights, the branches of the trees scratching the windows sounded like someone trying to break in. The terrace was directly above the bedroom, and the stacked furniture creaked and groaned all night long as if people were on the deck. I was spooked. I wondered what on earth had made me think an isolated farmhouse was a good idea. View or no view. Which without the terrace, I realized, was no view.

When I woke up in the morning after a restless night, the storm was still raging, and I couldn't get an internet connection anywhere in the cold stone house. I wished Kathleen and Stephanie, or anyone else for that matter, were with me to commiserate. Damn them for having lives and families that got in the way of travel, I thought selfishly. But there was nothing I could do about it. One thing was for certain, though: I was not about to stay there another night. I called my host and told her I was leaving. I took my suitcase out to the SUV and got in. I had no idea where to go. The dark sky and falling rain made me feel like I was in a horror movie.

I retraced my route back to the center of the small town and the freeway I'd driven in on. I pulled into a parking lot where I had phone service and looked at the GPS on the dashboard, useless with no address to enter. I berated myself for not buying a map of the country in Lisbon. All I knew was that the ocean was close and to the west, while port wine country was several hours to the east. Looking on my phone, I could see the town of Vila Real in the middle of wine country, so I set the GPS for there and set off. I'd figure out where to stay later.

Driving in the stormy weather added to my stress each time I passed a truck and lost visibility from the spray. I felt lost and hopeless, not carefree and blown by the wind. Traveling without knowing where I was going had no appeal when I had to be alone to navigate, read road signs in Portuguese, drive, and make every decision about every single thing. Some vagabond I was.

I stopped to fill the gas tank and get a bite to eat. With a pastry and cup of tea in hand, I searched the internet for a room for that night. I found a highly rated agritourism hotel on the edge of Vila Real and booked a room for one night, not wanting to make the same mistake twice. I got back on the freeway and felt better knowing I had a place to sleep. As I eventually neared Vila Real, I wondered if the GPS would send me on another wild goose chase, but I found the hotel easily on the first try.

"We've upgraded you to one of our cottages; it has a small kitchen," the receptionist said when I checked in. She also confirmed that the cottage was available for the next several nights in case I wanted to stay.

Things were looking up. The storm had even abated.

My stone cottage, a short distance down the lane from the main building, was as charming as the previous night's place had been dreary. Everything appeared new and fresh. A fire had been laid in the wood-burning fireplace, two big windows overlooked the garden and the hills in the distance, and there was plenty of space for yoga on the wide-planked wood floor. To top it off, the internet connection was fast and steady.

When I finally went to sleep that night, nestled in crisp linens on a big bed near dying embers in the fireplace, I resolved to stay a few more days. My decision was sealed the next morning when I found a loaf of freshly baked bread hanging from the nail above my door.

———————

I loved being in a place long enough to actually unpack, which didn't take long since I had only one suitcase. I'd been wearing the same clothes for six months, with a few minor additions and subtractions, but was proud of how little I had and how useful each piece was. That closetful of clothes I thought essential for my life in Portland was a distant memory.

After a good night's sleep, I felt rested, relaxed and ready to venture out and enjoy the sunny day. I decided to take a drive in the countryside to explore my new surroundings. I set the GPS for the nearby town of Pinhão in the heart of port wine country. I wanted a scenic back-road trip, so I unchecked the box for motorways, put on my sunglasses, and was off.

Two hours later, I regretted everything. The GPS had indeed taken me on small roads through little towns, mostly deserted but for the occasional general store with a few old men sitting outside. But then the roads became even narrower, and I found myself on a sidehill in a steep vineyard, boxed into a roofless tunnel of four-foot-high rock walls. Golden grape leaves clung to harvested vines. I hadn't seen another car or person for at least ten miles. I knew I'd made a big mistake when the road dead-ended in a muddy field. What was it with this Portuguese GPS?

There wasn't enough room to turn around, and I didn't want to get stuck in the mud, so I slowly backed up, not my strongest driving skill, while the car's proximity sensors pinged wildly. Yes, I know I'm about to hit the wall, I shouted pointlessly. Damn that upgrade to an SUV. I put the windows down and pulled in the side mirrors. Maybe that would buy me more room. I was sweating with anxiety. Denting the rental car would cost me a fortune! What if I couldn't get out of here? Where was my Mustang calm?

After what seemed like an eternity, I was out of the rock wall tunnel and able to turn around and return to the last major intersection. I took the left fork instead of the right and within two minutes saw a sign pointing straight ahead to Pinhão. I'd had it with the GPS and vowed to never take it off "motorways" again. About thirty minutes later, I arrived in Pinhão. It had been almost four hours since I'd left Vila Real. I found a café and sat at a table with a view of the Douro River.

"How far is it from here to Vila Real?" I asked the waitress after she took my sandwich order.

"The best way is to drive west about thirty minutes along the river to Peso da Régua. Then another twenty minutes on the freeway," the waitress said. "It's an easy and beautiful drive."

"That's great news," I said. "I'll have a glass of red wine with that sandwich after all."

The drive back to Vila Real was as easy and scenic as the waitress had promised, with steep hillsides of grapes tumbling straight down into the Douro River. I really liked the feel of the town of Peso da Régua as I drove through, with its charming tourist area along a river greenbelt and its location in the midst of vineyards, so I decided it would be my next stop. Back at the cottage, I searched the internet and found a cute short-term rental apartment.

"We should meet at the train station," Antonio, the owner of the rental, suggested in his confirmation email. "Then you can follow me to the apartment. Sunday at 1:00." After my GPS misadventures, I considered that a brilliant idea.

Antonio was a dark-haired thirty-something man dressed casually in pressed jeans, a collared shirt, and a V-neck sweater. Marinete, the pretty petite woman with him, wore jeans and a light sweater, a ceramic necklace, and black boots, completing my vision of European chic—looking stylish without effort. Neither spoke English well, but Antonio was quick to pull out an iPad with Google Translate.

"Please join us for tapas lunch, then we will show you the apartment," Antonio said in halting English.

Over plates of octopus salad, pork sausages, cheese and bread, cod croquettes, scrambled eggs, and olives, and a bottle of crisp white wine, I learned that Antonio worked for the Port Wine Institute and had a side business in vineyard management. Marinete was a general practice lawyer.

"You know," Antonio said, "the Douro wine region is the oldest demarcated wine area in the world. The wineries are called *quintas* and mostly sit high on the ridges. The vines are planted on steep hillsides."

"Yes, I drove through some of those steep hillsides the other day." They laughed when I told my rock wall story.

"In the old days, the port wine was made at the quinta, then taken in the rabelo boats to Porto, where it was stored before shipment to England," Antonio said, reading the words from the translation program on the computer. I'd seen the quaint wooden flat-bottomed cargo boats now used for scenic tours on the river. "I will make appointments for you to visit the quintas if you like."

"Yes, please," I said, grateful for the help and advice.

After lunch, we drove to the apartment high above town and I settled in. The unit was large and beautifully decorated, with a small front porch that looked out over a hillside vineyard tended by Antonio. Maybe I hadn't lost my touch of seeing behind the internet pictures after all. The best part was the washer and dryer. I had been handwashing all my laundry since leaving my apartment in Poland. Antonio and Marinete lived on the floor above.

My days fell into a regular rhythm, starting with reading emails and the news while sipping coffee on my terrace. Trying to regain my Mustang calm, I meditated, did yoga, and took long walks up the steep hill behind the apartment. In the afternoon, I'd visit a quinta where Antonio had made me an appointment or find a fun lunch restaurant. Sometimes Antonio and I would share a glass of wine, helping each other with English and Portuguese pronunciations, before Marinete got home from work. Other evenings, I'd relax alone on the terrace before making a simple dinner (I didn't like to drive at night, so I always ate in).

I thought about how different this alone time was from the ten days I'd spent at the hotel in Romania. In Peso da Régua, when I went wine tasting by myself, I missed having a companion, but I also had interesting conversations with strangers and locals. In Romania, there was no conversation. Was that the key? Or was it the availability of restaurants, wineries, and shops instead of being in a small village in the middle of nowhere? Ironically, I felt more like a vagabond now that I had a nice apartment. And I hadn't made any plans beyond extending my stay for a week in Peso da Régua.

One day, I visited Quinta do Tedo for a wine tasting. The young woman serving me told me the story of the owners, Kay and Vincent, who'd met in California. They'd owned the quinta since 1992 and split their time between there and Napa Valley while raising three children. It was midafternoon by the time I finished tasting. I asked the server about the five guest rooms on the property, thinking it would be a fun place to spend a few nights. A slim, dark-haired woman heard my American accent and stopped to say hello. She was the owner, Kay.

"I wish we could talk longer," Kay said after a few minutes of chitchat, "but I was just on my way to Armamar. I've heard about a bakery that makes wonderful apple fritters. I'm not exactly sure where it is and it will probably take at least an hour, but do you want to join me?"

"Of course!" I said, surprised, but pleased by the invitation.

We got into her car and Kay drove uphill away from the river to Armamar, which sat on a high plateau planted with apple orchards. Near the center of town, we found the bakery, named the English word Apple, and devoured two fritters quickly.

"These live up to the reputation," I said, licking my fingers.

"Yes, I'm going to ask them to supply me regularly for the guest rooms," Kay said. "There's also an apple cider producer up here somewhere that I've been trying to find," Kay said. "I know it's getting late, but . . ."

I didn't wait for her to finish. "I've got time—let's go."

We drove through forest and orchards, sometimes in circles, until we finally found a sign for the cider farm on a locked gate with a low rock wall on either side. We couldn't see any buildings beyond a curve in the downward-sloping driveway.

"There might be somebody there," Kay said. "What do you say we hop the wall and walk down there?"

I shrugged. "Why not? It'd be an adventure to get arrested for trespassing in Portugal."

We followed the driveway for a few hundred meters before coming to a barn and a small house. The barn door was ajar, and we could see crates of freshly picked apples inside. But there was no sign of any people.

"Darn," Kay said. "I guess I'll have to come back another time. But at least now I know where it is."

Later, as I drove alone back to Peso da Régua, I thought about how much fun it was to hang out with a person of my own generation who wasn't a guide. I felt sorry for myself that Kathleen and Stephanie weren't there. Yet, I knew I'd only been on this escapade because I was alone.

———

Much as I liked the Douro Valley and having a home base, I felt the itch to get on the road again and started to make plans. I was in my element, searching the web, making reservations, buying plane tickets, and, well, *planning*. I realized this approach made me much happier than being a totally free spirit. I got my anchor points in place with reservations and decided having open space between those points gave me enough spontaneity to feed my vagabond urge. And, of course, almost anything could be canceled or changed if I really wanted.

I decided to drive through the middle of Portugal to the Algarve, the far southern coast renowned for golf courses, sandy beaches, and warm weather. I'd spend a week there, then drive back to Lisbon to fly to Barcelona, a city I'd always wanted to see. Once in Spain, I could next fly to Seville and travel around the southern white hill towns, continuing to enjoy warm Mediterranean weather if possible. I booked flights, cars, and hotels.

And as long as I was planning, why not think about November? I saw an Instagram post by Nina, a travel writer I had met at a lodge in Zambia, about a trip she had just taken to Morocco. The exoticism of a North African country appealed to me, but I didn't feel comfortable traveling to my first Muslim country alone.

I contacted Nina, who put me in touch with Carol, an Aussie who organized bespoke Moroccan tours. Carol and I hit it off immediately when we talked, so I asked her to craft an itinerary for me. After spending so much time organizing my Portugal and Spain travels, I found it a luxury to have somebody else do the work. Especially somebody who intimately knew the country. I marveled again at the value of connecting and staying in touch with other travelers.

I bought a discount plane ticket from Seville to Marrakesh but had no idea where to go after Morocco and felt that I should schedule something for the holidays in December. As if by magic, or maybe karma, I got an email from Gretchen, my fellow Mustang trekker, inviting me to her Phuket, Thailand, beach house for Christmas. "You can come to Bangkok whenever you like and use it as a jumping-off point to explore Southeast Asia. We'll head to Phuket on the twenty-third and stay a few days into the new year," she wrote. I booked a ticket from Morocco to Bangkok in early December and decided to work out the details later. Now this was how a vagabond was supposed to travel.

"Welcome to the Hilton," the receptionist said as I checked into the resort hotel in the Algarve town of Vilamoura. I hadn't been staying in chain hotels since I started traveling, opting instead for local charm, but I'd accumulated so many loyalty points during my corporate career that I could stay at the Hilton for virtually nothing. The free week would let me splurge a bit in Morocco and still stay within my budget for the year.

When I was traveling for work, places like this Hilton were normal fare for business conventions and, in fact, a convention was taking place at the hotel when I arrived. It was also a holiday week for school kids in Britain. My room was standard issue, with a balcony that overlooked the noisy pool area. I golfed a few days and found the adults-only pool. I walked on the beach, but it was too cold to swim.

I contacted Jayne, the woman who had arranged my Zambia trip and surprised me at the airport with flowers for my birthday. It turned out she lived only fifteen minutes from my hotel, so we arranged to meet. The night we had dinner together brightened an otherwise dull week, especially when she told me the story of how she had been charged by an elephant while managing the Zambezi River camp where I had stayed with Gayle. My conversation with Jayne about travel and living as an expat was a refreshing change from the short exchanges I'd had with conventioneers or British families on holiday in the work/vacation setting of my hotel.

By the end of the week, I was ready for a few days in Lisbon before heading to Spain. Despite my experience at the creepy farmhouse in the north, the craziness of the GPS, and this somewhat dull time in the

Algarve, I really liked the easygoing vibe of Portugal. I decided it was a place I could happily come back to, maybe next time visiting Porto. And maybe next time with friends.

CHAPTER 16

SPAIN

NOVEMBER 2015

I arrived at my Barcelona B&B in late afternoon. The days were getting shorter, so I went out for a walk while there was still daylight. On one street, a line of old townhouses with wrought iron balconies created a stark contrast to the ultrachic stores on the other side. Dark, low clouds hung over the city, and the dim light made the businessmen drinking coffee at sidewalk cafés seem a bit sinister, despite my feeling perfectly safe.

I came upon a bookstore and, having learned from my experience in Portugal, bought a Spain guidebook that was in English. As dark descended, I went back to my room for a few hours to read before adapting my schedule to the Spanish pace of life, which included going to a nearby tapas restaurant for dinner at 10 p.m.

An overcast sky again greeted me the next morning, so I borrowed an umbrella from the hotel and hoped for the best. I soon abandoned the large, four-lane boulevards, preferring to wander into the old town labyrinth of pedestrian walkways lined with three-story buildings, each with a unique carved or colorful doorway. I maneuvered past other pedestrians with open umbrellas in an unchoreographed dance. I stopped in artisanal shops and dawdled over pastry and coffee, lingering longer when the rain showers got heavy.

A few hours passed before I realized I could no longer find any familiar landmarks on either of my paper or phone maps. My feet hurt from walking in rain-damp shoes, I was worn out from window shopping, and my stomach growled from snacking instead of eating a meal. When the dark sky got even darker and the rain came down in buckets, I knew it was time to head back to the B&B. The only problem was, I didn't know where I was.

I ducked into an alcove and waited for the worst of the rain to lessen. I splashed through a few puddles to a bigger street that allowed vehicle traffic, which I hoped included a taxi that could take me to my hotel. It didn't matter that I didn't know where I was, as long as I knew where I was going.

I stuck my arm out in my best imitation of a New Yorker, but to no avail. The rain didn't make it any easier. Down the block I saw a hotel with a cab stand and made a beeline for it. Thankfully, within a few minutes, I was sitting comfortably in the back of a taxi.

"Please take me to this address," I said in halting Spanish, as I handed the driver a card with the B&B's address on it.

He looked at it quizzically and said something in Spanish or Catalan, I couldn't tell which.

"I'm sorry, I don't speak Spanish. English?" I said hopefully.

"No," he responded. Then rattled off something again, pointing across the street. Maybe he didn't want to take me.

"Por favor. Esta address." I pointed at the card, not realizing the Spanish word for address was *dirección*.

"Okay," he said, shrugging his shoulders.

He put the car in drive, inched into the traffic, and made an immediate left turn. At the end of that short block, he turned left again. Then stopped. I was in front of my building. Just one block—or about a three-minute walk—from where I'd gotten in the cab.

I laughed and tried to tell the cabbie that I hadn't realized where I was, but from the expression on his face, I could tell he thought I was a crazy or lazy American tourist. I gave him a twenty-euro note for the two-euro ride and resolved to pay more attention to where I was in the future.

———————

The next day, I decided that even if I got lost, I was going to set out to see Gaudí's Sagrada Familia. I was pretty burned out on cathedrals, monasteries, and temples, but this was Gaudí's pièce de résistance, or whatever the word for masterpiece was in Spanish. My B&B host had advised me to buy advance tickets online. The metro was easy to navigate, so I didn't get lost and arrived with enough time to examine the perimeter of the building. I scrunched up my nose at the melting ice cream cone spires topped with colorful fruit baskets—not my taste in architecture—but at my scheduled time, I paid for the headphone tour and entered the cathedral.

I learned that Gaudí's design of the cathedral was inspired by a forest. The soaring ceiling was supported by columns that grew up like trees, thick at the bottom and branching randomly into space to hold up the structure. Afternoon light, filtered through avant-garde stained-glass windows of green and orange, dappled the floor as if coming through leaves. Lovely. Like nature itself, the design was simultaneously simple and complex. In striking contrast to the immense scale of the cathedral forest, I could make out small bugs, beetles, and lizards subtly carved into the massive wooden entry doors.

I sat in one of the pews and reflected on the variety of religious sites I'd seen on my travels. I had dutifully admired the architecture and the art (even when repulsed by the subject matter), but I had never felt drawn in, had remained a dispassionate observer.

But there was something different about this church. Without images of God or Jesus or Buddha or any number of other deities, and without paintings or sculptures of suffering or beheadings or crucifixions, Gaudí had evoked a sense of awe by emulating nature. How simple.

After a couple of hours in the Sagrada Familia, I began to feel my Mustang calm return. I realized how easy it was for that feeling to get buried under the pressures of travel, be they navigating airports, getting lost, finding food and lodging, or just living day to day. As I watched the light play on the walls and floor, I felt thankful for the life I led and overcome by a deep sense of joy. I wondered if maybe this feeling of personal calmness and inner joy, rather than the worship of an external being, was why people came to church.

But apparently Gaudí's masterpiece did not inspire quiet introspection for everyone. I watched visitors snap selfies, check the photo, then move on quickly, seeming to never actually look at what they were photographing. As I took a few cell phone photos myself, I thought about the heavy camera equipment I had left back in my hotel room and realized my pendulum had swung fully away from my photo-a-day project of January. I suspected my pendulum had swung in other ways too, but those changes had been too gradual to notice.

———————

After four days in Barcelona, I flew to Seville, where I rented a car and drove south to stay for a week in a condo on a golf course. I'd enjoyed playing a few rounds of golf in the Algarve in Portugal and liked the idea of playing a few more times in Spain. I also planned to explore the famous white hill towns of the Andalusian area. But since it was now early November, there was practically no tourist traffic, which meant the hill towns were lovely but very quiet, and the golf resort was empty. I golfed for four days, playing two balls at once since I was completely alone on the course. Everything seemed dead and dull. I realized I felt the same way I had in the Algarve—misplaced, and wondering how to recapture the joy of travel. Maybe traveling to normally busy places in the off-season wasn't always a good idea.

At the end of the week, I returned to Seville to spend a few days in the city. I had booked a room in a boutique hotel on a pedestrian street and had to lug my bag across the ancient cobblestones to the twelve-foot-high, thick wooden front door. When I stepped inside, I left behind the sights, sounds, and smells of the rest of the world. Small fountains burbled soothingly in a central courtyard, and instead of checking in at a characterless reception desk, I was led to a small round table and served a glass of red wine along with the registration paperwork. I heard the low hum of people coming and going or simply sitting in the lobby relaxing. I felt back in my normal groove again, eager to enjoy my surroundings and to go out and see the city.

The next day, I decided to take a free walking tour to get oriented instead of resorting to my usual aimless wandering. The group met at La Giralda, the bell tower for the Seville Cathedral, reputedly the third-largest church in the world. Our perky twenty-something female guide pointed out a small domed area next to the bell tower and told us that the original building was a mosque built in 1184 by North African Moors, Muslims of Berber and Arab descent. In 1248, the mosque was "Christianized" when Ferdinand III conquered Seville; the construction of the cathedral began in 1402. Apparently, the original mosque was so beautiful nobody wanted to destroy it, which was unusual in those days of razing the structures of opposing religions.

The walking tour group included a motley crew of Brits, Aussies, a few other Americans, and a Canadian named Keith. I guessed he was about fifteen years younger than me. We discovered we had both recently been in Bulgaria, quite a coincidence. And we were both traveling for an indefinite period around the world, he while taking a break from his career as a record company executive.

Keith asked if I wanted to have lunch after the tour, and after crossing a bridge to the Jewish quarter and wandering the back alleys, we eventually found an outdoor café where we ordered lunch and beers. I asked him what music genre was his specialty.

"Punk rock," he said. "In addition to my corporate job, I also play guitar in a punk rock band."

Well, that was something different. I told him I never listened to punk and, in fact, wasn't much of a music person at all. I knew what I liked but didn't really pay attention. He shrugged off my comments and suggested we go to a flamenco show that night. Now that was more like it. We walked back to my hotel, where the concierge reserved us two tickets.

The small theater consisted of about forty folding chairs lined up in front of a 10′ x 10′ stage. The dancers stomped and clapped and sinuously moved their bodies around every corner of the tiny stage without falling off. I could see Keith's fingers slightly moving in his lap as he played along with the intricate guitar solos. After the show, we went to dinner at a local bar, where ham hocks hung from the ceiling.

"Look," Keith said after I'd had some wine, "I know punk isn't your thing, but there's a concert tomorrow night I'd like to take you to. There are several local bands, but the headliner is a famous band from Denmark."

I had no desire to go to the concert, but I was enjoying his company and thought, why not? We were both leaving Seville the day after, so time was limited.

"Aren't we too old?" I asked.

Keith laughed. "Oh, the kids will think we're somebody's parents. We'll stand in the back and drink and watch the scene. If you wear black, you'll fit right in. Besides, punk rockers are very accepting people. Oh, and don't forget to bring earplugs."

The next night, after having spent the day sightseeing with Keith, I put on my black jeans, black sweater, black leather jacket, and a colorful pair of earrings. Keith was dressed the same way, minus the earrings.

After an early dinner we took a cab to an industrial area a few miles out of the center city. I put aside my sixty-year-old sensible questions like how will we get home, what if it isn't in a safe area, and what if I hate it? Keith seemed perfectly comfortable.

"You and I might be the only people here without a tattoo," I whispered to Keith as we stood in line to get our hands stamped. "How can you play in a punk band without a tattoo?"

"The thing about punk is that everyone is trying to be different. I'm different because I don't look like the rest of them. So, very punk."

I got a glass of cheap wine and listened to the warm-up band, called The Mutant Sperms. The music was so loud that, even with earplugs, conversation was impossible. I must admit that I kind of got into it; we stayed until 3:00 a.m. If, a year before, anyone had told me that I'd be at a punk rock concert in Seville until the wee hours with a rather younger man I'd just met, I'd have told them they were nuts. But then, maybe doing things that were kind of nuts was part of the joy of travel.

CHAPTER 17

MOROCCO

NOVEMBER 2015

"Welcome to Morocco. I'm Soufiane, your guide," said a swarthy man in his mid-thirties, dressed like a hip European in loafers, jeans, and a sweater jacket. After some small talk, he added, "Please let me say I am so sorry about the Paris attack. The people who do those things give my religion a bad name. Islam is a peaceful religion. Please do not judge us by those events."

Two days prior to my arrival in Morocco, members of the Islamic State had killed 130 people in Paris and injured hundreds more. "Thank you for that," I said. "People everywhere, not just followers of Islam, do terrible things in the name of religion."

Before leaving the terminal, I got a SIM card and some cash to cover the two weeks we'd be on the road before returning for a week in Marrakesh. At the parking garage I was pleased to see that our transportation was a new black SUV; Soufiane would be the driver and guide. We headed out at dusk toward the Atlas Mountains, to a boutique hotel where I had a reservation. We drove north for an hour and a half until we reached a village that was dark except for a few random lights in small adobe buildings. Seeing a sign indicating we were in Ourigane, I commented on its similarity to Oregon, where I was from. "It's pronounced Weer-gan," Soufiane said as we approached an empty intersection.

"Close enough," I said. I needed a good omen to quash my fear that I was once again headed to a too-far-from-civilization place to stay. Soufiane turned right at the intersection and drove down a dusty dirt street with a ten-foot-high wall bordering the left side.

"Here we are," Soufiane said as the headlights illuminated an unassuming sign announcing the hotel entrance. In Morocco, as I would soon learn, outward appearances did not reflect what was found inside. Behind the high wall and metal gate I beheld a sleek, glass-fronted building and delicately lit landscaping. The owner, a French woman, met us on the doorstep and offered me a glass of champagne, which I gratefully accepted.

"Welcome," she said. "I'll show you to your room. Dinner will be served in half an hour."

My trip from Spain to Morocco had been short and easy, but suddenly I felt tired and overwhelmed with the prospect of venturing into and learning about yet another foreign country. Maybe I was moving around too much, or maybe I was suffering from the late nights out in Seville. Whatever the reason, I hoped that three nights of R&R to celebrate my birthday at a nice hotel would perk me up before Soufiane and I set out to see the rest of the country. I thanked Soufiane, and he wished me a happy birthday before driving away into the dark night.

The next morning, I awoke to a landscape of red earth hills covered with pine forests. My room had a large private terrace, so I made a cup of coffee and settled into a lounge chair, enveloped in the smell of dewy sage. I thought about my birthday a year earlier and the joy of seeing cheetahs in South Africa. I had been on safari, getting ready to change my life—and boy, had I! I thought about the many places I had been since then, the experiences I'd had, and the people I'd met. I certainly had broadened my perspective and had a lot of fun. I hadn't set out with any goals, but I wondered how deeply my experiences had impacted my core being and beliefs.

Before, I was a successful urban professional with a two-bedroom house and a closetful of clothes and shoes. Now I lived out of a single suitcase. I used to be adamant about going to the gym to stay fit but now realized how absurd that concept seemed in much of the world; walking and yoga were serving me just fine. I had learned that not only could I survive without the internet every day, but I enjoyed being disconnected. Yes, I was living a different life, but was it a more meaningful life? Was I a better person than before? And what did it mean to be a better person anyway?

I had become more patient with people and accepting of the unforeseen challenges of continuous travel, especially after Nepal. I was perhaps even more curious about the world and was enjoying laughing and sharing stories and ideas with people from different cultures and backgrounds. I tried to buy local and keep a small environmental footprint. And, although I was still firm in my conviction that formal religions were not for me, I felt that my experiences were making me a kinder, more compassionate, and more spiritual person.

On the other hand, I knew I was sometimes self-centered and annoyed when I didn't get what I took for granted I would have—a fan, a clean guesthouse, or a GPS that worked. And even though I wasn't buying material goods, I indulged myself with guides, hairdressers, and nice hotels like this one.

As I thought about all that I'd seen, I felt a twinge of guilt about staying in a beautiful hotel when there was so much need in the world. But why should I feel guilty? I'd worked damn hard my whole life, used my intellect to live responsibly, taken care of myself financially, and put the opportunities I was given to good use, I thought. I was generous and charitable. Did being a good person have to mean not enjoying the finer things in life, or traveling on a shoestring budget? I didn't think so. After all, the owner of this hotel had to make a living too.

Maybe the question I needed to ask was whether my travels were helping me stay open to different ways of thinking or living. And, more importantly, was I having a positive impact on others as I moved through the world?

As I finished my coffee, now another year older, I was fairly certain the answer was yes.

———

I got dressed for the day's hike in this Muslim country in long pants and a long-sleeved shirt, a big scarf wrapped loosely around my neck in case I needed a head covering. Luckily, it was a cool day. After a hearty breakfast of scrambled eggs, berry crepes, and fresh-baked bread, I met my hiking guide for the day: Mohammed, a local Berber man of about thirty who lived in a nearby village and spoke perfect English. We walked directly from the hotel and soon were on a dusty trail leading to Mohammed's village in the mountains.

"The Berber culture is over four thousand years old," Mohammed said. "Even the Moors of Spain were originally of Berber descent."

"The main thing I know about Berbers is that you make beautiful carpets," I said.

"Yes. The women weave the rugs, and the men tend the flocks to provide the wool." Mohammed pointed at a herd of sheep ahead on a hillside.

"I was recently in Bhutan, where the weavers follow traditional patterns. Is it the same here?"

Mohammed laughed. "Quite the opposite. Berber women never use patterns. No two rugs are alike. The weaving is a way of telling their own stories. They don't even know the design until they begin weaving and the story tells them what to say."

We walked up steep paths and down dry ravines. We passed through orchards and pine groves, and occasionally small villages that seemed to consist solely of a handful of houses and usually a small mosque. Passing one mosque, I could hear a spindly chorus of children's voices repeating phrases after the teacher.

"It's a Koranic school for the youngest children," Mohammed said. "When they get older, they will go to school in bigger villages."

"What will the children be told about the Paris bombings?" Mohammed and I had been talking about terrorism earlier, so I didn't feel the question was inappropriate.

"They will be told that it is not Islam. We do not condone killing others. The radical sects give us a bad name."

A few hours into the hike, we reached Mohammed's village. "We will have lunch here at my mother's house," he said.

Although Mohammed's mother prepared the meal, she never appeared on the thatch-covered rooftop deck where we ate a tomato-pepper-and-onion salad and traditional Moroccan chicken tagine. She had made the latter in the eponymous clay domed cooking vessel and served it with fresh-baked bread. For dessert, we drank mint tea from a silver tea service and ate almonds and walnuts from the family's backyard trees. The meal was delicious, and I was pleased when Mohammed agreed I could meet his mother and see the humble kitchen where she cooked. I wished I could spend the rest of the day on that tranquil rooftop dozing in the sunshine, but we had a two-hour walk back to the hotel.

———————

Because it was my birthday, my tour organizer, Carol, had booked me for a hammam at the hotel at five o'clock. I wasn't sure what a hammam was but knew it involved a massage and steam bath. I was tired from the hike and couldn't wait to be pampered.

Yasmine, a middle-aged woman with lovely brown eyes, ushered me into a small, dark room. We walked past the massage table to a small dressing area with a bench and hooks for my clothes. Something smelled like fresh flowers, although I couldn't see any. "I am sorry I have little English," she said.

Not a problem, I thought. I liked my massages quiet. I undressed while she stood and waited by an arched door. When I was naked, she led me into a bread-loaf-shaped vault filled with steam. A large marble or granite slab—I couldn't tell which—filled the middle of the room. Yasmine told me to lie down face-up. I eased myself onto the slab, focused on breathing the hot steamy air, and closed my eyes. Yasmine was in the corner playing with faucets, trying to regulate the steam, I thought.

"Yow!" I sputtered as I was doused with a bucket of warm water. Despite the surprise, I enjoyed the sensation. I closed my eyes when I saw Yasmine approach with a second bucket. I closed them a third time and waited again, but this time I felt her soapy hands washing my feet, then my legs, then my entire body. She instructed me to roll over and washed my back side. Let's just say that she didn't miss a single spot.

"Back in ten minutes," she said, and left the room.

The heat and sweat felt fabulous. Yasmine returned and scrubbed off the outer layer of my skin with something that felt like sandpaper. (I later learned it was a mitt called a *kessa*.)

"You have much dead skin," she said. "You need hammam more often. In Morocco, we have once a week." Well, no wonder I had a lot of dead skin—I'd been accumulating it my whole life instead of getting it scrubbed off every week. Yasmine left again.

When she returned, she applied a black mud from the nearby hills, then left me to marinate. If I moved, I slithered on the slab like an egg white, so I stayed still. When she returned for the final time, Yasmine turned off the steam before helping me sit up on the edge of the slab, where she threw buckets of cool water all over me. "Stand up now," she commanded. She rinsed the clay from my nether regions with more buckets of cool water. I sat down on the slab while she washed my hair, kneaded argan oil into it, then rinsed me again. She stepped outside to grab several towels, then had me stand spread-eagled so she could dry me. I was finally ready for the massage.

"Follow me," Yasmine said, leaving the steam chamber. She quickly changed into a dry linen sheath, while I stood stark naked. She offered no towel or robe. I found it interesting that in a culture where women are heavily covered in public, they are comfortable being naked with other women.

I lay down on the massage table, closed my eyes, and relaxed as Yasmine's strong hands easily manipulated my wet-noodle body. I gave in to the blissful coma of massage, hoping my leg muscles would firm up in time for me to walk to my birthday dinner, and wondering if part of being a better person at sixty-one could include a weekly hammam.

"Our route is a loop that will take us southeast through Ouarzazate, Todgha Gorge, and Aït Benhaddou," Soufiane said at the start of our two-week road trip. "Then across the desert to the coast and north to Essaouira before returning to Marrakesh." I loved hearing the exotic names.

The miles passed easily as we drove through pine forests, deep gorges, and oceans of palm trees. Dusty brown desert towns blended seamlessly into the landscape. I stayed in small *riads*, which looked like drab hotels on the outside but offered lush inner courtyards and plush rooms. I quickly realized that Soufiane was one of those special guides who knew his stuff and was a genial companion to boot.

Along the way, we stopped at outdoor markets where vendors sold potatoes, peppers, onions, pomegranates, cucumbers, and dates. The markets included stinky live animal stalls filled with sheep, goats, and chickens that were still much easier to take than the strong smell of the butchered meat section. Soufiane walked beside me, translating if I had questions, and I was usually the only foreigner. I was also usually the only woman and felt conspicuous despite the fact that I wore long pants and a tunic and scarf loosely tied around my hair. In fact, I realized I rarely saw women at all, even when we drove through the towns and villages.

"There are no women shopkeepers, no women sitting at the cafés drinking coffee, few women walking on the streets," I said to Soufiane. "Why is that?"

"Oh, they take the children to school in the morning and pick them up again in the afternoon. Other than that, women stay within their homes or visit with each other. It's not like in the city, where women have more freedom. You will see a big difference when we get to Marrakesh."

"The dunes are always moving, and there is no road," Soufiane told me when we stopped in Hamid, a dusty outpost on the edge of the Sahara Desert that reminded me of the Wild West. "That's why we need a local guide to find our camp." Soufiane went into a small store for supplies and returned with a traditional white Berber headscarf for me to use in the desert. I was touched.

Yousef, our local guide, was tall, dark skinned, and handsome, his blue eyes made bluer by the indigo scarf wrapped around his head. We drove for three hours along a rough track, Yousef pointing the way around sand dunes. I could see why we needed a guide.

"How do you know how to get to the camp if the dunes are always moving?" I asked.

"I grew up in this desert," he said. "I navigate by landmarks like the mountain ridge to the north, the major dunes to the south that move slowly, and the sun or stars, which are always there since it is a desert and we rarely have clouds."

"If you grew up in the desert, where did you go to school, and how did you learn English?"

Yousef laughed. "I went to school in Hamid. My family were nomads, but we all had to go to school as children. I learned Arabic and French in school but taught myself English once I became a guide."

"That's amazing. You speak English very well," I said. "Do you have a family?" I hoped I wasn't rude, asking a personal question.

"I'm thirty-nine years old but I've never been married," he said. I couldn't imagine why not, he was so good-looking and such a nice man.

We finally arrived at camp around four o'clock. Of course, there was no cell coverage, but otherwise the camp was quite luxurious. The Brits who owned the camp had made alcohol readily available with a help-yourself cooler filled with beer, wine, gin, vodka, and whiskey. And ice! Apparently there was a generator somewhere. Soufiane and Yousef went to retrieve my luggage from the car, so I drank a cold gin and tonic alone while sitting on a deep sofa in the three-sided "living room tent." This tent even had coffee tables with checkers and chess games set up ready to be played. In front of me, high dunes served as a backdrop for seven sleeping tents, three on each side of a long red Moroccan wool carpet running across the sand like a hotel hallway. At the very end stood one larger tent, which turned out to be mine.

When the men returned, I followed them to the far tent and opened the "door," a flap secured by a rope through a ring. No keys here. Inside I found a king-sized bed covered in a thick white down comforter, with a red-and-gold woven blanket folded at the bottom of the bed. It had been warm all day, but that night, when the temperature dipped into the forties Fahrenheit, I needed every layer of the blankets, plus the hot water bottle someone had slipped under the covers while I ate dinner.

Although there were a few other guests at the camp when I arrived, they all left the next morning, so I had the place to myself. Soufiane suggested a camel ride, so I climbed aboard a white, curly-haired camel covered with flies. The saddle wasn't very comfortable, and my butt hurt after a short while. A Berber boy led the camel up, over, and around dunes until I was completely turned around and surprised when the camp came back into view.

That afternoon, I reveled in the solitude of the camp when the staff disappeared for the equivalent of siesta. I swung in a hammock, reading a book and drinking cold water from the cooler. As the sun dipped lower in the sky and the air cooled, I decided to climb a nearby tall dune. I stuck my point-and-shoot camera in my pocket and headed up. It was slow going, walking in the sand, and although I thought I was going straight up, when I looked back, I couldn't see the camp anymore. I'd have to be careful to follow my footsteps back down, I thought.

I crested a ridge and decided I'd gone far enough. Dunes stretched out in every direction, and a slight wind sent infinitesimal grains of sand into my ears and eyes. For protection, I wrapped my headscarf like Yousef had shown me and snapped a few photos of the expansive desert scene before the camera became hopelessly jammed with sand. The changing colors of the sky mesmerized me, but soon I realized that I'd better head down so I could get to camp before the sun dropped below the horizon.

I stood up, looking for my footsteps to follow down the dune, but they had already disappeared under the shifting sand. I thought about all the times I'd gotten lost in the past year. What a dummy I was, thinking I could navigate the desert alone. I started down in the direction of camp and hoped for the best.

What a huge relief when halfway down I saw Yousef coming up to meet me. I was saved.

"I wanted to make sure you found your way back," he said. "It's easy to get disoriented here in the dunes."

"How did you know I was here?" I asked.

He laughed. "Just because I am not visible to you does not mean you are invisible. I've been watching you since you left the camp to make sure you were okay. I hope you enjoyed the sunset." Instead of feeling my privacy was violated like when I was in Bhutan, I felt comforted.

That night I went outside my tent to look at the stars. I was sure nobody was watching me then since it was two a.m. The quiet was unlike anything I'd ever heard—or not heard—before. In a forest or the mountains, there were always little noises, leaves moving in a breeze, night animals scurrying, or even the hooting of an owl or call of a coyote. But on this night in the desert there was no wind, so not even the sand was moving. I felt I could almost hear the shooting stars, which were flying across the sky as if I'd thrown confetti in the air. The Milky Way formed a thick river, and the sky seemed more light than dark. The only thing missing was my old friend, the full moon.

Along with hearing the frogs and seeing Chomolungma, this experience would be added to my "best-ever" list. I was overcome with a feeling of intense peace and serenity that was different from the Mustang calm that had been helping me navigate the real world. This feeling was more ethereal, a sense that my life was a thread in the universe, woven into a pattern as intricate as that of the rug I was standing on. I was meant to be there, at that moment, the boundless intelligence of the universe talking directly to my soul, telling me I was on the right path.

I have no idea how long I stood there before I started shivering from the cold. Reluctantly, I returned to the warmth of the huge bed in the lavish tent at the end of the red carpet laid on the sand in the middle of the Sahara Desert beneath a billion stars.

———————

My final week in Morocco I spent in Marrakesh, staying near the main square in a riad that provided an oasis of calm amid the bustling city. The first order of business was to get my hair colored at a chic salon where Soufiane had made me an appointment. The Islamic female hair stylists wore full headscarves with only a few bangs showing, although they also had on tight jeans with modest hip-length tops. Soufiane gave the "no orange" speech for me in Arabic and, luckily, the color turned out perfect.

The next day, Soufiane, in his usual blue jeans and sweater, arrived at the hotel with a local guide who was, like fifty percent of the men I had met in Morocco, named Mohammed. This Mohammed was a George Clooney look-alike college history professor. He wore a traditional *djellaba* (a loose-fitting outer robe with a hood) over Western slacks and shoes; somewhere in the folds of the robe he kept his cell phone. Our destination was the souk, or market, but we weren't going to the finished-product tourist souk; we were going into the bowels where the products were actually made.

The ancient part of the souk was a labyrinth of dark alleyways, crowded with stalls, vendors, and buyers. We watched an auction of goat, sheep, and cow hides tied with twine, which buyers carted off in wheelbarrows. We followed the hide buyers to the leatherworking "street," where men in djellabas sharpened the knives they used to cut shapes out of the hides, then sat and hand-stitched shoes, purses, and belts.

We explored a pungent alley where long skeins of raw wool hung above and inside huge vats of beautiful, deep-colored dyes. "The wool will be sold to artisans in another section of the souk, where it will be woven into rugs," Mohammed said. Down another "street," tailors sat at treadle-powered sewing machines and made both custom and off-the-rack clothing.

In the metalworking alley, the heat was palpable. Some blacksmiths made large frames for furniture, while others shaped precision pieces for intricate lampshades or chandeliers. Most wore flimsy sandals, and some went barefoot, despite the red-hot metal and heavy tools. One of the last alleys we ventured down was the woodworking area. Men traced intricate patterns onto the wood, then painstakingly carved each tiny piece with precision knives and chisels, making tables and boxes inlaid with different woods or mother-of-pearl.

I found being behind the scenes and watching the artisans infinitely more interesting than merely seeing finished products. But selling finished products was also a purpose of the souk, so before we left each "street," Mohammed would take me to the shop selling what he said was the finest-quality finished product. I was certain he had arrangements with each place to get a cut of anything bought by someone he brought into the store. Which only seemed fair.

"Surely Soufiane has told you I'm traveling for an extended time and don't even have a home right now. So I'm not buying, even though I've seen some fabulous things."

"Yes, I know," he said. "But if you see something you must have, it can be shipped."

I hadn't seen anything I couldn't live without.

We were almost out of the woodworkers' alley when Mohammed directed me into a small store. I was looking politely at the goods when a very large bowl, two feet in diameter, seemed to cast a spell over me. The outside featured burnished wood; the inside revealed some of the most intricate and beautiful mosaic work I had seen. When the shopkeeper quoted a price, I did a quick conversion in my head from dirham to dollars. I was reluctant to spend the money at all, and the price was higher than I expected, but after a negotiation involving Mohammed as a go-between, the shopkeeper came down to a price I thought reasonable. The bowl would be shipped to my friend Kathleen, who'd store it for me until my return to the States.

"I will also send one of these inlaid boxes to you," the shopkeeper said, pointing at a display of jewelry boxes. "Please choose the one you like. It is a gift."

I looked at Mohammed. Had I overpaid so much that the shopkeeper felt guilty? No, merchants in the souk traditionally offered a gift in gratitude for the first sale of the day, which would portend a good day overall. I remembered my recent thoughts about becoming a better person and wondered if starting each day with gratitude might help. In any case, I was grateful to have had this fun experience of bargaining in the souk. It wasn't until I looked at my credit card bill a few weeks later that I realized I'd miscalculated the exchange rate conversion. I'd paid more than twice as much as I thought for the bowl. Of course, by then the money didn't matter.

CHAPTER 18

Thailand/USA/Thailand

DECEMBER 2015–JANUARY 2016

The journey from Morocco to Bangkok had taken almost twenty hours, and my back was throbbing from sitting on a plane too long. When I stepped outside the airport, the tropical climate made my clothes stick to my body despite it being the cool season, and I knew my hair was limp and stringy. My mood wasn't helped when I finally got to the front of the taxi line and the cabbie, who didn't speak English, made it clear that he had no idea how to get to the address I had given him. Well, Gretchen's house *was* in a residential area in a city of ten million, but I was still annoyed. Eventually, he handed me over to another driver, who I had to trust knew the way.

To my relief, he found the house on a small side street so quiet and calm I couldn't believe I was still in the bustling, raucous Asian city I'd just been driven through. It was my first time traveling in this part of the world and I was looking forward to being introduced to it by someone who knew it well. But because it was Wednesday afternoon, Gretchen was working, so I wouldn't see her until that evening. When we had been trekking in Nepal, Gretchen had explained to me that many expats in Bangkok had live-in help, so her housekeeper would meet me when I arrived. The diminutive Thai woman who opened the door looked to be my age. She understood some of my English, but despite my protestations, she carried my suitcase upstairs, where she showed me to a deliciously air-conditioned guest room comfortably furnished with Thai antiques. I took a long shower, lay down on the bed, and felt the breeze of the ceiling fan on my upturned face. Although there was only a seven-hour time difference between Morocco and Thailand, I was drained and fell promptly asleep.

About an hour later, I awoke refreshed and went to the patio with my computer to check emails. Before I could even ask, the housekeeper showed up with a glass of iced tea and a tray of little snacks. I wondered what it would be like to have someone cleaning, cooking, and serving me food every day.

I logged in and immediately saw bad news from Pennsylvania, where my mother lived. Apparently, just as I had left Morocco, my mother's husband had suffered a serious stroke and was in the hospital. The message was from my brother, who had flown across the country from Idaho to be with her. It was the middle of the night there, so I couldn't pick up the phone and call. I suddenly felt very far away.

All I could do was send emails and wait for my family members to wake up the next morning and give me a more detailed report.

When I finally spoke to my mother, she admitted that she needed help, which surprised me. Like me, my mother had always prided herself on being a self-sufficient woman. She and her husband (they had married late in life, so I never called him my stepfather even though I loved him as a member of the family) were both in their late eighties and lived independently in a ranch house in a rural area. The doctors told her that he would be in a rehab facility for the next three months, so she'd be on her own for the winter. She asked if I could fly to Pennsylvania to help her for a week or two. Of course, I said yes and said I'd stay for as long as she needed me.

I bought an expensive ticket to leave Bangkok three days later on Sunday—a one-way ticket since I didn't know whether I'd be coming back to Thailand. Then I canceled the side trips to Myanmar and Cambodia that I had scheduled for early December. When Gretchen came home from work that evening and I told her the developments, she said she was sorry, of course, but also that she would take off work the next day, Friday, so we would have two days to see Bangkok before I had to leave.

———————

Friday morning, Gretchen and I drank coffee on the patio, reading the papers and planning the day's activities. Headlines in the Bangkok newspaper were all about the King of Thailand's eighty-eighth birthday celebrations that week. Affectionately known to his subjects as "Dad," the king apparently enjoyed enormous popularity, despite the military coups in recent years that had put generals in charge. Whether his popularity was genuine was hard to discern, since Thailand had strict lese-majesté laws calling for up to fifteen years in prison for each count of insulting the king.

"You mustn't make any jokes or sarcastic comments while we are out in public. You never know who is listening and might turn you in," Gretchen said as we ate breakfast. I thought about the whisperers in the dining room of my lodge in Romania.

"Even an American tourist?"

"Yes, anyone. You must take me seriously on this. It can be very dangerous." She picked up a section of *The International New York Times* from the coffee table and showed me a page on which the bottom third was blank space. "This is a censored article. If the local publisher deems something offensive to the king or Thailand, it's not printed; the blank space lets you see how much you aren't seeing. They wouldn't think twice about detaining you if you insulted the king, especially the week of his birthday."

"I had the impression Thailand was a democratic nation that welcomed tourists to its miles of beaches," I said. "I had no idea there was such repression."

"As is often the case, what the tourist sees isn't necessarily reality," Gretchen said. I remembered that Goma Air Lady in Kathmandu had said much the same thing.

We headed out to visit the Wat Pho (Temple of the Reclining Buddha). We rode a trolley packed with people of all ages wearing bright yellow T-shirts with sky-blue sleeves and the slogan "Bike for Dad" emblazoned on the front in both Thai and English; citizens would celebrate the king's actual birthday with a bike parade. On the sidewalks, makeshift shrines with large photos of the king as a younger man were draped with bright yellow banners. (Gretchen told me that yellow was the king's color.)

After seeing the remarkable Reclining Buddha statue, which is 50 feet high and 150 feet long and totally covered in gold leaf, we treated ourselves to an hour-long foot massage nearby. To escape the heat, we visited an orchid garden hidden in a quiet neighborhood. Since Gretchen owned a lifestyle magazine, she knew all the best places to eat, so we feasted on local delicacies like spicy shrimp soup and green chicken curry. When we finally got home at the end of the evening, the housekeeper had left sweets and a chilled bottle of white wine on the veranda. I was stimulated by the culture that was so different from other places I had visited and sad that I wouldn't get to spend more time with Gretchen or in this part of the world. I knew I wanted to come back.

I selfishly wished I didn't have to travel to the States, especially to the bone-chilling cold of Pennsylvania. But I wanted to be with my mother to support her. My emotions rose and fell like waves on the ocean. Her husband's condition had stabilized, but it wasn't yet clear what the long-term damage would be. I didn't want to admit that my mother was old too; it could have happened to her. I was afraid of what my stepfather's stroke meant for the future, both for him and for her as a potential caretaker. Thinking about how kids like me came to the rescue of parents who needed help, I wondered who would be there for me when I was her age. I pushed all those feelings aside and did what I expected my mother was doing: Buck up and deal with it.

———

I was surprised how easy it was to fall into a comfortable daily routine with my mother once I arrived in Pennsylvania. We shared coffee in the mornings, she spent the afternoons with her husband while I went for a walk or did yoga, and we enjoyed evenings together watching *Jeopardy!*, eating take-out, and just talking. Sometimes my mother the teetotaler even drank a glass of wine with me.

Ever since I'd left for college in Utah over forty years before, we hadn't lived near each other and, when we did have a visit, there was always a spouse along (hers or mine), or other family members. I loved spending time alone with her and felt like I was getting to know her better than I ever had. With her husband's stroke, there was the constant reminder that things can change in an instance, which made me relish our time together even more, not knowing how much of it we'd have in the future.

As much as I enjoyed being with my mom, I definitely didn't like being in northeastern Pennsylvania. The days were short, the weather cold and dreary, and the sky always gray, even when the sun was shining. The economy seemed as depressed as when I was growing up there in the 1950s and 1960s, since no major industry had replaced the coal mining jobs. I had lunch with two friends from high school that I hadn't seen in a long time, but other than that, I hunkered down with my mom and didn't venture out.

By the end of my second week there, my mother told me she was optimistic about her husband's situation and felt comfortable managing the house for the winter until he came home. "I'm so happy you were able to be here," she said, "but I'm ready to get back to my regular routine. You don't need to stay any longer."

I appreciated her candor and independence and suspected she, like most of us, tired of having a constant guest, even one she loved. And I had to admit I was ready to get back to traveling. Gretchen had told me I could rejoin her in Phuket at any time and had extended her invitation for me to stay at her house into January, even though she would have to return to Bangkok and work. I bought another expensive one-way plane ticket for the day after Christmas, both sad to leave and happy to go.

At the Phuket airport, tourists were dressed in colorful flowered shirts and flowy dresses, straw hats, and flip-flops. I could hear European languages, British and American English, and lots of Russian. Apparently, the heat and lush vegetation made Phuket a popular place to escape the Siberian cold and the relentless white of snow. I felt the same sense of escape after my two weeks in cold and dark Pennsylvania. Gretchen picked me up at the airport and we drove to Mai Khao Beach where she owned a triplex with two other friends.

It had been almost exactly eleven years earlier when a tsunami had hit Phuket and thousands of people died, many of them tourists, but I didn't see any hint that it had ever happened. I recalled a business dinner with a French couple a few years after the disaster; I was making small talk with the wife and asked how many children she had. Her face went blank as she flatly said, "We had three but lost a daughter and a son in the tsunami when we were on Christmas holiday in Phuket. It's still difficult for me to talk about, so please excuse me." Her eyes stared straight ahead, and I thought I'd never seen such sadness before. I also remembered my conversation in Dubrovnik when Marco said it wasn't good for the tourist business to remind people of the war. Gretchen confirmed that Thailand's tourist industry had quickly moved on.

I was pleasantly surprised when we arrived at Gretchen's triplex. From the outside, the building was unassuming, but inside it was the perfect beach house. Concrete floors made it easy to sweep out the sand that inevitably got tracked in. Ceiling fans kept the tropical air moving in the dining/living/kitchen area. The best part was the million-dollar view facing the turquoise waters of the Andaman Sea through floor-to-ceiling sliding glass doors on two sides. When the doors were open, inside and out felt identical.

As if that weren't enough, a deep infinity pool ran the length of the front of the building. Beyond the pool, sea morning glory vines blanketed the path from the house to the six-mile-long beach. Tall pine trees hid any other buildings close by. The ocean breeze soothingly ruffled the landscaping and brought the salt smell into the house. I felt like I'd arrived in heaven.

Gretchen's friend Cait from New York had been there since before Christmas and would stay until after New Year's Day. We spent the week walking the beach every morning before it got too hot, then swimming, writing, reading, and eating fresh seafood for the rest of the day. The caretakers for the property came every morning to clean up and sweep the concrete floors. They did the grocery shopping and cooked for us on market days, stir-frying fresh fish and vegetables into fantastic feasts that were simple, yet elegant. Life was quite idyllic.

On New Year's Eve, Gretchen hosted a party where I met more of her friends, mostly American or British journalists covering the Asia beat. Although I had been traveling nonstop for over a year, I was an Asia neophyte and felt the least worldly of all the guests. The conversation ranged from the state of the king's health (poor) to the influence of China in Asia (massive) to the economics of a regional tourist culture (problematic). I loved listening to the insider cocktail chatter. When we set off fireworks on the beach at midnight, I made a New Year's resolution for the first time in decades. I resolved to avoid becoming jaded or America-centric; to remember that the world is full of fascinating, diverse people and places; and to never to be smug about being a world traveler—it didn't mean I knew a thing.

———————

A few days into the New Year, Gretchen and Cait left to return to work. I'd be alone at the house for the rest of my stay, except for the housekeepers whom I engaged to buy food and cook for me three nights a week.

Freed of the need to grocery shop or do any errands, I continued my early morning walks and spent the afternoons swimming, writing, and reading. I loved the solitude of the beach house with the beautiful view and even had fantasies about becoming an expat in Phuket. I talked to my mother every other day and was happy to hear that both she and her husband seemed to be doing as well as could be expected.

One night I sat on the patio with a cold drink to watch the mai-tai sun drop into the quiet turquoise ocean, as I had each night for the past two weeks. Fishing skiffs made their way back to shore, their running lights blinking in the growing darkness. Condensation on the outside of my cocktail glass pooled on the coffee table. The temperature was about 85°F, and the weather forecast for the next seven days was the same as it had been since I'd arrived in Phuket: sunshine, with highs of 93 and lows of 75. I munched fresh peanuts, smiled at my good karma, and began thinking about what the new year had in store for me.

I was scheduled to leave the beach house the next week to meet Kathleen in Australia for a couple of weeks. She had invited me to join her back in December, but since I didn't know how long I'd be in Pennsylvania, I'd only tentatively accepted. Once I got to Thailand, I'd bought a one-way ticket to Sydney, not sure where I'd go after Kathleen left. Other than setting a date to meet, we hadn't settled any other details for our trip yet, remembering how our Portugal plans had been canceled at the last minute.

I had no idea what I wanted to do after Australia, either. I'd been thinking I wanted to catch the end of the U.S. ski season, but wasn't that being lazy about seeing the world? There were still so many experiences I wanted to have and places to see, why not go somewhere new? I picked up my computer and scanned the internet for ideas, conscious that I had less than six months left in my vagabond journey before the lease ran out on my house in Portland. The internet was a bad idea—far too many choices. Suddenly I felt overwhelmed, like when I first faced the idea of traveling for a year or when I left the cold, viewless farmhouse in Portugal with no destination, no plan, and nobody to help me decide on one.

That night I tossed and turned, unable to sleep. The lease on my house ran out in June. Should I continue to rent it, sell it, or move back in? Did I want to keep traveling alone? If so, to where? Or was I, as my mother often asked me, "tired of being on vacation"? Should I be finding a different place in the States to settle down? Would my life be even better if I finally found and kept a partner? And, more immediately, where would Kathleen and I go in Australia?

Magically, the universe intervened to soothe my worries. Over the next few days, my email inbox overflowed with ideas and invitations. Kathleen had found a cool spa in Australia where we could unwind and catch up. Carol, the woman who had organized my Morocco trip, invited me and Kathleen to stay at her house in the Blue Mountains for a few days after we left the spa. At that point, Kathleen was returning to the States, and I'd be on my own. Then Nina, the travel writer I'd met in Zambia, invited me to visit her family winery in the Hunter Valley north of Sydney. A friend who worked for The Nature Conservancy, a worldwide conservation group I avidly supported, invited me to join her in Kenya in February to visit two wildlife conservancies where they did work. Friends in the States wanted me to join their ski trips in March and April.

I accepted all the invitations and ideas and dove headfirst into booking flights and organizing my calendar. My final night in Phuket, I made myself a vodka tonic and watched the tangerine sun slide toward the dark blue horizon of the sea. When the orb reached the water, it appeared to melt into a puddle on the surface, then disappeared. The horizon glowed crimson, orange, and dark pink.

I took a sip of my drink, refreshing and cool, a sharp contrast to the sizzling heat of the day. The ceiling fans in the living room whirred, slowly moving the sultry air. Geckos called randomly from their favorite spots on the walls, and the sea cicadas chirped more wildly and loudly than usual, reminding me of that sunset in the Danube Delta and those deafening frog calls.

I sat in the dark, listening to the sounds of the night, thinking how lucky I was to be alive—and in this place, thanks to the generosity of my friend Gretchen, whom I'd never have met if I hadn't gone to Mustang. Of all the joys travel brought me, perhaps making new friends was the very best. Eventually the cicadas quieted, and I could hear the soothing sound of the waves lapping at the shore. Which, of course, had been there all along.

CHAPTER 19

AUSTRALIA

JANUARY–FEBRUARY 2016

This time, when I booked my ticket to Australia, I remembered to get a visa. After landing in Sydney, I picked up a small white Toyota rental car, rejecting an offer to upgrade to an SUV, and hit the road heading north. It would be a couple of weeks before I met Kathleen at the spa, so I had accepted Nina's invitation to visit her and her husband in the Hunter Valley for some yoga, travel talk, and wine drinking. After spending a delightful few days with this couple I barely knew (it had been more than a year since I had met Nina when in Zambia), I continued on to a more obscure (at least to me) wine region a few hours away: Orange and Mudgee. How could I resist those place names?

Most of the wineries in the area were small, often located at the end of long dirt roads, nestled in rolling hills covered in grapevines. The famous Australian hospitality was everywhere and, as had happened in New Zealand a year earlier, Oregon wine connections often meant that I left with a free bottle of wine in addition to those I bought. In fact, both the landscape and the vibe of Orange reminded me of Oregon's Willamette Valley.

One of my favorite stops was at De Salis winery a few miles outside of downtown Orange. I arrived at 3:45, not realizing the tasting room closed at 4:00. I was about to leave, but when I mentioned to the young man behind the counter that I was from Oregon, he immediately insisted that I stay to try their Pinot Noir, knowing Pinot was a specialty of many Oregon vineyards. He poured me a glass; it was rich and earthy.

We talked wine while I tasted a few more samples. A rugged-looking older man who had been tinkering with a forklift across the room came and sat on the stool next to me at the bar, introducing himself as Charlie, the owner. Mitch, the server, was his son.

"I see you like our Pinot Noir," Charlie said. "Mitch, pour me a glass of what you have open, but then go and get a bottle of the 2006 for her to try." When I left an hour and a half later, they gave me another bottle to take home and enjoy with dinner.

The next day I drove the two hours from Orange to Mudgee past gum trees and sandstone gorges, stopping at a few wineries before arriving at the renovated Victorian building that was my boutique hotel. After a shower and a quick nap, I went in search of dinner to a highly rated (on the internet) Aussie country tavern that served wine instead of beer. The receptionist told me I could eat in the bar, my preference when I was alone, and the bartender said I could sit anywhere since nobody else was there. There were only eight barstools, but in front of one was a bottle of wine and a half-full glass, so I took a seat a few barstools away and was looking at the menu when a tall, tan, wrinkled man with a bulbous nose came in and sat on the stool in front of the bottle. He was probably my age.

"Watch out for Gary here," the tattooed bartender with a shaved head said to me. "He's a fixture at the bar who knows his wines."

"Hi, I'm Cheryl." I introduced myself to both men.

Gary raised his glass and said to the bartender, "Peter, pour Cheryl a glass of this one to taste." He motioned to his bottle, and the bartender poured me a glass of a silky, smooth red. Gary was a colorful raconteur, but I suspected little of what he said was true, especially when he told me he hadn't eaten since 1973. "The thing is, Cheryl, I'm gay, and so it's very important for me to stay thin and attractive. It's just too hard if you waste calories on eating instead of drinking."

I was still laughing when a movie-star handsome man who looked to be in his fifties came in and sat on the other side of Gary. He introduced himself as Scott. The bartender recognized him as a TV personality from Sydney. TV star or not, Scott was easy going, without an ounce of pretension. Soon Scott was drinking some of Gary's bottle, and had ordered one of his own.

The next to join our group at the bar was Craig, a thirty-something hipster with a stringy blond beard. By then, Scott was pouring from his bottle for the rest of us. Craig said he owned a store in town where he engraved trophies and sold vinyl records, a weird combo that fit the motley nature of our crew. We ordered food and shared plates, and I bought a bottle for the four of us to end the night, glad I was only a three-block walk from my hotel.

———

From Mudgee, I drove two hours to the Sydney airport to catch a flight to Byron Bay, where I would meet Kathleen at the spa retreat near there. The shuttle dropped me off at the entrance, where a young woman met me. "This is an ancient and sacred space, a healing space," she said. "The spirit of the Buddha will help you feel calm and relaxed in mind and body." A large Buddha statue sat on top of a manicured hill looking out at the ocean. If the possible result was anything like my Mustang calm or Sahara serenity, I was all in.

Spa days were both structured and not. I went to yoga class every morning, Kathleen and I attended a drawing class, and sometimes we lounged at the pool. Although in my travels I had been meeting fascinating people and making new friends, it sure was nice to have an old friend to talk to. I had hoped when I started my journey that other longtime friends would join me, but so far, Kathleen was the only one who had been able to.

Other than hanging out with Kathleen, the best part of the spa package was the daily "treatment" chosen from a menu of health consultations, scrubs, and massages. The massages weren't the typical fare. Usually they had a holistic description that didn't always make sense, so we chose our options somewhat blindly. I hoped for some relief from the intermittent pain in my right hip that had been bothering me more than usual lately.

My first appointment was with a healer whose bio said she opened emotional energy blockages that contributed to bodily aches and pain. "Each body is like a keyboard," she told me when I got onto the massage table. "I have no idea what will happen when we start the session, but I will read your energy and we'll go from there."

Well, we didn't go very far. She ran her hands lightly over my head and spine for about ten minutes before telling me my energy flow, which starts at the head, was blocked at my neck because I analyzed too much instead of feeling. I didn't say anything, but as she went on and on about the importance of letting emotions flow and didn't even start the massage, I became annoyed and thought, what a waste of money. I already knew I could be overly analytical and was good at stifling emotions I didn't like, but I considered that a strength. I wanted a massage, not a touchy-feely lecture. The therapist cupped the back of my head with her hands and pressed.

"You're very skeptical of my skills and don't want to deal with why your flow is blocked," she said. I felt guilty that she could read my mind and tried frantically to think good thoughts about her. "Your head is about to explode with all that analysis, and it is causing stiffness in your body. I recommend you use your time at our retreat to work on letting go of trying to control things you cannot. Our time is done." I'd signed up for an hour but had only been there thirty minutes. I'd never been kicked out of a massage before.

The next day I went for what I hoped would be a true deep tissue massage. I was disappointed when the therapist asked me to start by visualizing a golden stream emanating from the crown of my head and flowing to my toes. But I'd done that kind of work before during meditations and gave it a shot. After a few minutes, she told me my energy flow was blocked just below my shoulders. Well, at least I'd gotten it past my neck! Or she had misread the notes from the therapist the day before (that I assumed they shared) and was supposed to say neck. I kept visualizing, while trying not to think about wanting the massage to start. I didn't want to get kicked out again.

"Good work. There's a trickle going down your spine," she said, after ten minutes of light touches along my arms and legs. I did feel that some indefinable thing was shifting in my body. "You have tremendous energy overall, but there is anger in your right hip." I hadn't mentioned the hip pain to her, so how did she pinpoint that? She talked me through more visualization as she gave me a deep and satisfying massage, telling me at the end that my pain and stiffness would lessen if I didn't hold myself to such a high standard and accepted things as they were.

The next day's session was a health consultation with a psychic naturopath.

"You are in excellent health but should drink more lemon water and less alcohol," she said. Okay, I would add lemon water to my routine but ignore the other advice. "You're in the process of transforming. You've always been a striver, but now you are in a different place in your life, right?"

"Yes," I admitted, thinking she meant the transformation from working to retirement and travel. "I've always thought that anything worth doing is worth doing well. I had a successful career, but now I'm striving to be a better person." Even though I hadn't yet figured out what that meant.

"It's time to let go of striving and be happy with who you are. Then you will be a better person."

Mmmhh. I thought all the advice I'd gotten so far sounded a lot like that of Goma Air Lady when she told me serenity comes when you trade expectations for acceptance.

Our last full day at the spa, the morning dawned dark and ominous. By afternoon, lightning and thunder accompanied the downpour of rain. What a perfect setting for the massage of the day: The Big Kahuna, described as a combination of dance, rhythm, breath, and energy, where Polynesian ancestors spoke through the masseuse. I wasn't sure the island ancestors would have anything to offer to an American of Polish-Slovak descent, but why not?

As I climbed onto the massage table, Kate, a small masseuse who didn't look the slightest bit Polynesian, explained how the session would go. "I will sing and chant to the ancestors, and we will have a conversation," Kate said. "I'll tell you what they say, and the massage will progress depending on what they tell me to do. After we finish, the ancestors will give me a message to relay to you." I told her about my hip, suggesting that she might already know about it from the other therapist, but she claimed none of them ever shared information and protected each person's privacy.

"I'll ask the ancestors about your hip. And by the way, the room is soundproofed because sometimes the ancestors and I become quite noisy. So feel free to vocalize along with me if you want, since it is often very cathartic." No way was I going to sing or make noise, I thought, but when Kate started chanting, I was quickly transported to a different place and felt compelled to hum softly along with her. She cradled my arms and legs and worked my scalp and neck with powerful fingers, sometimes chanting, sometimes singing, sometimes being quiet— when, I assumed, she was listening to the ancestors.

Kate brushed her arms along my right side from head to toe and then put her hands on my hip. I was suddenly awash in negative images from my career in a male-dominated profession, the sexist actions and remarks, the glass ceiling and lower pay. The intensity of my anger overwhelmed me, and I realized I was groaning loudly as Kate sang a sorrowful tune.

"The female ancestors are telling you to let it go," she said, massaging my hip.

"Let what go?"

"The male energy you hold. You needed that energy to protect yourself in your work years, but you don't need that shield anymore. They say to let it go."

How could Kate possibly have known anything about my work life? I hadn't said a word about it during my entire time at the spa. She leaned into the massage, and my body could feel her energy ebb and flow. I let the anger course through me as my groaning turned into a low, slow vibration in my throat. Kate's chanting became more melodic as she finished the session by sweeping a sarong lightly across the length of my body, then told me to take my time before coming out to receive the message the ancestors would give her for me.

I felt emotionally spent and stayed on the table for a while, wondering what the hell had just happened. The experience had been very powerful and unexpected. I composed myself, dressed, and joined her outside the massage room. Kate embraced me. "It's highly unusual," she said, "but the ancestors have given me two messages for you. Use them as guides for your future."

"Okay," I said, hoping for something that resonated with me after the intense "massage."

"The first message is 'Find the freedom in the feminine flow.' You need to dance with abandon and nurture your feminine side, which the ancestors believe has taken a back seat for too long. Your female strength is impressive and should be released. Including allowing yourself to feel your emotions more fully." Well, that resonated, and it mirrored what the therapists had been telling me all week long.

"What's the second message?" I asked with trepidation.

"Allow yourself to know yourself in a whole new way." Kate paused to let the message sink in. "If you drop the masculine shield like the ancestors said, you will not only discover the feminine flow, but also will experience deep joy and sorrow in ways you never have before."

Wow. Those were quite the messages. That "masculine shield" had served me well for most of my life, however, and I wasn't sure I wanted to give up what it represented: rationality, emotional control, independence, and even adventuresomeness. But I could see the wisdom in letting myself become fully realized and merged, not occupying a strictly masculine or feminine box.

That evening, Kathleen and I compared stories about our equally mind-blowing Kahuna massages. The week at the spa had offered far more than the relaxing chance to catch up we'd originally hoped for. We'd both had insights that would change the way we approached the world and our lives in the future. I vowed to dance more often, even if only in my head, and to embrace my emotions. I'd also work on giving up that urge to control, and instead, accept things the way they were. It wouldn't be easy, but I felt I would have a head start if I incorporated the Buddhist teachings of a few months before.

The next morning, at my final early-morning yoga class, I realized that the pain in my right hip that had prevented me from doing certain poses all week had completely evaporated. Maybe I was on the right track.

When Kathleen and I flew from the spa back to Sydney, we picked up a rental car and drove two hours west to the Blue Mountains National Park town of Leura, where we were to stay with Carol, who, despite many conversations while planning Morocco, I'd never met in person. She had invited us for two nights, but once we were there, Carol asked if we would house-sit and take care of her cat for the rest of the week while she went on a business trip. We gladly agreed to her request.

After our intense spa experiences, Kathleen and I found Leura the perfect location for letting our lessons sink in as we explored the area, known for its dramatic sandstone cliffs, waterfalls, and the eucalyptus forests that make the mountains look blue. We drove the scenic byways and stopped to hike to dramatic lookout points.

On a short hike to a red rock canyon lookout called Sublime Point, we came upon a man unsuccessfully trying to photograph two butterflies that flitted around him, never landing. A black XXL T-shirt barely covered his copious beer belly. He introduced himself as Craig.

"I work for the coal company," he explained, when I asked about a logo on his baseball cap. "We're mining just outside the park, so I'm stationed here temporarily." He went on to say he lived "up past Orange—in the aboriginal village." He looked as white as me, and he must have noticed my raised eyebrows. "My mom is aboriginal, but Dad wasn't. She raised me." The butterflies kept flitting around him.

"Too bad you can't get a butterfly to land on you for your photo," I said.

"Oh, it's okay. They land on me all the time," he said. "Sometimes it's my brother's spirit come back to tell me he's okay. When that happens, the butterfly lands on my right shoulder." He patted the spot. "That's where my brother's skin cancer was first found, so that's how I know it's him."

We murmured the right words to be polite, then started down the path. Craig followed as if we'd invited him to join us. My "is this safe?" antennae raised for a moment since no other hikers were around, but my gut said there was nothing threatening about Craig. He continued his story as we walked.

"My brother was afraid to die. He was still young and didn't want to go. In our culture, there's an in-between place where souls who hang on too much get stuck. I didn't want him to end up there."

The midday sun was hot, causing sweat to drip from all our brows. Neither Kathleen nor I had thought to wear a hat when we started our walk in the shade of the trees. The three of us crossed a small bridge over a narrow ravine, arriving at a rock outcropping with a staggering view across the Blue Mountains and into the valley below.

"This is incredibly beautiful," Kathleen said as we snapped photos of each other and the view. Craig was silent and took his own photos, not speaking again until we asked him to tell us more about his brother. Craig looked happy that we asked.

"My brother was in the hospital, not happy about it, but not wanting to die. I sat with him one day and told him it was okay to pass over. That we'd all miss him, but he needed to go. He confessed that he was afraid to be put in the ground." Craig's tough-guy miner appearance was at odds with his deeply sensitive and riveting story.

"I told him that only his body was going into the ground. His soul was going to heaven, where he'd meet all of our aunties and uncles and the grandparents that had passed before him. My brother said that wouldn't be so bad, and seemed to relax. Shortly after, he drew his last breath."

After a moment, Kathleen quietly thanked him for sharing his story, then we all stared at the view in silence a little longer before starting back up the trail. Craig huffed and puffed as he hauled his big body uphill to a flat resting spot. He sat on a big rock, sweat rings under his arms, and we sat on smaller rocks nearby. I thought Craig had finished telling the story of his brother's death, but he continued.

"A couple of weeks after he died, I was going home from the mine for the weekend, thinking about him while on a long stretch of highway and watching the storm clouds in the distance. I missed him so much, and I was worried about him, that he might still be in the in-between place. I asked my brother to give me a sign he was okay. Just then, one cloud took the shape of my favorite auntie's face. Then a big black cloud split in two and created a sort of stage. All of my relatives came out onto the stage—I recognized them. Aunties and uncles and grandparents and my parents—even my white father. There was a flash of thunder, and my brother walked onto the stage, where everybody hugged him."

"So he was okay," I said, my words inadequate.

"Yes. My brother smiled at me and waved, then the clouds came together again as if nothing had happened. I pulled over to the side of the road and cried like a baby. I know it sounds strange, but it's true."

We sat in silence while a trio of giggling teenage girls bounded down the trail, breaking the spell. Craig said he was going on a side trail to take more photos, and we bade him good-bye. As I thought about the message from my grandmother in Poland to stop poking around in her life, the message at the creepy temple in Nepal to get out of there, and the messages from the Polynesian ancestors at the spa, I wondered how many other messages had been sent to me that I didn't hear for lack of listening and awareness.

As Craig walked away, I couldn't help but notice that a butterfly was following him.

KENYA

FEBRUARY 2016

"READER DISCRETION ADVISED: This magazine contains content with images and themes that may be considered offensive." The large sticker was strategically placed over the Vogue cover model's breasts. At least Qatar Airways was offering reading material for the fourteen-hour journey from Melbourne to Doha. I would then have another eight hours before arriving in Nairobi.

After two nights recovering from jet lag in Nairobi, I flew to Loisaba, a wildlife conservancy in Northern Kenya, a day before my friend Lauren, with The Nature Conservancy, was due to arrive. My driver/guide met me at the small airstrip in native tribal dress: a red cloth draped over his shoulder and wrapped around his waist, a beaded headband, and beaded bracelets. We drove in the equatorial heat from the dry, dusty airstrip to the camp, past acacia trees, rocky outcrops, herds of impala, Grévy's zebra, elephants, and even an emu. As always, the sight of the exotic animals in their natural environment thrilled me. I succumbed again to the spell of Africa, as had so many writers I admired from Isak Dinesen to Beryl Markham to Paul Theroux.

When we arrived at the camp, the manager showed me to my room in one of the four guest structures on the property. I call it a "structure" because it was a simple wooden deck built on stilts, with a thatch roof.

The rear "wall" was the natural rock of the cliff. There were two side walls, but the front was open to the elements, with a bird's-eye view of the watering hole below. One highlight of Loisaba was the Star Bed, a queen-sized, mosquito-net-canopied contraption on wheels that could be rolled out at night onto the open deck. You could watch the Southern Cross move across the dark sky even with only one eye open. I felt comforted knowing an electric fence surrounded the lodge to keep the stealthy leopards from seeking a midnight snack.

I had a few hours before the evening game drive, so I wandered over to the main lodge, where a man in khaki shorts and shirt was intently typing on his computer. I guessed he was in his early forties. He introduced himself as David, a giraffe researcher from California. He had been setting up a network of trap cameras at Loisaba and two other camps to learn about the giraffes' range and movements.

"Surprisingly, we don't know much about giraffes," David said. "And since seven of the nine species of giraffe are in serious trouble from habitat loss and poaching, we need to find out more, and fast."

"I'd love to help with the cameras if you need it," I said, thinking how cool it would be to work with a researcher.

"I wish you'd been here a few days ago when I was trying to secure the cameras to the trees and keep my data straight at the same time," he laughed. "But I'm done now and leaving tomorrow. Still, why don't we share a car for tonight's game drive? Do our part for the planet by saving some gas."

It wasn't research, but I knew it would still be fun to get some insider information, so of course I said yes. After an evening of lots of laughs and seeing colorful birds, elephants at a watering hole, and scores of giraffes, I decided that saying yes was a habit I needed to continue to cultivate.

———

After a few days at Loisaba, filled with game viewing and learning firsthand about The Nature Conservancy's work, Lauren and I went on to another camp in a tiny four-seater plane. Flying at less than 10,000 feet for over an hour, we had a bird's-eye view of elephants maneuvering through scrub brush, zebras and impalas grazing on grassy plains, and warthog families running from the sound of the plane's engine. We flew over the 8,000-foot-high peaks of the Mathews Range and into the huge wilderness of the Namunyak Wildlife Conservancy.

The area was home to the seminomadic Samburu Tribe, who raise their cattle among the wildlife. The Namunyak Conservancy was established in 1995, in cooperation with the local communities of Samburu, to combat extensive poaching like what had occurred between 1977 and 1995, when over 30,000 elephants were killed for their ivory. Once the elephants were gone, the entire ecosystem was upended, and the Grévy's zebra and reticulated giraffe left too. By the time I got there, twenty years later, 4,000 elephants had returned, and other species were following. I wondered if we'd actually see any of the small number of animals, given such a large area.

My tent (Lauren was staying in staff accommodations) was at the end of a sandy path. The canvas structure was furnished with a king-sized bed, two armchairs, and a small table and chairs. The en-suite bathroom had an outdoor shower with a killer view out over the valley. I curled up on one of the lounge chairs on the patio and listened to the midafternoon quiet for a few moments before falling asleep. I awoke half an hour later to see a Diederik hornbill in a nearby tree watching me intently. At teatime, I made my way to the main lodge, an oval open-air, thatched building with a wildlife watering hole a few yards downslope from the deck and pool. The place was empty except for an older British couple, James and Penny, who invited me to join them. They were delightful conversationalists, and James was a skilled storyteller.

"We've been coming to this lodge for over thirty years," James said. He and Penny had moved to Portugal from England when they were newly married and owned a port wine business in Porto.

"I spent a month in Portugal last fall," I said. "I loved it. But I didn't get to spend time in Porto. I plan to go back."

"You must look us up," Penny said, writing their email address on a piece of paper before excusing herself to get ready for the evening game drive.

Half an hour later, a thin, young man in a bright red wrap skirt and tire-tread sandals came up to me. He was bare chested except for a magnificent, beaded necklace of vibrant red, yellow, blue, and white that flowed down to the middle of his chest like a shield, then spread out in two thin strands that wrapped around his waist and crossed in back.

"Hello," he said. "I'm Philip, and I will be your guide." He wore five thick beaded bracelets on both his right and left arms. White discs had been inserted in his earlobes, reminding me of the current fad in the States. But those punk boys had no idea they were copying an ancient Samburu style.

"Are you from this area?" I asked.

"Yes," he said with a wide, engaging smile. "I'm Samburu and grew up here. Our tracker is Samburu also." He pointed at the safari vehicle, where a man in an army-green uniform with a rifle over his shoulder sat on the roof. Another vehicle was pulling in behind ours. Lauren, who had been in her room catching up on work, had joined me by now. We gathered our binoculars and backpacks.

"Cheryl!" I heard, and looked around.

It was David, the giraffe researcher. He wasn't due here for another few days, but apparently his schedule had changed. I felt like I was greeting an old friend instead of somebody I'd met only a few days before. Travel does that to you, seeing a familiar face in a strange place.

"We were just leaving for a game drive," I said after hugs and hellos. "Want to join us?"

"Of course," David said. "I'll drop my stuff at the room and be right back."

A few minutes later we were bumping along the dirt roads, identifying birds and watching for big game.

"We know little about how giraffe interact with and are utilized by the Samburu," David said. "What can you tell us, Philip?"

"We Samburu know where they go and how to kill them for bush meat if we need it. But compared to what we know about elephants and lions, you are right. Giraffe are not well studied."

"For my research project," David said, "we plan to engage the community and analyze the data together. We want to make sure there's local ownership and knowledge about the resource and conservation efforts. That's the only way we can stop the poaching in the Conservancy."

"Yes, the poaching is a problem," Philip said. "But many people use the giraffe as an important source of meat for the family, so we will need an alternative source of food for the effort to succeed."

I loved being part of a conservation discussion with someone directly affected by the resource, rather than from an ivory tower viewpoint. (No elephant ivory pun intended.) Although David was busy installing cameras during the day, he joined us for game drives the next two nights and taught us how to identify giraffes by the pattern of their patches. "Like human fingerprints," David said, "no two are alike."

For our final full day at the lodge, Philip said he had planned something special. By then, David had left, so it was just me and Lauren.

"We will walk an hour to what we call the singing wells," he said. "I'll explain more when we get there. Be sure your water bottles are full. The vehicle will meet us at the site."

The coolness of the early morning wore off quickly, and we sucked our water bottles dry as the temperature rose. The path was a rough two-track through the bush. Philip led and the tracker walked behind, both very much on guard as we traversed an area where we'd seen both lions and leopards during our game drives.

Finally, we got to a grove of shade trees on the bank of the dry riverbed and sat down. On the bank directly opposite us, four lanky Samburu teenage boys stood waist deep in two holes in the sand, splashing water at each other. "No photos are allowed," Philip said.

"The digging of the wells is not a tourist attraction, and we are privileged to watch." We put our cameras away.

"Are they doing laundry?" I asked, seeing four pieces of cloth draped over the low bushes on the bank.

"No," Philip explained, "they are digging their wells. They will dig until they hit the water table." He pointed out a hollowed half tree trunk in front of each hole. "They'll use the tree as a trough and fill it with water for their cattle."

I could see sand flying.

Philip continued, "Each family has a designated spot that has been theirs for generations. You can see now that other boys are coming to start their digging." I stood to look and saw a few more people further down the riverbed. I also saw two of the boys across the river climb out of their holes. They were naked.

"Should we not look?" Lauren asked. We were about fifty or sixty yards away.

Philip laughed. "Because they are naked? They don't care! We Samburu will wear what you call a sarong, but we call a *kikoi*, to protect ourselves from the shrubs and branches, but we are also comfortable in our skin."

"Don't the boys have to go to school?" Lauren asked.

"Some boys do," Philip said. "But if you are a good and smart boy, you are rewarded by getting to tend the cattle. It's the best job in the world—other than guiding." He smiled his huge smile and even the tracker, sitting off to the side of us, laughed in agreement. "You are outside all day with your friends, then at night you take your cattle to the *boma*, the thatch-fenced area, to sit by the fire, protected from the leopards and other night hunters. Success in our culture is measured differently than in yours. A successful Samburu has many cows and many sons to tend them." He left out a fact I learned much later that the Samburu were also polygamous.

A half hour passed, with other groups of young men arriving at the river and digging. Soon we could hear the unmistakable sound of cowbells. As the cattle made their way to the riverbed, one boy jumped into the family well, now deep enough to hide him completely, and handed a bucket of water up to another on the rim, who poured it into the trough. Then the singing began.

Each family had a distinctive song, chanted melodically and hypnotically by the boys. As the cattle approached the troughs, they stood waiting patiently in line as the different songs floated through the air—clearly distinct, but not competing with one another, almost like a cappella choirs. No cow left its line to go to another trough, and when one was done drinking, it moved aside to let the next one in. Everything was quite orderly. The Samburu kept refilling the trough until all the animals were watered.

"The songs are all different," Philip explained, "but the words are similar. They tell the cattle how much they are loved and appreciated and depended upon. It is a great honor to tend the cows."

We watched the primal scene from beneath our tree until, eventually, Philip took us across the dry wash to the wells. He greeted the boys, who smiled and waved to us, seemingly unconcerned with our presence and intent on their task. I liked the feeling of participating without my camera getting in the way.

As we were leaving, I noticed a lanky young man up on the bank squatting by a bush. I looked away at first, assuming he was taking care of personal needs, but as we walked nearer, I could hear rock music. He was fiddling with a cell phone. I was quite surprised.

"Philip, does everyone have a cell phone?" Philip had one, but I had assumed it was provided by the lodge as a safety measure.

"No, but more and more boys save their money to get one. There isn't signal everywhere, but the bigger problem is how to charge them. I charge mine at the lodge, but electricity in the villages is scarce. Installation of solar panels is changing that, though."

"Access to the internet will change these young men," I said. "What do you think about that?"

"We can't stand still," Philip said. "But our culture and history are strong. We like our way of life. Although some young people might be lured away, I think we can withstand the pressures of progress."

Later that night we drove back to the same spot under the big trees that had shaded us that morning. We sat on the roof of the Land Rover having sundowners, and as the sun set and the sky darkened, we watched elephants playing in the wells, showering each other with water. After dark, a leopard emerged from the opposite bank and took a quiet drink.

"The humans help the animals survive by digging the wells and providing water," Philip said. "Even though the wildlife kick sand into the holes, creating more work again the next day, the Samburu would never consider fencing the wells to keep the animals out."

The next morning, we took a short game drive before flying to Nairobi, where I'd spend the night in an airport hotel and fly to the States in the morning. I relished the feel of the equatorial sun on my shoulders, knowing I'd soon be in the middle of an Idaho winter, with plenty of decisions to make. But here in Africa I didn't want to think about any of that.

Philip stopped the car near a small clearing where, about thirty yards away, a resting cheetah let out a big yawn, rolled over a few times, then posed for photos, its big eyes staring straight at me. For once, I was happy to have the camera and big lens I'd been toting around the world with me. It had been more than a year since I'd seen my first cheetah, and this cat was just as special, as were each of the conservation areas I'd visited.

Although my career had been dedicated to sustainability and environmental regulation, the work had focused on reducing the footprint of people and businesses on the environment, not on conserving wild spaces for other species to thrive. This visit to Kenya brought home the importance of conservation efforts around the world, especially in this time of overdevelopment, climate change, exploitation of natural resources, and yes, even overtourism. At the same time, I knew that eco-tourism was a proven method of helping local economies as well as wildlife and natural environments. My travels so far had cemented for me the need to continue to avoid the places where "everyone else goes," while at the same time being ever mindful of my own footprint, both positive and negative, in the places that I did go.

CHAPTER 21

USA

MARCH–AUGUST 2016

Boise, Idaho, was as cold as I thought it would be. And as white—and I don't mean just the snow. Especially after coming directly from Africa. And even though I'd been through the United States only two months before, I was struck, as always when returning to my home country, by the number of obese people. America might be the land of plenty, but we don't always manage it well.

I had returned to catch the end of ski season. After my brother, Victor, picked me up at the airport, we headed to Cascade, Idaho, a little over an hour north of Boise, where he lived in an idyllic rural valley with his wife, Paula, two horses, four goats, three cats, three guinea pigs, four dogs, and a miniature donkey. He also had two pickup trucks, an SUV, and a Subaru sedan. He graciously offered to loan me the Subaru for the next few months until I had figured out what to do with my house. Until I made a decision, I wasn't going to plan any other international trips.

"I'm going to put a lot of miles on it," I said. "How about I buy it, then if you want it back, I'll sell it to you when I'm settled?"

"I don't want to sell it. You can pay for the maintenance and insurance and buy new tires if you wear these out. If you take it now, I won't have to plow around it all winter."

After a few days of hanging out with Victor and Paula and getting reacclimated to American food and TV, I drove east to ski with my friends Marty and Ken who lived in Wyoming near Jackson Hole. I was eager to hit the slopes again, but as I drove across the expanse of Idaho, I felt a sense of loss at not being an international traveler anymore. As if I had lost my identity. Somehow, being in the States seemed less exciting and, therefore, maybe I was too.

During the next two months, I again lived the ski bum life—only with better snow than I'd had the year before. I drove ten thousand miles through the western United States and Canada, staying with friends or in rented condos in ski towns. Looking for companionship, I tried internet dating, thinking maybe there was another vagabond out there somewhere whom I could meet on the road, but men seemed to be frightened away by the fact that I didn't live anywhere. Instead of dating, I drank whiskey with local cowboys and wine with urbanites on ski vacations. I agonized for hours over whether to go home to Portland or make a change. When I rode the ski lift with strangers, I had trouble answering the question "Where are you from?"

By the end of April, I knew that I wasn't from Portland anymore. I had left that life behind. I didn't yet know whether my path was to keep traveling or to find a place to settle down as a retiree, but I had plenty of time to figure that out over the summer. As usual, once I made the decision to leave Portland, I didn't look back and moved forward quickly. I put my house on the market, the renter decided to leave early, and by June I had closed on the house, as well as on my seventeen years in Oregon. Now I was really a vagabond.

That summer, I came to grips with traveling in America rather than the world, enjoying the freedom of knowing the territory as well as the language. I house-sat for Gayle in Idaho, dog-sat Stella (best dog ever) in Colorado and enjoyed long visits and hikes with other friends. Marty and Ken let me crash in their guestroom for a few weeks and I joined them on a week-long horse-packing trip into the Wind River Mountains, where a clap of thunder made my horse rear like the Lone Ranger's, except that I fell off, which really screwed up my back. I put another twenty thousand miles on my brother's Subaru, driving through mountain passes in Idaho, Montana, and Colorado and on long, straight high desert roads in Wyoming, Nevada, and New Mexico. The vast distances and big landscapes sometimes made me feel like I was back in the Mustang region of Nepal, until I remembered I was in a car on a paved road and could easily get a cold drink with ice.

Every month I saw my old friend, the full moon, in the clear Western skies and felt connected to the rest of the world. I was working on feeling the feminine flow and noticed that I hadn't had hip pain since the Big Kahuna massage, even though now my back pain was worse. Not once did I regret my decision to sell the house in Portland.

Toward the end of the summer, I followed the famous Route 66 west from Albuquerque to Flagstaff, sharing the road with families in SUVs and groups of grey-haired motorcyclists, marveling, as I always did, at the red rock scenery of the Southwest. I loved stopping in the dusty small towns of 1950s motels, Navajo jewelry and weaving stores, and Route 66's schlocky souvenir shops. When I got to Flagstaff, I turned north toward the Grand Canyon.

I normally avoided the National Parks during the busy summer season, but I'd never been to the south rim of the Grand Canyon, and a few days earlier, I thought I'd at least check to see if a room was available in the Park. I knew it was a long shot on such short notice, but there must have been a cancellation as I was able to book a historic cabin at Bright Angel Lodge for one night. Good karma, I thought.

The Park was as crowded as I expected; I sat in a line of cars at the entrance. I drove to the lodge, checked in to the small log cabin not far from the rim, then chatted up a ranger before asking for a recommendation for an uncrowded hike where I might see the endangered condors that had been successfully nesting in the Park.

"You sound like an experienced hiker," the grizzled ranger said. "If you're comfortable with heights and a less-maintained trail, take this one." He used a yellow marker to delineate a path on a map. "You might see condors. But in any case, there is an evening presentation about the condor recovery program at six."

"Thanks for the tip," I said. "Anything else you might recommend?"

"Well"—he scratched his chin—"most people aren't interested in this, but tonight is the Perseid meteor shower."

"Fantastic!" I said. "I love the Perseids." I remembered the first time I'd heard about the Perseid shower, when I was still in high school. I convinced my brother to drive out of town in the family's pickup truck with me. Lying in the bed of the truck, we counted shooting stars until midnight curfew.

"You're the first person today who'd even heard of it," the ranger said. "Nice to know somebody is still paying attention to nature instead of selfies."

The hike was perfect, and I only saw three people on the trail. The views down to the Colorado River were plentiful, and the colors of the two-billion-year-old rocks changed with every passing cloud. I didn't see any condors, so that evening I joined a small group at the outdoor amphitheater on the rim and listened to a ranger's story about the incredible captive breeding program that had brought the species from nine birds in 1985 up to around four hundred birds, half of them now in the wild.

Just as the ranger was telling the group about the bird's nine-foot wingspan, as if on cue, two condors appeared from below the canyon rim and soared effortlessly, directly above us. The birds were, to say the least, magnificent. Another life-lister for me!

After dinner in the lodge, I prepared for watching the Perseid shower later. The almost full moon would dilute the stargazing until shortly after midnight, when it would set. I got my folding camp chair out of the car, put a full water bottle and an extra pillow from the bed into my daypack, and set the chair and pack by the door of the cabin. Then I set the alarm for one in the morning and went to sleep.

I was groggy when the alarm went off and almost rolled over to go back to sleep. But the urge to experience one of nature's grand shows took over. This year the meteor shower was predicted to have a macroburst, which wouldn't happen again until 2027. Instead of the usual sixty shooting stars per hour, there could be as many as two hundred. And, to top it off, the Grand Canyon was a designated International Dark Sky area, with night lighting minimized.

I checked my phone and could see the temperature outside was about 45°F. I put on my down jacket, wool hat, gloves, and heavy socks, then grabbed the pack and chair and headed out to the rim trail. I walked about fifteen minutes out of sight of the buildings and the already dim lights to a relatively flat spot on a small hill a few feet above the trail. I set up the chair so that when I leaned back, I had a full view of millions of stars. Even with the Dark Sky designation, I noted, the sky seemed to be filled with only half the number of stars that I'd seen in the Sahara Desert. But that didn't matter, since as soon as I settled in, shooting stars zipped left and right, some faint with short tails, others dragging a brilliant light stream behind them.

After I'd counted a hundred shooting stars, I checked my phone and realized I'd only been watching for forty-five minutes. Spectacular. I stopped counting for the next half hour and then felt myself nodding off. Five more meteors, I told myself. Then you can go.

I stared without focus at the sky and saw two more stars almost instantly. But I also saw movement in my peripheral vision. I froze, then slowly turned my head. I wasn't scared but felt a shiver go down my spine—either from the cold or from being startled, I thought.

There was a shadow, a form, silently and slowly coming toward me on the path. I tried to focus. A big dog, perhaps? It was golden, almost translucent, as if the moon were shining on it, but the moon had set. Why would a tourist let their dog out, unleashed, in this environment?

If it was a dog, why didn't it smell me and come over to investigate? The creature trotted by on the path below me, seemingly oblivious to my presence, and I imagined it was floating, not walking. I watched its haunches disappear into the darkness and decided it was a coyote.

Another bright star with a long tail flew across the sky. I shivered again. Three was enough. I couldn't wait for five, and although no ancestors seemed to be talking to me, I sensed a strong message. I packed up my things and warily walked back to the cabin.

The next morning, I wondered whether I had actually seen a coyote walk, or float, four feet in front of me without paying me any heed. Maybe the animal was a ghost coyote, or a protective spirit animal, or even a vision warning me to go inside to avoid Navajo Skinwalker night spirits. Or perhaps it was simply a reminder of the wonders of nature.

———————

While I was traveling throughout the West, I examined every town I visited as a possible place to settle down. When I house-sat or visited people I knew, I thought about moving to those places with a built-in friend base. But I was also willing to move where I didn't know anyone, especially since I'd had eighteen months of practice making friends from scratch. I did want to be near a decent ski area (I was now retired and could ski midweek!) and a major airport (so I could easily keep traveling). I quickly eliminated large urban areas like Salt Lake City and Las Vegas, despite their big airports, because I was done with city life. I also eliminated ski resort towns like Sun Valley, Taos, or Aspen as unaffordable. I scoured Best Places to Retire lists and looked at flyers posted in windows of Main Street realtor offices. Nothing seemed to fit the bill.

I thought hard about moving somewhere abroad, but that didn't feel right. After traveling through so many countries with oppressive policies, regimes, or religions, I appreciated the advantages and freedoms of America, despite the political schisms that seemed to be at an all-time high. I loved seeing the incredible landscapes of the world, but the natural scenery of the United States was equally grand and unique. I would still always want to travel abroad to experience other cultures, but I also enjoyed the local flavors of regional cultures of America. And I could speak the language. While I aspired to be a citizen of the world, America was my home for now.

So I kept looking, and could have compromised on my criteria, but the more I saw, the more I realized that my international wanderlust hadn't yet been satisfied and I wasn't ready to settle down. I wanted to keep traveling. Maybe because I had been considering nesting, I decided to go overseas and stay in one place for three months, working on the first draft of a book about my travels. Since I'd started traveling, I'd lived in Poland for six weeks, stayed in Phuket for three weeks, and had a few three- or four-week stints housesitting in the States, but otherwise I'd been on the move.

I thought about all the places I had yet to see, and all the places I'd already been, and finally chose Porto, Portugal. I rented an apartment at the beach for the first month, then an apartment in the city center for the next six weeks. I booked my one-way flight for September. After that . . . I had no idea.

CHAPTER 22

PORTUGAL

Coming through for me once again, my friend Kathleen accompanied me to Portugal. We spent ten days traveling in the north and east of the country, staying in old monasteries turned boutique hotels and at the Quinta do Tedo guesthouse (sadly, Kay, my apple hunting friend, wasn't there). We also spent a few days at Antonio and Marinete's apartment rental, being chauffeured around to wine tastings by Antonio as if we were long-lost friends.

After our excursion through the countryside, we drove to the three-bedroom beach apartment I'd rented. Technically, it was in the town of Vila Nova de Gaia, across the Duoro River from Porto, but the area had the advantage of miles of boardwalk going south along the coast for daily walks, as well as a path along the river to the area across where all the famous port wine companies were located.

Kathleen's partner, Richard, who had previously joined us in Transylvania, decided to join us for a few days before they would fly back to Portland together. We walked the boardwalk, exploring cafés and beachside cocktail bars. We toured a port house and tasted the wine. By the time they left, I had a good feel for my new neighborhood.

Now it was time to buckle down and write. I had a serious talk with myself to get into a routine, adding incentives. If I wrote for two hours in the morning, I would let myself have a long walk on the beach. If I wrote for another two hours in the afternoon and did an hour of yoga, I could have an extra glass of wine.

By the end of the fourth and final week, the late October weather was colder and windier, but my discipline was paying off. I'd made progress on the book, was up to eight miles for my beach walk, and felt limber from my almost daily yoga. (I wanted that extra wine every night.) I packed my things and moved to my two-bedroom apartment in the city.

The solitude and routine of the beach had satisfied my inner introvert; I was ready to be around people again. Acquaintances from Portland, Laura and Kevin, had seen my social media posts and wanted to get together the next week when they were traveling through Porto, so I invited them to stay with me. I sent James and Penny, the British couple I'd met in Kenya, an email with my phone number, asking if they'd like to meet for lunch.

When it rains it pours, I thought, when James called and offered to host me for lunch at their port house restaurant on a day Laura and Kevin would be in town. After a month with little contact with people and absolutely no commitments, now I had a conflict. I explained my schedule to James and asked if we could meet later, but instead he invited Laura and Kevin to join us, adding that "tasting is always more fun with more people."

I wasn't sure whether Laura and Kevin had any interest in port but accepted the invitation for them. Who wouldn't want to visit a port house in Porto, hosted by the owners? Over lunch, James regaled us with the story of how, shortly after marrying Penny in 1960, he joined the family business that had begun after his nineteen-year-old grandfather was sent to Porto in 1882 to learn the trade. He also showed us memorabilia from the family history, including thank-you notes written after visits from British royalty and American presidents. I wished my family history offered a bit more excitement than a secretive grandmother.

Kevin, Laura, and I spent another couple of days exploring Porto. The final night of their visit was my birthday, so we went to a neighborhood restaurant across the street from the apartment. We drank cocktails at the bar and tried to converse with the patrons, mostly succeeding only through sign language or translations by the bartender. We feasted on the Portuguese specialties of cod, octopus, and tuna. As we toasted my sixty-second birthday, I told stories about my sixtieth in Zambia and South Africa and my sixty-first in Morocco.

My conclusion at the end of the night was that, so far, my sixties were pretty damn fun.

After Kevin and Laura left, I continued to explore the city on my daily walks. I found a place to get my hair colored. I had my favorite markets for fresh fish and vegetables and became a regular at my birthday restaurant. As I had hoped, living in a place felt different from passing through, with perhaps the biggest difference being not frequenting places where other tourists were. The combination of traveling while staying in place was working out great, but I was again ready to move on.

With winter approaching, I thought about staying in Europe to ski, but I liked skiing in the American West better. I decided to continue the stay-in-one-place lifestyle and rented two Teton Valley, Idaho, condos for the ski season. (I'd waited too long to reserve a single place and would have to move over the Christmas holiday.) Teton Valley was where I'd lived in the 1990s, was near my friends Marty and Ken, and was a candidate for my eventual settling down, so living there for the ski season would be a good trial run.

My final week in Porto, I accepted an invitation from James and Penny to lunch at their house in the tony western area of Porto. The cab dropped me off in front of an elegant old stone building with a beautiful garden, where I could see several workers trimming bushes and weeding.

"Welcome," James said, ushering me into a living room where there was a fire in the fireplace and two springer spaniels waiting patiently to be petted. The room was furnished conventionally but for two large bean bag chairs on either side of the couch. James plopped down in one with a comment about how he and Penny loved the chairs. I took a seat on the couch and was scratching the dogs behind the ears when Penny came in, carrying a tray of snacks and three glasses of white wine.

We drank the wine and ate chips and olives while they told me how they had bought this classic old house as a young couple. "It was in such disrepair," Penny said. "That corner by the fireplace was like a waterfall when it rained because we couldn't afford to fix a leak in the roof. We were so poor then, and just starting out. Now, even though the kids are gone and it's too big for us, we can't bear to sell it."

Of course, now they were successful business owners who regularly went on safari in Kenya and had hired help.

When we finished the wine, James suggested we head to the kitchen for lunch. "We're quite casual here," he said, which I had already gathered from the bean bag chairs. We walked past a wood-paneled formal dining room, with a table for twelve and a huge chandelier, and into an inviting country-style kitchen, with a small table and four chairs.

Two women were just finishing putting food on the table. We sat down to a huge bowl of several dozen iced shrimp, a loaf of still slightly steaming bread next to one bowl of dark yellow butter and another with rough sea salt, and a wooden salad bowl filled with fresh greens and bright red radishes. An open bottle of white wine sat beside a cruet of vinaigrette. The meal was simple and elegant.

When we sat down, Penny handed me a second napkin. "We don't stand on ceremony here. Just grab a handful of shrimp. There is the bowl for the shells, and a finger bowl to clean your hands. I hope you don't mind the messiness."

"It's perfect," I said as I dug into the shrimp.

Halfway through the meal, James opened a bottle of red wine that he wanted me to taste. "We're working on our red wine selections. Port is our main thing, but there are grapes here that, with the right attention, can be made into high-end wines. Portugal is known for its cheap wines, but that is changing."

We tasted the wine. "It's delicious and tastes very high-end," I said honestly. The wine was dry and minerally, with a unique taste different from that of Spain, France, or Italy. After we finished the shrimp and salad, Penny opened a cupboard and brought out a Portuguese salted almond cake. James opened a bottle of Six Grapes port. We ate and drank and talked until it was almost four o'clock, when James finally called me a cab.

"I've overstayed my welcome," I said, feeling slightly tipsy as we made our way to the front door.

"Not at all," James said. "It was delightful. This is for you." He handed me a small shopping bag with a box inside.

"Thank you for lunch, the great time, and the goody bag," I said, holding it up.

"It's just some hooch," James said. "Be in touch, and we hope to see you again sometime."

Once in the cab, I opened the bag to find an expensive bottle of port inside. Hooch, indeed.

CHAPTER 23

USA

DECEMBER 2016–SEPTEMBER 2017

I relished being back in the mountains of Idaho, but I was struggling to find a place to stay over the holidays during the gap between my two condo rentals. I had assumed I would find something once I got to Teton Valley, but nothing was available locally that wouldn't break the budget I had so carefully followed all year.

I kicked myself for being such a vagabond that I had not planned ahead for the holiday. After a few hours of dead-end internet searching for a place to go at the last minute, I decided I needed to find a pre-organized trip that might have one slot open. I felt lucky when I found a group Christmas-to-New-Year's hiking trip in Death Valley. I'd never been there.

Hiking in the warm desert weather was a welcome respite from snowy Idaho. The group turned out to be a friendly batch of solitary misfits (except for one delightful, grounded couple), each of us without someone special to spend the holidays with. I didn't know why, but I felt a restlessness I couldn't quite name. Was it holiday blues? Loneliness? I figured it would fade when I got back to the ski slopes.

Back in Idaho early in January 2017, I moved into my second condo and skiing almost every day did perk me up. On the ski lift I met a local man whom I dated for a while, but we morphed into being good friends instead. I continued halfheartedly working on the book but was losing steam and motivation. As the season wore on, that sense of ennui and restlessness returned. I wasn't sure whether it was because I wanted to travel again or to buy a place and settle down. You'd think that after two years, I would have made up my mind already.

After the ski area closed in mid-April, I road-tripped around the western United States again, comparing locations against Teton Valley but not coming up with anything better. I made my way to Portland to put my winter gear and skis in my storage unit, still packed to the gills with furniture and other stuff. I could see my bar stools perched on a stack of boxes, a huge wardrobe box that had who knew what forgotten clothing in it, and my bicycle, tennis racquet, and golf clubs right in front, ready in case I needed them. Somewhere in the bowels of the storage unit were my dishes, pots and pans, artwork, furniture, and even a few cases of wine I'd bought for aging and hadn't wanted to drink before my departure two years earlier.

Everything could stay exactly where it was for another year, but why? If I wasn't going to stay in one place and wanted to be unfettered, I should sell everything and start over whenever I was ready. I tried to remember the messages from the Polynesian ancestors about my feminine flow and knowing myself in a new way, and realized it was okay to say I missed having a home. I did want to have a home base. Though I would always enjoy travel, it didn't need to be constant.

I went back to Teton Valley, contacted a realtor, and looked for a place that was small enough for one person, but of the quality that I wanted. It turned out, however, that available homes were either big five-bedroom ski houses or smaller homes or condos more suitable for first-time buyers or use as rental units. Though discouraged, I tried to look at the bright side. Maybe I was being sent a message that it wasn't my destiny to be a retired woman living alone in a small town, doing nothing more ambitious or creative than skiing and hiking. So I changed my mind. I would travel internationally again, maybe for another year. I'd think about settling down later.

By the middle of July, I had an autumn of travel planned with both structure and flexibility. My itinerary would be partly dependent on organized tours and partly independent. The anchor was a three-week trip to Mongolia in September, a place foreign and desolate, not yet on the major tourist map. Just my cup of tea, I thought, traveling somewhere most people don't go. To get there, I had to fly through Seoul, a place I'd never been. A long-lost law school buddy lived there, so I arranged to visit him and his wife for a week on my way to Mongolia. Kevin and Laura wanted to trek in Nepal, so I agreed to join them after Mongolia.

Within days of finishing various travel arrangements (except for buying a return ticket to the States), I got a call from my realtor about a house that had just come on the market.

"The house is twice as big as you want," she said, "but it's a good deal and I think you should see it."

"I'm going traveling again," I said. "I leave late August to visit my mom in Pennsylvania, then in September I'm going overseas for a few months."

"Let's go see it anyway," she said.

We met at the house, which had good bones and a lot of windows. The price was right, and I did some quick calculations in my head. I could stretch my budget for a few months to both travel and pay a mortgage. If I acted fast, I could close in time to move my things from storage to the house, then unpack whenever I got back to the States. Buying a house would be a good investment, and I could always sell or rent the place if I didn't want to live there permanently.

"Write up an offer," I said to the realtor, surprising even myself.

Shortly after the offer was accepted, I got an email from the friend in Portland who I had sold my beloved Volvo to back in 2014. She was letting me know she planned to sell the car. I took all of three minutes to respond and buy it back. I drove to my brother's house to return his Subaru, then flew to Portland to oversee the loading of a moving van at my storage unit, picked up my new old car, and drove to my newly purchased house in Idaho. When the moving van arrived a few days later, I had the movers put the furniture in place and stack the boxes in the relevant rooms. I unpacked the kitchen, prepared a guest room, and arranged for a friend in transition to house-sit while I was gone. The rest of the unpacking I left for some undetermined date in the future, as if the new house were merely a different storage unit.

I slept in my own bed in my new home for six nights, then boarded a plane to Seoul.

SEOUL, SOUTH KOREA

SEPTEMBER 2017

"What's with the outfits?" I asked my friend David, as we watched the changing of the guards at the Gyeongbokgung Palace in Seoul. Groups of Korean young people were dressed in fancy garb from centuries ago. The girls wore high-waisted, ankle-length hoop-skirt dresses and carried tiny matching purses. The boys were in flowy-sleeved white shirts, topped with a hip-length vestment over baggy pants. If they were a couple, the outfits were in matching colors, as if at a wedding. It was very humid, and the costumes looked hot, but nobody seemed to mind; we saw a lot of posing and selfie-taking.

"Shops rent these costumes," David said. "The palace is a popular tourist attraction for Koreans as well as foreigners. The young people honor their ancestors by renting old-fashioned clothing for a few hours, while they take the tour and then go get lunch. It's a traditional Saturday afternoon date."

The goose-stepping guards at the palace were also wearing traditional dress, complete with swords in decorated scabbards swinging on their hips. The groups of young people lined the cordoned-off walkway. I realized I could frame a camera shot with nobody in it wearing modern-day clothes, emphasizing the foreignness of this country that seemed very alien to me anyway; I'd never traveled in East Asia and had only been to Southeast Asia when I went to Thailand two years earlier to visit Gretchen. But despite the heat and humidity, I felt great to be traveling again, seeing new places and cultures.

I'd landed in Seoul the day before and taken a bus to David and Angela's neighborhood. I had assumed David hadn't offered to pick me up because he was still working, but after an hour and a half traveling through Seoul's metropolitan area of twenty-five million, I understood that the airport was simply too damn far; the bus was easier. When I finally got to my stop and met Angela, we took a cab to their house. She said they didn't own a car and always used public transport or taxis. Another reason he didn't pick me up and a reminder that everyone doesn't live like most Americans.

The taxi dropped us off in front of a government house on a U.S. military base that was an oasis of green in the city. David had spent his career in the Foreign Service, evidenced by his impressive collection of batiks from Indonesia, paintings from Japan, and artifacts from China. Even though I hadn't seen David since we graduated from law school almost thirty years earlier, we had no problem connecting and catching up with lively conversation.

The morning after our palace visit, I realized that the Visa debit card I was using for all ATM cash withdrawals would expire at the end of the month. Damn. I would need that card over the next three months and felt really stupid making such a rookie mistake after all this time traveling. I tried to call my bank, but because South Korea's time zone was fifteen hours ahead, it was only Saturday night in the United States. I'd have to wait two more days to reach them, and by then I'd almost be on my way to Mongolia.

There was nothing to do except enjoy the rest of the weekend. David, Angela, and I went to the forested park at the Seoul Tower, a landmark high on a hill. The park boasted a great view all the way to the DMZ and North Korea, which it turned out was only about thirty miles away. But after a steep, sweaty walk to the top, we found the air pollution so thick that we couldn't see a thing; instead we went to an air-conditioned bar and drank beer. On Sunday we focused on indoor activities, like visiting museums and art galleries, trying to beat the heat.

On Tuesday morning, I got through to my bank and was told a replacement card could be sent FedEx to arrive within two to three business days. Great news, except I was leaving for Mongolia on Thursday. No problem, the representative said, we will send it to your hotel in Mongolia. Right then, I loved the global economy that made such a thing possible. I crossed my fingers that the timing was right and the package would be in Ulaanbaatar when I arrived.

During my few days in Seoul, I got a good taste of the contrasts of the country. Mega high-rises and shiny business districts were interspersed with Buddhist temples and crowded street markets. We ate take-out at David's house, noodles in little cafeterias, and a few dinners in fancy restaurants. The streets were always packed with people, and every conceivable space held some sort of business or combination of businesses. One store with a name printed only in Korean had a sign in the window that read, in English, "Home Spa Cosmetic Store, Make Shopping and Having Tea Simultaneously." In the grocery stores, pieces of fruit were individually wrapped with ribbons and bows, displayed as if in an art gallery. And art galleries were tony affairs, as in any Western country, with hardwood floors and aloof proprietors.

By the end of the week, I was ready to be done with the heat, humidity, and crowds of this dense but complicated city. I couldn't wait to get to Mongolia and its wide, open spaces. Little did I know I should be careful what I wished for.

CHAPTER 25

MONGOLIA

SEPTEMBER 2017

I had arranged the trip to Mongolia through an Australian company specializing in offbeat travel. Maybe I should have realized that the company's target audience was young people traveling in a group, not solo older women, but the itinerary sounded perfect. After two days in Ulaanbaatar (which, I learned, everyone called UB), I would go south to the Gobi Desert for a week, followed by twelve days of hiking in the western Altai Mountains, home of the famed eagle hunters. The Golden Eagle Festival at the end of the trip would be the highlight for me. I knew I would be roughing it and, for the first time, didn't take the Romanian yoga mat with its now heavily duct-taped carrying case. After decades of camping and now three years of travel sleeping in all sorts of different conditions, I thought I was prepared for anything. I was wrong.

There was nothing wide or open about Ulaanbaatar, Mongolia's capital of one million people. I had been met at the airport by Tuvshin, my twenty-something guide, and Buchay, our driver, and now we were stuck in rush-hour traffic, trying to get to the hotel in the city center. Tuvshin, who had been sniffling constantly, hadn't said much, and I wasn't too thrilled about spending the next two days with a guide nursing a cold. When we passed a cluster of yurts next to the freeway that looked like a suburban tent town, I told Tuvshin I thought yurts were for herders.

"They are called *gers*," he said shortly. "It is where the people live."

I tried a few other questions about the city but got similarly terse answers. I gave him the benefit of the doubt that he wasn't feeling well, but it wasn't usual guide behavior. He finally volunteered one piece of information as we neared the hotel.

"That's a statue of Chinggis Khan," he said, pointing at a huge bronze statue of a man sprawled in an armchair. I had noticed when I'd flown in to Chinggis Khan International Airport that Mongolians used a different spelling than Genghis Khan.

We finally arrived at a Western-style high-rise hotel, where I checked into a room on the fifteenth floor. Unfortunately, my FedEx package with the debit card had not yet arrived. Tuvshin told me that he and Buchay would return at seven to take me to a Mongolian BBQ restaurant for dinner. I was dubious, since I had filled out the company's questionnaire saying I preferred not to eat meat, but I didn't want to make waves my first night in the country.

When we arrived at the restaurant, my heart sank. The all-you-can-eat BBQ restaurant had mostly long tables to seat twenty people at a time, and it was packed with international soccer teams of young men in town for a tournament. The main attraction was a huge center grill, surrounded by four chefs tossing and spinning knives as they moved slabs of meat. The rest of the meal consisted of a self-serve buffet with hot and cold noodle and vegetable dishes. Not exactly my favorite way to eat, but it was quite typical for a theme restaurant catering to big groups or families.

Tuvshin and I were seated at one of the few tables for two at the front of the restaurant. After we filled our plates at the buffet (I got a small portion of meat to try it) and sat down, I said I would like a glass of wine. I could see a bartender behind a well-stocked bar, but there were no waiters or waitresses in sight.

"Yes, okay," Tuvshin said, shoveling food into his mouth as if he hadn't eaten for days. He was quite chubby, so I didn't think he hadn't been getting enough to eat.

"Do I need a waiter to order wine?" I asked after a few minutes, hoping that Tuvshin would offer to go to the bar for me, since I had no idea whether the staff spoke English.

"You can go to the buffet as often as you want," Tuvshin said, looking like he might be going for seconds soon.

"I'd like a glass of wine with my meal," I said, trying different words in case the problem was my English. I even tried using the more universal word "vino," since that was also the way to say it in Russian.

"Of course," he said. Not making a move.

Figuring I could make myself understood somehow, I pulled out my wallet, walked to the bar, and bought a glass of wine. Tuvshin never stopped eating except to blow his nose. Thank goodness he would be my guide only for my two days in UB.

We began with a day of sightseeing, driving outside the city to visit a huge aluminum statue of Chinggis Khan on horseback that made the statue downtown seem tiny. Back in town, we went to the winter palace of the Bogd Khan, the eighth living Buddha and last king of Mongolia, who had lost power in 1919 when the Chinese invaded. The palace, a small two-story structure, was not only decrepit, but creepy, since the Khan had kept a zoo of exotic animals that were now stuffed, as if they were pieces of furniture. I was the only tourist at either attraction.

I told Tuvshin I needed to buy a warm coat for the second part of my trip, so he and Buchay took me to a multistory department store and told me they'd wait in the car while I shopped. Great, I thought, happy Tuvshin wouldn't be trailing behind me. I knew how to shop without speaking the language.

To my surprise, the first-floor makeup and perfume departments could have been at a Macy's in the States, offering the same brands and the same layout. On the second floor, all women's clothing, I quickly found an inexpensive, Chinese-made fiberfill coat that fit the bill. I also bought a Mongolian cashmere sweater and leggings for a quarter of what I would have paid elsewhere. On the way back to the hotel, I had Buchay stop at a liquor store so I could buy an emergency bottle of vodka to take with me to the desert, just in case.

I was extremely relieved to find the FedEx package with my debit card waiting for me at the front desk. I could have accessed cash with my credit card, but I never did that, so I wasn't sure I'd remember the password. I made a withdrawal of Mongolian Tugrik at the hotel ATM and felt better heading into the wilds of the country with some cold, hard cash. Now all I had to do was get through one more dinner with Tuvshin.

The restaurant that night was a big improvement, with white tablecloths, hip young waiters who spoke English with a Russian accent, an international menu with pastas and fresh salads, and a wine list. Tuvshin, dressed in baggy pants and a faded T-shirt, devoured his food as soon as it arrived, while I savored mine, wondering what food would be like in the desert and drinking several glasses of wine in case I wouldn't be able to order any for a while. My two evenings with Tuvshin had been like a bad internet date—except, in my experience, the bad date would have talked nonstop instead of barely saying a word. The phrase "get me out of here" kept running through my mind; I couldn't wait to be rid of Tuvshin the next day when I flew to the Gobi Desert.

The next morning at the airport, when Tuvshin told me he was also my guide for the week in the Gobi, I felt like crying. Buchay had driven the car south overnight and would pick us up at the airstrip. What could

I do? Call the company in Australia and ask for a new guide? Maybe in some places, but it didn't seem possible here.

I'd had such high hopes for my time in the wide, open spaces of the Gobi, but the week seemed like a month in the dour company of Tuvshin and Buchay. I felt like I was in solitary confinement in the most vast and unpopulated landscape I'd ever experienced. There were few trees or bushes, and the wind blew constantly. We'd drive for hundreds of kilometers on barely visible dirt tracks, rarely seeing another vehicle and never a fence or printed sign of any sort. Horned larks flitted beside the car as we drove, but there were no other birds and no wildlife. Every couple of hours we'd see large herds of goats and sheep, with a clutch of a herder's gers off in the distance.

Each day, the two would take me to a "tourist attraction," where Buchay would park and Tuvshin would get out and say, "Now we walk." I climbed a sand dune, scrambled up a hillside to see ancient petroglyphs, hiked into a canyon with lammergeiers soaring overhead, and visited a sandstone escarpment where the first dinosaur eggs in the world were found in 1923 (a fact I learned from the guidebook I'd read while planning the trip, not Tuvshin). After the mind-numbing hours in the car, these excursions were a welcome break, despite the nonstop wind.

Each night we'd stay in a ger hotel, described in travel brochures and Instagram posts as romantic and cozy. In fact, the ger camps were like trailer parks set on gravel in the middle of nowhere. Each "room" was a separate ger, in which a short door led into a grim, windowless round space with a teepee-like center pole. The bathrooms were always in a separate building, usually made of cement, probably so they didn't blow away in the wind. At least when I went out to pee at night, it was easy to see by the light of a gazillion stars, just like in the Sahara. Even the wind couldn't diminish that spectacular view.

Dinner took place in a large common ger, and, since I had asked for no red meat, I was the only person not eating greasy stew. Instead, I received chicken in a spicy red sauce, the same recipe everywhere. At least I could get beer with my meal, but there was no bar where I might meet the few Chinese and Korean tourists, and I heard no one speaking English anyway. Thank goodness I had my private stash of vodka back in the room to help pass the time.

I was feeling the same "should-be-loving-this-but-don't" feeling as when I was in New Zealand almost two years earlier. I focused on relishing the solitude by channeling my inner introvert, but to no avail. I was still annoyed by the wind, the food, and Tuvshin.

I realized how lucky I'd been over the past three years, with guides like Bruce, Brani, and Soufiane and new friends like Antonio, Nima, and Gretchen. They made my travels come alive and helped me see and experience things I wouldn't otherwise. Tuvshin did redeem himself slightly when, on the way back to UB, he found me a flock of a hundred demoiselle cranes, I bird I never thought I'd see. But otherwise, the Gobi was a bust.

Chinggis Khan conquered China, Vietnam, Korea, Thailand, Cambodia, Iran, Pakistan, Afghanistan, Turkistan, Uzbekistan, Tajikistan, and Armenia, as well as parts of Russia, India, and Hungary. After a week in the Gobi, I was convinced he was merely trying to get out of the incessant wind, find some different food, and maybe ditch a bad guide.

"It's not normal to be so cold this time of year, and the forecast for next week is not good," said Alembeck, my guide for the second part of my Mongolian adventure in the Altai Mountains. I guessed that the temperature was close to freezing. He put on a pair of gloves as he took me on a short walking tour of Bayan-Ulgii, where my flight had landed. Mostly Muslim Mongolian Kazakhs lived in this town of 30,000, home to the Golden Eagle Festival I'd attend at the end of the trip. I was grateful I'd bought the winter coat in UB and had packed my gloves and hat in my carry-on for easy access.

I was thrilled that Alembeck spoke excellent English and was personable, but I had other things to worry about. Despite taking daily Aleve while in the Gobi, the long hours bouncing on dirt tracks, no yoga, and sleeping on plywood slabs had taken a toll on my lower back, which had started seizing up. I was grateful that my hip hadn't bothered me even once in the past year and a half since the spa at Gaia experience, but my neck and shoulders were starting to ache. I wasn't sure how I would manage hiking and traveling for the next ten days, especially since our vehicle was an old Russian 4WD van packed with camping gear and food. I met the cook (a woman) and the driver (a man), neither of whom spoke more than a few words of English, but both smiled and laughed and talked to me (via Alembeck), clearly excited about our trip. They were all in their early to mid-thirties. Their enthusiasm was a welcome contrast to my time with Tuvshin.

Over a lunch of soup and bread, I told Alembeck about my back problem. "I don't know how well I will do in the van. Or camping," I said. "But we'll give it a try." I imagined him thinking I was a frail old lady.

He looked concerned but tried to reassure me it would all be okay. "The eagle hunter's house where we will stay for two nights is only a few hours away. We can stop as often as you like, and hopefully your back will feel better before we camp." What do young people know about bad backs, I thought?

The road out of town was paved for the first hour, then turned to dirt and eventually to a track before we arrived at our Kazakh family's house, a small stucco-and-wood building in a broad valley, treeless mountains rising on either side. I eased myself out of the van and tried to stretch my back. The air seemed even colder and windier than in town.

We were met outside by the patriarch eagle hunter, his wife, two teenage daughters, and a four-year-old boy or girl, I couldn't tell. Two sons in their twenties wouldn't join us until dinner.

The mother ushered us into a small entry space. A large room on the left had ten cots around the perimeter and a few cupboards. The smaller room on the right had a kitchen at one end, two cots at the other, and, in the middle, a low-to-the-ground table (no chairs) and a yak-dung-burning stove with a large pot of meat simmering on top. I wasn't sure where I would sleep in this tiny house, but I hoped it wasn't in the big room with a bunch of snoring men.

"I need to use the bathroom," I said. "It was a long drive."

After asking the mother, Alembeck pointed toward a short rock wall fifty yards downwind. When I got there, I saw a pit with two wooden planks to stand on surrounded by a rock wall barely two feet high. I squatted as best I could and looked out at an expanse of nothingness, not able to get low enough to keep my backside out of the cold wind—nor out of sight of those in the house. I resolved not to drink anything that evening so I wouldn't have to go out in the middle of the night.

Once back at the house, I wanted to wash my hands, but there was no running water or even a basin, so I used a bottle of sanitizer I'd brought with me. By then, Alembeck had worked out the sleeping arrangements and told me that the cook and I would sleep in the two cots in the kitchen; he and the driver would sleep in the bigger room with the rest of the family. After the long day of traveling, I wanted to take off my bra, but people were in both rooms, so I turned my back and slipped the bra off under my shirt, hoping nobody noticed or cared. There certainly wasn't any private place for them to undress either.

For dinner, our cook prepared a tomato-and-cucumber salad and potatoes to go with the huge yak roast that had been cooking on the stove. When dinner was ready, the patriarch eagle hunter came in with his two sons and three older men and sat cross-legged on the floor. Even when I was doing yoga every day, I had trouble sitting in that lotus position, so I kicked my feet out to the side and wished I had a backrest. After the men were seated, the other children joined us.

"This yak roast and the additional guests are in your honor," Alembeck said when the mother brought a huge piece of meat to the table. I was humbled by the opportunity to be there, but wondered why neither the additional men nor the sons had been introduced to me.

The hunter picked up the roast with one bare hand (I hadn't seen any sign of handwashing since I had arrived) and a large knife with the other and began carving slices as if the meat was on a vertical rotisserie. Once he had a big pile on the platter, he handed out portions to the men, who took them with their bare hands. After all the men were served, he handed me a piece. I knew I'd have to eat some to be polite, but my dislike of red meat was nothing compared to my discomfort over where the hunter's unwashed hands might have been that day.

I swallowed my fears of contamination along with pieces of the lean and gamey yak meat, which wasn't all that bad. The men talked convivially, while the women served milky tea and then cleaned up. The Kazakh nomads were legendary for their hospitality, but the men utterly ignored me and I felt that I was only there as the excuse to have a party. Sometimes I'd ask Alembeck what was being said, but he was having trouble following the dialect. Maybe the hospitality meant something to eat and a place to sleep, and nothing more.

When the dinner party broke up, I grimaced as I contorted my spine to a standing position, went outside to brush my teeth in the frigid air, visited the two planks again, washed my hands with hand sanitizer and cold water from my bottle, and wondered why I thought this kind of travel was fun.

I went back inside, kept on most of my clothes, and tried out the cot. The springs were so old that the skinny mattress sank almost to the floor under my weight. If I moved, I could feel every coil. At least I had a bed, I thought. And the burning stove would keep me warm, but I had no idea how long yak dung burned and wondered whether I was supposed to get up at night to stoke it. I was still wide awake when the two teenage girls and the four-year-old came into the room, rolled out blankets on the wooden floor, and curled up under thick quilts. It could have been a slumber party, but nobody talked. Listening to their steady breathing, I finally fell asleep.

———————

I felt like I barely slept but was somehow fast asleep when I heard one of the teenage girls shoveling yak dung into the stove. She already had a big pot of water boiling on top, even though I could tell it was just past dawn. The cook, in the cot across from me, rolled over and pulled the covers over her head.

A few minutes later, the patriarch and his sons came in, fully dressed, and sat on the floor around the table. The teenager immediately poured tea and served them. They did not try to be quiet. When I swung my legs over the side of the cot (thankful that I'd slept in my pants) and stepped around them to go outside to pee, they never even gave me a glance.

When I got back to the house, the teen had placed a cup of tea and a hard biscuit on the table for me. I downed an anti-inflammatory pill with the tea, since my night on the cot hadn't helped my back one bit. I was quite surprised when the girl asked me—using perfect English!—to join her in milking the yaks. Blushing, she said she and her sister studied English at school, but she was clearly uncomfortable speaking it. I knew that feeling.

I put on my coat, hat, and gloves and followed the girls outside to a pasture of grassy tufts filled with thirty yaks. The girl's mother, in a heavy coat and flowered headscarf, sat on a stool milking a yak. The other girl was herding the beasts to the milking spot, using sticks and clucking noises. Craggy mountains rose behind the pasture, treeless flanks shining golden in the early sunlight, a light dusting of snow on top. The beauty of the scene took my breath away. Or maybe it was the intense cold.

About half an hour later, when the milking was done, the teenagers took me to see their dog, which was chained to a stake in the ground. As we neared the animal, it jumped up and pulled at the far reach of the chain, ready to attack.

"It is a young wolf," the older girl said, concentrating on using the right words. "My father stole it from the mother."

"Why does he want a wolf?" I asked, feeling terrible for the poor wolf, but fascinated to see it.

"For the Eagle Festival," she said, in a tone that clearly conveyed the unspoken teenage Kazakh equivalent of "duh." I guessed I'd find out more when I saw the festival.

We made our way back to the house, where the hunter was bringing an eagle out of a nearby small stone enclosure. The bird was hooded and calm. Alembeck was standing by the van.

"The eagle hunter is taking you into the mountains so you can watch the bird practice," he said. "His son has already left on horseback, and we will go in the van."

I went inside, packed my backpack with an extra fleece layer, water bottle, and camera, including the telephoto lens. I had mostly given up traveling with the bulky lens but had brought it on this trip especially for the festival. Getting to photograph a practice session would be even better.

The patriarch got into the front passenger seat of the van with an eagle so big it filled the space between him and the windshield. The bird sat calmly, as if riding in a car were standard fare, even though I hadn't seen any cars near the house. It was exhilarating to be so close to the great bird.

We drove on a sketchy two-track up a ridge to a rocky outcropping overlooking the valley. When we reached the top and got out of the van, Alembeck pointed out a cluster of buildings on the valley floor that included a small store and the school. "The herders move to high country pastures for the summer," he said, "but stay in the valley in winter so the children can go to school." It was the beginning of the school year, and the hunter's family had only been back for two weeks before I arrived.

The hunter and his son worked the bird, releasing it to soar, then calling it in with a whistle and yell. The son dragged a rabbit pelt behind the running horse for the eagle to pounce on, and if the bird was successful, the hunter would reach into his coat pocket and pull out what looked like a raw chicken thigh for the bird's reward.

I was fascinated by the entire process and took a lot of photos, but the wind had picked up and I was getting cold. From the ridge I could see dark clouds over the high peaks in the distance.

"There's a storm coming," Alembeck translated the hunter's warning. "He wants you to take a picture before we go." The hunter stepped up on a rock outcropping with the bird on his gloved hand and posed regally. He didn't put the hood on the bird, which watched everything intently, including the ridge in the distance, in case there was any prey. I moved around as well as my creaky back would allow and shot from every angle.

"He wants to see the pictures," Alembeck said when the hunter handed the bird to his son. When I showed him the digital images, the hunter smiled for the first time since I'd met him.

Dinner that night was leftover yak roast, but at least Alembeck had remembered there were camp chairs in the van and brought one in for me so I didn't exacerbate my back issues by sitting on the floor. I spent another fitful night on the coils and woke up the next morning grateful that we were leaving for a week of camping and hiking in a national park high in the mountains. I could hardly believe I thought sleeping on the ground would be better than the cot, but I did. I didn't even mind getting up at dawn since it meant I could get out of that uncomfortable bed.

A few inches of fresh snow covered the ground as I went outside to the pit toilet, and I could tell the temperature had dropped substantially overnight. The sky was still dark and overcast and, back at the house, I drank two cups of hot tea before feeling warm. I wasn't sure what time we were leaving, so I nibbled at a biscuit, edited my photos from the day before, repacked the few things I'd taken out of my backpack (my suitcase had stayed in the car, since there was no room for it in the kitchen), and was ready to go. The family paid me no mind, going about their daily chores.

I went out to the van, where Alembeck was pacing with one hand pressing his cell phone to his ear and the other under his armpit to keep it warm. I put my backpack into the back seat, and he motioned to me to wait. He finished the call and put the phone into his pocket.

"There's a problem," he said. "The temperatures for this week are predicted to be minus seventeen at night, rising only to minus nine in the daytime." I tried to convert from Celsius to Fahrenheit in my head. Zero at night and fifteen or sixteen in the day?

"That's too cold to camp, Alembeck," I said. I had seen the lightweight polyfill sleeping bags in the van and, having winter-camped when I was younger, knew we weren't even close to having the gear we needed.

"I know," he said. "Also, the road into the park where we were going is closed by the storm. My boss suggests we drive in the valleys around here, since we can't go to the mountains."

"Where will we stay? And what will we do?" I was trying to keep an open mind and reminded myself that sometimes the worst circumstances made way for the most memorable experiences.

"We will ask to sleep in Kazakh herders' homes since it will be too cold to camp even at low elevations." Alembeck tried to look optimistic. "Herders will always make room for travelers, and we have plenty of food."

I thought about the prospect of a cold week sleeping on cots or the floors of other houses. It was bad enough here, where they were prepared to host us. What would accommodations be like for surprise visitors? In years past, I might have considered such a venture a fabulous opportunity. But not now. I didn't care how far I'd traveled to get to Mongolia. I was tired, hungry, cold, and in pain. I didn't need to experience the Mongolian Kazakh lifestyle any longer. I was even willing to give up the Eagle Festival, since I'd gotten a taste of eagle hunting the day before. Despite an intense feeling that I was giving up, something I was generally loath to do, I couldn't shut out the refrain in my brain: Get me out of here.

"I don't want to do that, and I'm not sure my back can take it," I said to Alembeck. I was becoming increasingly aware how much easier it was to deal with adverse conditions if I felt healthy, but my back was only part of the excuse. I hadn't expected luxury, but I simply was not enjoying the lack of basic amenities of this lifestyle or the increasingly harsh weather.

"Please tell your boss we will cut the trip short and return to Bayan-Ulgii today. If possible, I would like to fly to UB tomorrow. And don't worry, I will insist that you and the team still get paid."

Alembeck spent the rest of the morning either on the phone or talking to the hunter while I swatted a volleyball in a circle with the girls. By noon, he had proposed a new plan.

"The hunter has agreed that we can stay here again tonight. Tomorrow there is a small one-day eagle festival nearby, a warm-up for the three-day festival in Bayan-Ulgii you were supposed to attend. Instead of a hundred competitors, there will only be about twenty. But at least you will have seen what you came to Mongolia to see."

It was a good compromise. I could manage one more day, I thought. And even another night in the coiled-spring torture chamber of the cot.

The next morning, we left early for the mini-festival being held an hour's drive from the hunter's house in an open field surrounded on three sides by high ridges. The driver parked the Russian van next to about twenty other vehicles on a ridge with a great view of the field. The wind shook the van as I added my grey winter coat to the five layers I already had on, including my new cashmere leggings under my jeans. I wrapped a scarf around my head and pulled on the wool beanie I'd brought. Alembeck and I were going to walk down to the field, where the competition had started; the cook and driver decided to stay with the van. I stepped out into a blast of frigid wind and wondered if I should rejoin them.

Alembeck had been talking to a man from the vehicle beside us. "His car has a thermometer," he said. "It's minus twelve." About ten degrees Fahrenheit. Without the wind chill. No wonder I was shivering already.

About twenty eagle hunters stood at the edge of the field, each wearing a thick coat lined with fur, a silver-studded leather belt, a fur-and-felt hat with earflaps, heavy boots, and elbow-length leather gloves to protect against the eagles' talons. The hunters' families sat on the rock outcrops huddled in fur and leather coats and hats. They all looked plenty warm.

"Here's your ticket," Alembeck said, handing me a handwritten badge in a cheap plastic folder, strung on a thin piece of red twine. "They are calling this the first annual Eagle Release Festival. A bird will be released after the competition, in honor of the service the eagles provide." I put the badge around my neck. "The organizers are proud that eleven tourists are here today."

Ten other nuts like me, I thought. I braved the cold for about half an hour of the first event, where eagles came to their owner's arm when called in from soaring, before I had to escape to the van to warm up. I ventured back and forth through the second event, eagles pouncing on pelts dragged behind a horse, which was what I'd watched the hunter practice two days earlier. Thankfully, there was not only a tent where women sold tea and bread patties slathered with butter, but also a makeshift latrine with wooden sides and a roof.

Even after hot tea and the warm van, as soon as I ventured outside my feet instantly became blocks of ice. I suggested to Alembeck that we should leave, but he insisted we stay for the final event. He pointed at the young wolf I'd seen at the hunter's house. It had been tied up near a truck all day. I watched two men put it into a burlap bag, then carry it out to the middle of the field. The hooded eagles had been taken to the top of the ridge by each hunter's assistant, while the hunters waited below on horseback.

The wolf was released and looked around for a nonexistent hiding place while the first eagle swooped down and caught the wolf's back in its talons. The eagle's owner galloped to the scene and jumped off his horse to disengage them, the objective being to achieve the shortest time from eagle release to wolf release. The hunter held the young wolf down until the two men ran out with the burlap bag and started the process over again. And again, and again.

I believe in the laws of nature. An eagle attacking a wolf in the wild is just fine with me. It's about the food chain and an honest fight. But this felt like the Colosseum and the gladiators in Rome. I'd had no idea that an eagle festival meant the eagles would be hunting live prey. I knew I shouldn't be put off by the reality of what eagle hunting (or falconry in general) entailed. But I felt stupid for romanticizing travel in Mongolia and told Alembeck I was ready to leave. He convinced me to go to the tent for another cup of tea, telling me the final ceremony was something I should see.

I killed some time in the tent, watching women roll out and fry the bread dough. When I returned to the van, Alembeck told me that the competition was almost over but all tourist visitors were being asked to come out to the stage for the award presentations. Warmed by the tea and fire in the tent, I agreed.

The hunters were still on their horses and pranced to the stage to accept their various awards, announced by a man with a microphone in both Kazakh and, surprisingly, English. The other tourists seemed to be Asian.

"We are so honored to have foreign guests for our first annual Eagle Release Festival," he said, after all the awards had been given. "One lucky person will be chosen to release the eagle." He put his hand into a jar with eleven slips of paper and pulled one out.

"Number three," he said. My number!

The swarm of eagle-holding men on horseback surrounded me. I was grateful I had learned to say *"rackmet sizge"* (thank you, in the local language). The horsemen moved aside, and I was led by my eagle hunter host up a steep hill to a rocky outcrop, numb from the cold but newly exhilarated. Breathless from the climb, I extended my arm so the hunter could put his thick leather bird-handling glove onto my hand before transferring the bird, which danced on my arm for what seemed like a minute. I realized the eagle was the same one I had watched the hunter practice with a few days before. What a miracle that I would be the one to release the captive bird I'd ridden with in a car.

"Go fly, my friend," I said. "Be free and be happy." The magnificent eagle faced into the wind and took off. She soared above for too short a time, then flew away, far, far away, out of sight.

A few tears of joy trickled onto my cheeks and instantly froze, but at that moment, all the hardships of the trip felt worth it.

"Didn't you tell me I'd be staying in the best hotel in town?" I asked Alembeck after we'd driven from the festival to the regional capital of Bayan-Ulgii and parked in front of a decaying building.

"This is it," he said, and I was instantly embarrassed. I had no right to have been so judgmental about the tourist offerings ever since I'd arrived. I traveled to understand how other people lived, not to complain about it. I needed to buck up and be grateful for being here. Inside the hotel, the carpet was frayed and the lobby dimly lit. Since dinner and breakfast were included with the room price, Alembeck showed me a dark dining room just past the lobby. Then he told me he'd pick me up at nine in the morning to go to the airport, and left. The front desk clerk, who spoke no English, gave me the key to my second-floor room and pointed at the stairs.

The room was freezing cold, with stains on the carpet and a threadbare bedspread on the bed, but also a bathroom with running water and a radiator. Hot water came out of the tap and I washed up quickly, but when I tried to turn on the radiator, nothing happened. I went down to the desk to ask for help, but even with sign language and pretend shivering, all I earned was an extra bedspread and a long shoulder shrug. I called Alembeck.

"I can't get the heat to work. And I can't make myself understood at the front desk. Can you please call them and then tell me what I need to do?"

"I'm sorry, I should have told you. The power plant won't be turned on until the first of October. No place in town has heat until the government starts up the plant."

Really? In such a cold climate? Still, it was better than winter camping and it was only one more night. I went downstairs for dinner, dejected, but happy to be leaving the next day. I wondered about my sanity in choosing to travel to so many places where the weather was uncomfortably cold or hot. There wasn't a soul in the dining room, but my dinner of soup and bread tasted good. On my way back to my room, I ran into Alembeck coming into the hotel.

"I've brought a space heater from my brother's house," he said. Thank goodness there wasn't a Mongolian superstition about heaters like the Romanian one about fans. "But I also have other news."

We went upstairs to plug in the heater. The power cord was spliced together in three different places and looked like a fire waiting to happen. Oh well, I thought. I'll either die by fire from the heater or freeze to death, so what's the difference? I could hear the wind rattling the window.

"What's the news?" I asked.

"The weather forecast is for very high wind tonight and tomorrow. The airlines have canceled all flights for tomorrow. You will fly out on the same flight the next day instead, and tomorrow we will take you to see a beautiful lake." I'm sure my face showed my dismay. "I'm sorry," he said as he left.

I tried to channel Goma Air Lady and say all thing happened for a reason and I should be happy not to fly if conditions weren't good. But that strategy wasn't working. I sorely needed a shower after days without warm water. The doorless bathroom was a small square with marble-like tile on the floor and walls. I could see that when I turned on the shower, the entire room would get wet—as well as the space beyond the door, probably. I moved the heater to the other side of the room. I didn't need to add electrocution to my possible ways of dying that night.

I stood under a stream of gloriously hot water for a few minutes, just enjoying. Even though it appeared I was the only guest in the hotel, I feared the hot water might run out, so I reached for the soap on the sink and promptly slipped on the polished tile. I went down hard on my sit bones, the back of my head ricocheting off the tile wall. For a moment, I thought I had broken my back, but everything moved okay. I sat on the floor, water cascading onto me, holding the spot on my head that was already developing a bump, and burst into tears. It felt like the lowest point of my entire travels.

———————

Two days later, after a pleasant day driving to the lake on a snowy road and having a cold picnic inside one of the Russian military tents we were supposed to have been sleeping in, I was on a plane to UB. When I arrived, a tall man in his late thirties met me at the airport. I was grateful it wasn't Tuvshin.

"I'm Tebo," he said in English with a New York accent. He had a chiseled jaw and looked like he worked out regularly. "Do you need a wheelchair? What a bummer about your back being screwed up. I have a bed reserved at the hospital if you want to see a doctor."

"No, thank you, it's getting better." Maybe I'd overplayed the bad back.

Tebo took me to lunch instead of the hospital and told me he had spent his twenties and early thirties in the Mongolian military and as a mercenary.

"Yeah, I spent a few years in Iraq working with an American unit. The bros there taught me to speak English."

"They did a good job," I said. "You even know some slang."

"They specialized in slang," he said. "Not like the Russians I did some work for. They were all business, unless it was vodka time. I also speak Chinese, learned it in the army, but I would never work for them. They are bastards." I wondered what kind of work he had been doing in the military that required speaking all three languages.

"Why are you back in UB?"

"My mom is going blind. She can't work, and I'm the only child," he explained. "I used my language skills to get this job with the travel company as a guide and manager." I wished he, not Tuvshin, had been my guide in the Gobi. "I want to start my own business, guiding Americans and Aussies, driving them around in nice SUVs, not the Russian crap we drive here." That sounded like a good business venture.

After lunch, Tebo drove me to the same high-rise hotel I'd stayed in before, which now seemed ultraluxurious. I had six days before I was due in Hong Kong, and all I knew was that I did not want to spend them in Mongolia. I scoured the internet for nonstop flights from UB to nearby countries that didn't require a visa to enter and ended up booking an early morning flight to Siem Reap in Cambodia, a place I had intended to visit two years earlier but canceled when my mother's husband had the stroke.

That night, I had dinner on the twenty-eighth floor of the hotel, in a very nice Western-style restaurant filled with British and Russian businessmen. Pasta with salad, and two very welcome glasses of wine. I had to be up at four to get to the airport, so I turned in early.

At midnight the room spun, and I barely made it to the toilet to puke my guts out. Has to be food poisoning, I thought, glued to the floor by the toilet for the next three hours. I didn't care if I had to crawl to the airport, I was getting the hell out. This was the final straw.

When Tebo picked me up at four a.m., I tried to fake being okay to fly. I carried a bandanna in my hand just in case. I fervently hoped the flight wouldn't be turbulent. At the airport, Tebo stayed with me until I got in the security line.

"How big is your mother?" I asked.

"About your size," he said. "Why?"

I took off the heavy winter coat I'd bought when I arrived. I wouldn't need it in Cambodia. "Please give her this for me. Thank you, and good luck with your business idea."

Tebo looked pleased and gave me a hug. I went through security and waited for the boarding call. I felt a tug of defeat, of failing to meet the challenge of traveling in this country. I usually didn't walk away from hardship. I usually embraced off-the-beaten-track experiences, of which this was surely an extreme example. I'd had some incredible moments, like seeing demoiselle cranes and releasing a golden eagle, because I had stuck it out. What else might I be missing by leaving early?

I thought once more about the Polynesian ancestors at the Australian spa telling me to know myself differently. Maybe walking away represented not a failure but an accomplishment, a show of strength. I'd done it many times in my life: left a job, a relationship, or a situation that wasn't working for me. I had no reason to be embarrassed that I didn't want to stay in Mongolia. I was still the intrepid traveler I'd set out to be.

As the plane taxied down the runway, I felt a surge of relief—along with a resurgence of bile from the night before. I swallowed hard and watched Mongolia's landscape disappear beneath a layer of clouds. The sun was shining as we climbed high in the sky, and I knew something in me had shifted, even if I couldn't quite identify it just yet.

SIEM REAP, CAMBODIA, AND HONG KONG, CHINA

SEPTEMBER–OCTOBER 2017

"Would you like a cold towel?" asked a sweet-faced young man standing at the door of the boutique hotel. He held a tray of rolled towelettes and a yellow, flower-garnished drink in a stemmed glass. I accepted the towel gratefully but passed on the drink, still queasy from the food poisoning the night before. The heat and humidity of Siem Reap had sapped me after the frigid temperatures in Mongolia.

Inside the fan-cooled, open-air reception area, the sight and smell of tropical flowers climbing up the wall bombarded my senses. An inviting pool surrounded by palm trees, vines, and more flowers shimmered beyond the reception area.

"Your room is on the third floor," the receptionist said. "We have a spa on the first floor. Perhaps you would like to make an appointment for a massage?"

Perhaps? Had I died and gone to heaven? Mongolia was seeming farther away by the minute.

"Tomorrow, the guide we have arranged for you will be here at nine a.m."

"Just to confirm," I said, gun-shy after Tuvshin, "the guide will speak English, right?"

"Oh, yes."

Well, we will see, I thought, as I followed the bellhop up the stairs to my room. Still, no matter what, I was glad I had decided to pay a visit to Siem Reap before heading to my previously scheduled destination of Hong Kong.

———————

After a massage, which definitely helped my back, followed by a refreshing dip in the pool, I was ready to tackle my first task—buy an outfit or two fit for the steamy tropical climate. My only appropriate attire was a light silk dress I had taken to wear in Seoul, a sarong, and a couple of cotton shirts. The hotel had recommended that I take a motorbike-rickshaw taxi to a nearby night market.

The driver of the motorbike was very careful, and I felt safe in the open rickshaw even though we drove amidst cars and trucks. Within five minutes, we were driving down the middle of a street lined by open-air clothing shops, each stall containing identical racks of the baggy trousers worn by tourists and locals. I randomly picked a shop and asked the driver to stop. A tiny Cambodian woman rushed to help me, directing me away from the rack marked "Small" and toward the one marked "Large." Compared to her and the other Cambodian women I'd seen, she was right—I was much larger than they were. I chose a pair of yellow pants with elephants and a turquoise pair with lotus flowers, added two lightweight T-shirts, and bought the whole lot for the equivalent of fifteen dollars.

I went back to the hotel, had a simple dinner to make sure my stomach wouldn't react badly, and slept like a baby on a comfortable bed in my air-conditioned room.

My guide, Prak, turned out to be a delightful Siem Reap native who spoke excellent English. He was in his early fifties and exuded that Buddhist calm I had seen so often in Nepal.

"Angkor Wat means temple city," he explained. "Much of the reconstruction took place in the 1900s and continues today. Tourism has been a great benefit to our local economy, but some people complain that it has changed the character of our town."

"Amazing. I thought Angkor Wat was just a few buildings, not four hundred acres of twelfth-century ruins."

The complex was an amazing amalgam of more than fifty beautifully restored temples in the midst of the jungle that lurked ready, at a moment's notice, to envelop the buildings and grounds at the slightest hint of nonactivity. I wondered how much effort it had taken to clear the foliage from both the outside and inside of the structures.

We spent the better part of the day touring the ruins, Prak explaining the history and meaning of each building. "Tomorrow we will go to a shrine outside the city," he said. "The day after, we will come back and see more of Angkor Wat."

Since I had only a few days in Cambodia, I liked the idea of seeing the countryside in addition to the ancient city. The next day we drove an hour out of town into the jungle to visit a reclining Buddha statue which was big, but still small enough to have fit inside the leg of the huge reclining Buddha I'd seen in Bangkok. The shrine was complete with souvenir shops and concession stands selling coconuts, sugary drinks, and snacks I couldn't identify, so I bought bottles of water for me and Prak.

"This afternoon," Prak said, "we are going to the sacred mountain to see a very important elephant statue from the year 802. Cars cannot travel there, so we'll ride motorbikes. It will take about an hour." Two men with motorcycles were standing by our van.

I've never been a motorcycle person and wasn't too keen about riding behind some guy I didn't know, much less without a helmet. But I climbed on and hoped for the best. Prak and his driver took off in front of us, and we started up a decent two-track that soon turned into a steep, rutted, four-wheel-drive road and, finally, a rough mountain bike trail.

About half an hour in, the sky opened, dumping a thick, rain-forest rain on us. Prak gave me a plastic poncho to wear, but it barely helped. Soon we were crossing streams swollen by the rain. I held on for dear life, stranger or not.

We were sizing up a rushing torrent of water to cross when I told Prak I thought we should turn back.

"But it is a very important statue," Prak said. "Most tourists never see it."

I can see why, I thought. I hated to miss the opportunity to see something unique, but I was soaked, despite the poncho, and the water seemed to rise as we watched. The only good news was that it was so hot, there was no way I would get hypothermia. We turned back.

The return trip was an ordeal, skidding on the muddy downhill back to the parking lot. Once there, as I threw my leg over the bike to get off, the wet fabric of my new yellow elephant pants ripped open, leaving my purple underwear visible to the world. Holding the rear end of my pants together, I waddled to the van while Prak paid the cycle drivers. Luckily, I'd brought along a tunic-length overshirt and we were going from the temple directly to the hotel. So much for my bargain pants, I thought. And my pride.

———————

We returned to Angkor Wat on the third day of my visit. Prak guided me through shortcuts in the jungle that provided unique views of the buildings and avoided the crowded walkways. In the afternoon, we took a break sitting in the shade of an old wall, across from yet another magnificently carved building unlike anything I'd seen before. The walls of the structure crumbled slightly, but visitors leaned out of glassless windows, taking selfies or waving to friends taking photos below. I was, as I'd been for the past three days, sweating like I was in a sauna, and constantly worrying that my turquoise lotus pants from the market would split like the other pair.

We sipped from our water bottles while Prak, speaking with a deep familiarity, told more stories about the history of Angkor Wat.

"Your English is excellent," I said. "Did you learn as a boy?"

"No. I took classes when I decided I wanted to be a guide."

"Have you always worked as a guide?" I asked.

"No. I've only been guiding for fifteen years." He looked toward the building before us but seemed to stare far beyond.

"What did you do before that?" I asked.

"I worked for an import company. I didn't get an education when I was young, but in my twenties, I worked two jobs to pay for basic school and then university. Eventually I saved enough money to marry, and now I have two children."

"Why didn't you get an education as a boy? Isn't school mandatory in Cambodia?" I asked, wondering if the question was too personal.

Prak took a slow, deep breath, the kind you are taught at Toastmasters to take before a speech, or in yoga to calm the mind.

"When I was a boy," Prak said, "my parents were taken away and killed by the Khmer Rouge. My aunt tried to raise me, but I was forced to become a child soldier even though I was only thirteen. For several years, we used Angkor Wat as our base. I used to camp in these open spaces. That's why I know the area so well. We used whatever wood we could salvage from these temples for firewood. I was a child, so I didn't know any better, but the commanders should have. It was war. Bad things happen in wars."

"I'm so sorry," I said, not sure whether it would be more respectful to ask the hundreds of questions swirling in my brain or just be quiet. "Thank you for sharing your story, Prak."

He stood up. "Let's go see the inside of this temple. It's quite beautiful, and much more pleasant than talk of war."

I respected his privacy and took my once-again humbled ego to task. Here I was, a privileged American, grumbling about the heat and worrying whether my guide would speak English. But meeting people like Prak and being lucky enough to hear their stories was exactly why I traveled. To put my life in perspective and to give me a broader view of the world, which would, I hoped, make me more empathetic and understanding of others. I drank the last of the water in my bottle and decided the humidity wasn't so unbearable after all.

From Cambodia, I flew to Hong Kong for what I had originally planned as a luxury interlude between the rustic conditions of Mongolia and Nepal. But my time in Siem Reap had served the purpose of a break, so being in Hong Kong seemed superfluous, other than adding a new country for me. The hectic taxi ride from the airport on crowded freeways and narrow neighborhood streets confirmed that I was in a metropolis. I checked into my ultramodern corner room on a very high floor of an American chain hotel and got dizzy when I looked down at the busy street from the floor-to-ceiling windows.

When I'd made the reservation at the hotel, I had asked them to arrange a hair appointment for me at a salon where English was spoken. Fully expecting a replay of my Vienna most-expensive-hair-appointment-ever experience, I was pleasantly surprised when, despite the spa setting and the excellent color and cut, it cost less than half of the Viennese tab.

I didn't really want to go to Victoria Peak, the famous skyline observation point, but I must have been travel-weary as I let the front-desk receptionist convince me not only to go, but to take the local bus that left from in front of the hotel. The bus was, in fact, quite easy, despite my usual worry about taking buses and not being sure where to get off. The Peak was the terminus of the route, and I couldn't have missed it anyway because there were thousands of people there. I elbowed my way through the throngs of Chinese tourists and souvenir shops to the observation deck, where the view of the Hong Kong skyline and Victoria Harbor did not disappoint. But the tropical climate was, as usual, draining my energy. I took the obligatory photos, stood in a long line to take the tram back down to the city, and thought about having a cold drink when I got back to the hotel.

The one thing I did like about Hong Kong was the colorful and aromatic food. My visit coincided with the annual Moon Festival, a national holiday when families gathered to eat mooncakes and sing moon poems, so I made a reservation at a nice restaurant with a view to watch my old friend, the full moon. The exotic flavors of my meal delighted me and I made a point of not asking for translations of what I was eating. I couldn't help but notice that I was the only person dining alone during this family holiday, and it made me feel a bit melancholy, even though I'd spent plenty of time with my friends and family during the summer.

I walked back to the hotel along the crowded streets and felt hemmed in by the high-rise buildings. The next day, I found myself killing time in my air-conditioned hotel room, reading about other places to go instead of venturing out into the crush. Maybe it was the timing, but for me, experiencing one of the world's most famous cities felt like a chore. I couldn't wait to get back to the mountains of Nepal.

CHAPTER 27

NEPAL

OCTOBER 2017

Kathmandu didn't seem so foreign this time around. I was joining my Portland friends Laura and Kevin on a twelve-day trek of the Langtang-Gosainkunda circuit, a lesser-traveled area of the Himalayas than the Annapurna and Everest regions. Because it was their first time in Nepal, I convinced them that after the trek, we should go to Lukla to visit my friend Nima's guesthouse for a few days.

My Kathmandu-based friend Durga had organized the trip with Little Dawa as the leader, as well as two of our three porters from the Mustang trip. I liked seeing familiar faces and knowing what the routine would be, and I was happy to share it with Kevin and Laura, serious hikers who had no problem with the steep trails. The clear, sunny weather provided spectacular Himalayan views. We slept in guesthouses on the hard pallet platform beds I remembered from my previous trip, but, unlike in Mongolia, my back didn't bother me at all.

We had a few more days of hiking to go when Laura caught a bug. Our accommodation that night was a very comfortable hotel (bigger than a teahouse), with a nice view and a small restaurant with a warm stove. By the next morning, she felt worse and said there was no way she would be able to hike that day, especially since the destination was the famous Gosainkunda Lake, the highest elevation of the trek. But if we didn't hike, we wouldn't get to Kathmandu in time for our flight to Lukla.

By the time we had finished breakfast, Little Dawa had a solution. "Laura can stay here for the next two nights with one of the porters. Kevin, Cheryl, and I will take a porter to the Lake, and then, instead of continuing on toward Kathmandu, we will come back here. The next morning, we will hike to the nearby town of Dunche and catch a ride to Kathmandu in plenty of time for your flight the next day."

"That sounds like a good plan," Kevin said. "But I'll stay here with Laura." He was a good husband.

———————

Hindu legend has it that Gosainkunda Lake is the place where Lord Shiva stuck his holy trident into a mountain to get some water to flow. He needed the water to soothe his throat after saving mankind by swallowing the poison released into the world. Now he sleeps under the mountain. The trek wasn't heavily used by foreigners but was popular for Nepali and Indian Hindi pilgrimages to the lake.

The path to the lake was steeper and more difficult than most, and I was glad to be carrying only a small backpack with water and a snack. Although I had originally been sad that Kevin and Laura wouldn't be with me for two days, once on the trail I found I relished the solitude, with only Little Dawa silently hiking behind me and the young porter scampering ahead like a mountain goat with his light load.

When we arrived, the lake appeared calm, beautiful, and—perhaps because of the dark clouds that hung over us—somewhat mysterious. At 14,380 feet, I keenly felt the lack of air, despite my acclimatization. The day was bitterly cold, but thankfully there was no wind. On a bluff above the lake, a few wooden buildings served as guesthouses and restaurants. Little Dawa and I stopped for tea, then walked around the lake to a spot where a spigot had been stuck into the rock.

"Taking a drink of the water will wash away your sins," Little Dawa said. I thought maybe I'd better fill a big jug. I cupped my hands and took several big gulps of the deliciously refreshing water, but it made the inside of my mouth feel as cold as my hands did.

On the shore of the lake, several young men had stripped down to their shorts. One by one they jumped off a rock that jutted into the water, dunked their heads, then raced out to wrap themselves in towels.

"It's a tradition," Little Dawa said. I didn't find out until later that immersing yourself in the lake was the "true" way to absolve all sins, not drinking the water. I was thankful Little Dawa hadn't told me at the time; I might have been foolish enough to jump in.

My room that night was among the most primitive I'd ever stayed in. It seemed the "hotel" was built with plywood. There were no windows; the only light came through loose seams in the walls. A ratty mattress was folded atop a plywood frame. At the end of the hall was a single communal toilet, a hole in the ground with a wooden seat built over it. It was filthy, but still better than the wind-blasted outdoor pit in western Mongolia. There was no electricity.

Little Dawa and I ate noodles for dinner by candlelight in the main room of the hotel and I lingered by the wood stove for as long as I could before heading to the dismal room. I slept fitfully, partly because of the altitude and partly because of the lumpy pad on the plank bed. I woke when the slightest hint of light came through the crack in the wall. It was a long night.

But when I emerged from my dark nest, the morning was glorious. The ominous clouds had disappeared, and sunlight glinted off the water. I could see my breath and appreciated the cup of hot tea Little Dawa brought me when I got to the dining room.

Sipping my tea and watching the shadows disappear from the mountains as the sun rose, I tried to figure out why I felt so differently on this trip from when I was in Mongolia. I found the accommodations certainly no more luxurious than in Mongolia, maybe even less so. Was it because I had friends to talk to? Or because I had trekked in Nepal before? I couldn't put my finger on it. But I also realized that, although I did love the hiking and didn't feel stressed, I had not yet recaptured the Mustang calm I craved.

———————

"The flight to Lukla is now boarding," announced the PA system at the Kathmandu airport. I had looked in vain for my Goma Air friend when I arrived, finding only men at the check-in counter. I had really hoped to see her and her orange sari again, so I could tell her how much she had influenced my life and thinking. But no luck. Somebody had fixed the PA system so people could understand the announcements; maybe they didn't need her anymore. Everything seemed odd without her there. And, to top it off, was I really going to fly to Lukla on the first try and not have to wait through five days of canceled flights? Of course, I knew better than to get excited until the plane actually arrived in Lukla.

Nobody was more surprised than I when we landed at the world's most dangerous airport on the first try. Mingma and Diraj (the guide and porter from my previous trip) met me, Kevin and Laura, and after a quick stop for a cup of tea, we hiked in cool, sunny weather to Nima's guesthouse. Nima had arranged for an overnight camping trip on his family land behind the guesthouse where, he said, we would have a view of Mount Everest that tourists never see. What an unexpected opportunity!

The next morning, as we finished breakfast, Mingma and Diraj arrived with a teenage girl and another man as small as Diraj. None of our three porters could have weighed more than 110 pounds. Three large bundles sat on the deck, ready for the porters to carry to our campsite using tumplines around their foreheads so the weight was on their spine, not shoulders. Besides our individual duffels, the bundles included food and cooking gear, water, tents, and sleeping bags and pads. Each bundle was easily three and a half feet high, and who knows how much they weighed.

"I'd like to try lifting one of those packs with the tumpline. I've carried some heavy loads in backpacks, and I'd like to compare," Kevin said to Nima.

"Sure," Nima said, and placed one of the bundles on the short stone wall of the patio. "It will be easier if the load starts higher off the ground."

Kevin squatted in front of the bundle while Diraj arranged the tumpline around his forehead. Kevin stood up from the half squat slowly and smiled. "It's heavy," he said, as if that weren't obvious. As soon as he took a step forward, the bundle shifted and fell. The porters propped him up and straightened it. He tried again, the porters walking alongside to keep things steady. He managed a few steps before announcing he was done.

"I thought I was strong and in good shape," he said. "But you three are amazing!"

The teenage girl laughed the loudest as she picked up her load and started up the trail. Diraj and the other man easily hoisted their loads and followed her. All three of them wore flimsy sneakers. We laced our sturdy hiking shoes and slipped into our light backpacks to follow them up a relatively steep switchback cow path. Gradually, a better-worn path appeared, but it went straight up without switchbacks.

Now, I've hiked a lot in my life and climbed mountains, so I know what I'm talking about when I say that day's trek was some of the hardest hiking I've ever done. It was so steep we sometimes had to grab small tree trunks to haul ourselves up. I had no idea how the porters were managing it, but they were far ahead. We went relentlessly uphill for 4,000 vertical feet until we finally reached the campsite on a grassy plateau, where the porters had dropped the gear, set up the kitchen, and already started preparing dinner.

"The weather is supposed to be clear tomorrow," Mingma said. "We'll get up early to go to the Everest viewpoint."

We were all so tired that we were asleep by dark, barely having time to admire the star-filled sky. The next morning, I told Mingma that my legs were tired and maybe I shouldn't keep going.

"It's not as steep today," he said, which was small consolation. It was still another 2,000 vertical feet up. "And Chomolungma has been waiting patiently for you to return."

That did it. I put on my pack and started hiking. I couldn't let the Goddess Mother of the World down. As we went uphill, the vegetation changed from a forested hillside to sages, groundcover, and grasses. We maneuvered around large granite boulders and rocky outcrops. The air got thinner and cooler. We crested a ridge onto a small plateau and headed for some rocks. "There she is," Mingma said, pointing to a triangular peak far in the distance above the forested valleys and snow-covered ridges.

I've got to say, the sight of Chomolungma took my breath away, the same as it had before. Kevin and Laura seemed equally awed. The highest point on the planet. Seen by only a few. And from our vantage point, even fewer. My legs, though tired, were fine and I wondered again why I was so lucky. I tied a few prayer flags onto the bushes to keep the good karma coming, and felt the Mustang calm flow into my soul again.

CHAPTER 28

AUSTRALIA

NOVEMBER 2017

I flew from Kathmandu to Perth to meet my friend Katie, who had flown there from her hometown of Boise, Idaho. She was headed to visit friends in Sydney but had added a few weeks onto her trip to meet me. I'd known Katie for thirty years, and she had been an inspiration for me when, shortly after we met, she and her husband sold everything and bicycled around the world for two years. I'd joined her a couple of times as my annual vacation and always thought I'd like to do the same thing one day. And now I was, except not on a bike. She was my age, with a ready smile and striking short white hair that had been her trademark since she'd turned gray in her early thirties. We had rented a car for a road trip through Western Australia, an area I'd only scratched the surface of in two previous trips. Katie wanted to see the state's famous spring wildflower blooms.

We'd been on the road for a week, catching up with each other's lives and seeing plenty of flowers we couldn't identify, when we arrived at the entry village to Sterling Range National Park, which included the only major mountain range in the southern half of Western Australia. The highest peak was around 3,000 feet high, low by U.S. standards, but impressive since it rose out of a massive flat plain. But even more impressive was the fact that there were 1,500 species of plants and flowers in the small ecosystem, almost 90 of which were found nowhere else in the world.

We stopped at the coffee shop/diner/gift shop, where Katie asked the woman pouring the coffee about seeing wildflowers.

"If you are interested in flowers, you've got to talk to the guy at the table over there." She pointed at a grizzled old man with a gray goatee, wearing a freshly pressed khaki shirt and a tan, floppy-brimmed bush hat. He had a latte in front of him, the foam in a flower design. He scowled at the woman. "Eddie's the flower expert," she went on, ignoring his look.

Undeterred by the scowl, Katie went over to him and smiled broadly. "Hi, I'm Katie. This is our first time here. Can you give us any advice about where to go to see the best flowers?"

"Drive the scenic road and there will be plenty of flowers."

"Well, anything special or rare that we should be looking for?"

"Everything here is special," he said, the scowl never leaving his face. "Are you a botanist?"

"I'm not, but I do love to see orchids." Katie didn't mention her degree in agronomy. "We've been exploring for a week now, and they're my favorites. You must be a botanist. Are you a ranger here?"

The old man took a sip of his coffee and sighed. I imagined him thinking he'd never get rid of this pesky American tourist. I had made my way over and realized Eddie wasn't as old as I originally thought, more likely nearer our age.

"I am a ranger," he said. "Not trained as a botanist, but as good as one since I've been doing this for over thirty years. But today is my day off."

Hmm. He sure looked like he was dressed for work.

Katie persisted. "If you tell me where to see the best orchids, I'll let you get back to your coffee."

He finally gave in. "If you want to see a rare orchid, you can drive a few hundred yards down to the picnic area and walk around. They're everywhere."

We thanked him and went to the counter to pay. "You should ask Eddie about the orchid named after him," the woman behind the counter said in a low voice. I suspected he was in there every morning, drinking coffee and being a curmudgeon.

"Damn it, Marie, I can hear you. I've asked you not to blab about that." The scowl returned.

Katie couldn't resist returning to his table.

"Yeah, so I found an orchid never seen before. Documented as a brand-new species by the University in Sydney and the Botanical Society people. They named it after me." Almost as an afterthought, he added, "And no, I'm not going to take you to see it."

"Congratulations on the flower," Katie said. "Sorry to have bothered you, but can you tell me again where that picnic area is?" Katie asked.

"You really going to look for orchids there?" Eddie said, as if he were used to people asking for advice and then ignoring it.

"Of course," we said in unison.

Heaving an even bigger sigh, he slurped the remains of his coffee. "If you buy me a coffee for the road, I'll show you. I've got to go that way anyhow." I thought I saw a hint of a smile.

We spent the next few hours following Eddie around the Park to secret places where rare orchids grew, although he never did show us the one named after him. By the end of the afternoon, the three of us were singing along to Eddie's recordings of Australian country music, and I remembered the power of persistence and a smile.

Katie's friends, an American couple living in Sydney, had invited us to join them at a beach house for a week on Kangaroo Island, off the southern coast near Adelaide, so we made our way there. The kangaroos were plentiful and fun to see, but after driving long distances every day in Western Australia, I craved some down time. Katie went sightseeing and hiking with her friends while I stayed at the house lounging on the beach, swimming, writing, and reflecting.

Three years earlier, I had been in Zambia, trying to decide whether to change my life. At the time, I was reluctant to give up the creature comforts I'd worked so hard for as well as the fifteen years' worth of friends and routines I had gathered. But I was also a successful, financially independent, unfettered woman ready for a good time in new and different places, comfortable heading off on my own. Even though people often commented on how brave and adventuresome I was, I'd always had my safety nets, like making anchor plans for wherever I traveled, using my instincts to avoid getting into rough situations, and joining group travel or hiring private guides if I had any concern about navigating a place on my own. I hadn't set off on a journey of self-discovery per se; I was merely going to travel, be open to new experiences, and see what happened. But, of course, if you are an attentive traveler, you can't help but learn something about yourself.

I learned I could live out of a suitcase and call anywhere home (except maybe Mongolia). I found I enjoyed traveling alone and could even stick to a budget. I'd discovered a Mustang calm that could substitute for busyness and annoyance. I was working on freeing my emotions and feminine flow and I did dance more often. I had listened to the stories of individuals who had lived through unfathomably bad times and learned I could draw from their strength. I'd deepened my understanding of living sustainably, living spiritually, and living spontaneously. I had realized that, as I had gotten older, I wanted (and could afford) more creature comforts than I needed when I was young, and that it was okay to admit that. And, after all that, I thought I had become a better person, which meant I was more patient, accepting, thoughtful, and generous.

My incredible journey had been the result of both luck and discipline, and I knew I'd still need both in the future. In a few weeks, I was going back to the United States without a clear path ahead. But I wasn't the slightest bit worried. I felt more alive than I'd ever felt, possessing an inimitable spirit and curiosity about the world and more than sixty years of accumulated wisdom. Irrelevant or invisible? Not I.

I vowed to try hard to retain the lessons I'd learned on the road as I moved into the next chapter of my life, especially to avoid being rigid in my expectations and decisions. If I loved being in my mountain house, I would be okay not traveling so much. If I missed traveling, I'd be ready to lock and leave, for a week or for a year. Whether my future was to continue to fly solo or perhaps to meet a red-headed stranger, I'd accept either. No matter what, I knew I'd always carry gratitude for the life I'd been able to live and the experiences I'd enjoyed.

I'd gone deep into the mountains and jungles of the world, but I'd also gone deeper into the wilds of my own soul. The world had challenged me in ways I could never have predicted; sometimes I felt like the global citizen I aspired to be, sometimes I felt like an intrepid adventurer, and sometimes I felt like a complete fool. After three years of traveling, I knew I was an older, wiser, and more experienced me.

———————

From Kangaroo Island, Katie, her friends, and I flew to Sydney, where we went to dinner at a local Italian restaurant. It was my birthday, but I hadn't told anyone. At the end of our meal, I spied a waitress carrying a cake with a lit candle into the room.

"Is that for me?" I asked my dinner companions. "I didn't think you knew! Thank you!"

The waitress walked by and placed the cake in front a woman at a large table with her family.

"Knew what? Is it your birthday?" Katie said. "Why didn't you say something?"

"I didn't want anyone to make a fuss," I said.

We ordered a round of drinks to celebrate, and the waitress even brought me a cupcake with a candle. This was my fourth consecutive international birthday: South Africa in 2014, Morocco in 2015, Portugal in 2016, and now Australia in 2017. I announced to my friends that I was going to make it a tradition to be in a foreign country for every birthday that started with sixty. Why not? Spontaneity aside, sometimes it's good to have a plan.

TETON VALLEY, IDAHO, USA

SEPTEMBER 2021

A few weeks after my sixty-third birthday celebration in Sydney, I moved into the house I'd bought in the Teton Valley of Idaho, creating a new home base in the mountains I loved. I nested, skied, hiked, and even tried internet dating again, enjoying staying in one place. By the fall of 2018, I was ready to travel again, but not as a full-time gig. In addition to savoring numerous U.S. adventures and other international trips, I spent my sixty-fourth birthday in Bariloche, Argentina, and my sixty-fifth in Prague and Budapest, traveling with a man who shared my love of travel and had become my partner.

In 2020, because of Covid restrictions, I had to cancel several planned trips, and thought I'd be unable to keep my resolution about international birthdays. I was lucky to be living in my rural community, where my daily routine was mostly unaffected, except for wearing a mask to the grocery store. To adjust to the fact that I couldn't just get on a plane and go somewhere, I decided to work on the Buddhist notion of accepting what is and began approaching life in Idaho as if I were traveling in a foreign country.

While walking in my neighborhood, I talked to the neighbors I'd never met before, as I had with the people trimming roses in New Zealand. Instead of being annoyed by the influx of Americans seeking an outdoor experience at my favorite trailhead, I thought about hiking in Nepal and how welcoming the local people always were. At the weekly outdoor market, I asked farmers how to prepare vegetables I was unfamiliar with, as I'd done in Poland and Portugal when I was cooking for myself.

When countries started to open again late in 2020, I braved a trip to Kenya for my sixty-sixth. I celebrated with Samburu warriors dancing for me at Kalepo Camp in the north, owned by a couple I'd met years before while they were traveling in my backyard of Yellowstone National Park. The experience of traveling during the pandemic, when so many people didn't, required more planning (easy for me) and plenty of Mustang calm and patience (which I continued to work on). But it also reminded me of the power of connecting and staying in touch with special people I'd met around the world.

In 2021, with extensive planning and testing, I went overseas several times and spent my sixty-seventh birthday on a beach in Mexico, reflecting on how travel and the world had changed in ways nobody ever thought possible. I'm adapting, as we all must, choosing the risk level that is comfortable for me and waiting for the day when I can be spontaneous about travel again. I still get excited when the plane touches down on a runway in a country I've never been to or when I join a group journeying with knowledgeable guides and plenty of information. I have also learned to love moving at a slow pace, basking in a culture instead of checking off a tourist attraction, or savoring a glass of wine at an out-of-the-way café instead of rushing to a reservation at the latest farm-to-fork restaurant.

Going forward, when I make my travel choices, I will continue to consider the environment as well as my cumulative impact on the communities or cities I am visiting. I want to be more conscious about choosing to travel in countries that support human rights and strive for democratic ideals, patronizing local businesses and artisans whenever possible. And, hopefully not for much longer, I'll check the Covid statistics of the places I want to go so I can make an informed decision about my activities there and the risk level I'm comfortable with.

Travel remains an integral and precious part of my life, whether done with my partner, with friends, or solo. I believe in the importance of sharing ideas, cultures, and food as a way to bring the world closer together, to counteract isolationism and tribal us-vs.-them attitudes. Travel expands my mind and my attitudes, and I hope the people I meet while on the road are similarly enriched. So, I will unapologetically continue my journey to seek fresh experiences around the world.

After all, there are still more frogs to be heard, eagles to be released, and incredible indigo skies to be seen.

(NOT) THE END

ACKNOWLEDGMENTS

I must start by thanking every single person I met during my three years of traveling the world, especially since this book is as much about them as about me. Without these characters, there would be little story. Many people are named (I used first names only in case anybody didn't want to be identified), but there are so many others that I wish I could have included. But then the book would have been three times as long.

If you do find your name in the book, I hope you feel I have portrayed you accurately and fairly. If you met me but are not specifically identified, please know that you were just as important as others in contributing to my overall experience and observations.

Two people who do appear in the book deserve special mention: Kathleen Paul and Stephanie Hallock Cummins. Both are longtime friends, and without their encouragement to keep writing as the years flew by, this book would never have happened. They spent countless hours willingly reading endless drafts, as well as this final version. I reluctantly thank them for their brutal honesty when it was needed, something only true friends can provide. This book is as much a product of their early editing as of my writing. I cannot thank them enough for everything.

As for editing, I thank Jane Stuart, my copyeditor, who made the final words sing and taught me a lot about commas. Having fresh eyes near the end of the journey was so important, and Jane's thoughtful comments and edits will certainly add to the reader's enjoyment of the story. She gave me the confidence in my story to put this book out into the world.

For the production of the book, I thank The Book Makers—in particular Tracy Atkins, for internal design and shepherding the overall publication, and Tanja Prokop, for the beautiful cover design adapting one of my own photos from the Sahara Desert.

And finally, I thank each of you who have taken the leap of faith to read this account of my journey. Enjoy.

ABOUT THE AUTHOR

Cheryl Koshuta is an inveterate traveler. She relishes domestic and international journeys to experience—and learn from—different cultures and perspectives, as well as to indulge her passion for birding and exploring nature. When she's not on the road, she lives in the Teton Valley of Idaho, where she skis, hikes, and writes. Her first novel, *Saving Legacy Springs*, was published in 2013.

Author photo taken in the Lammergeier Valley of Mongolia.

CPSIA information can be obtained
at www.ICGtesting.com
Printed in the USA
BVHW031250230122
626950BV00005B/352